Spirit of Vengeance

Spirit of Vengeance

Nativism and Louisiana Justice, 1921–1924

John V. Baiamonte, Jr.

Louisiana State University Press
Baton Rouge and London

Designer: Albert Crochet
Typeface: Linotron Trump Mediaeval
Typesetter: G & S Typesetters, Inc.
Printer: Thomson-Shore, Inc.
Binder: John H. Dekker & Sons, Inc.

LIBRARY OF CONGRESS CATALOGING IN PUBLICATION DATA

Baiamonte, John V.
　Spirit of vengeance.

　Bibliography: p.
　Includes index.
　1. Rini, Joseph—Trials, litigation, etc.
2. Trials (Murder)—Louisiana—Tangipahoa Parish.
3. Mafia—Louisiana—History.　4. Ku Klux Klan
(1915–　　)—History.　I. Title.
KF224.R56B35　1986　　345.73'02523　　85-19143
ISBN 0-8071-1279-8　　347.3052523

To Pat

The great enemy of truth is very often not the lie—deliberate, contrived and dishonest—but the myth, persistent, persuasive and unrealistic.

—JOHN F. KENNEDY, 1962

Contents

Illustrations

Preface

I began this study in 1969, but I conducted no additional research on the subject until 1979, when I finally located the transcript of *State of Louisiana* v. *Joseph Rini et al.* in the Louisiana State Supreme Court Archives. After reading the newspaper accounts of the trial and finding the Dallas Calmes Scrapbook and the correspondence of Governor John M. Parker, Jr., I was certain that there was enough material for a monograph on what most law-enforcement authorities, some historians, and many journalists believe was a turning point in the early-twentieth-century development of the Italian criminal syndicates in the New Orleans area.

At first, *Rini et al.* appeared to be a "simple" trial of six men who were accused of killing a man while attempting to rob a bank in Independence, Louisiana, in 1921. However, further research revealed that some of the main characters had also been involved in the events of 1890–1891 surrounding the death of the New Orleans chief of police, David C. Hennessey. The involvement of the Ku Klux Klan and the belief that the crime was committed by members of the American "Mafia" complicated the case further. Finally, *Rini et al.* became a *cause célèbre*, both nationally and internationally.

In order to capture the human suffering and the drama of the case, I have often used dialogues, which I feel are crucial to an understanding of *Rini et al.* These conversations were, with a few exceptions, taken verbatim from reliable sources. The most credible documents are, of course, the official transcripts of the two trials. Then there are the newspaper accounts of conversations witnessed by the newspapermen. The reporters' transcriptions were for the most part quite accurate, as I found when I compared their accounts of courtroom testimony and the official records. In the interest of clarity, however, certain dialogues, especially those containing poorly structured sentences, erratic punctuation, and dialects, have been edited. Also, obscenities were sometimes omitted, and according to the context of the conversation, I restored them.

For various reasons, interviews were limited. Since *Rini et al.* concluded nearly sixty years ago, almost all of the main characters are now deceased, and many of those who are alive have failing memories. Further, some refused to discuss what was apparently a traumatic experience for them. And too often, those who were willing to talk about the case gave only theories and suspicions which could not be corroborated. Consequently, those few interviews utilized were tested for accuracy before being included as reliable sources.

A vast number of people have helped in the preparation of this study. First of all, I wish to thank Roman J. Heleniak for encouraging me to research the Italian-American experience in Louisiana. Also, Tom Gillen, who prompted me to complete this study by threatening to write the book himself, offered fresh insights and approaches to the story, and made his research files available to me. I am also gratefully indebted to Robert Tyler for legal-research assistance and to Michael Kurtz and John Williams, who read all of the manuscript and made valuable suggestions. I wish to thank Ruth Olson for her typing of several drafts. A personal note of gratitude is directed to my editors, Margaret Fisher Dalrymple and Barbara O'Neil Phillips, who labored patiently on the manuscript. Needless to say, without the sustained support of my wife, Pat, who typed and edited various drafts, this effort never would have seen the light of day.

Author's Note

According to Henner Hess's *Mafia and Mafiosi: The Structure of Power* and Anton Blok's *Mafia of a Sicilian Village, 1860–1960: A Study of Violent Peasant Entrepreneurs*, there was no single criminal organization in Sicily properly called the *mafia*. The term *mafia* was actually a trait of character, a philosophy of life, a moral code for all Sicilians. It required that Sicilians help each other, stand by their friends and family, fight common enemies, and divulge no secrets—*omertà*. Sicilians were also to stay clear of officials and the law and to protect their honor by means of violence. A man who practiced this philosophy was called *mafioso, uomo di rispetto* (man of respect).

The *mafia* mentality did not lead to a criminal organization. Instead, *cosche*, small groups of malefactors who obeyed a local leader, came into existence. They maintained relations with other *cosche*, sometimes arranging joint actions. In addition, these relationships were neither uniform nor regulated, and there were no initiation rites. Although Hess concluded that the Sicilian *mafia* was not a monolithic structure, the Italian government, sensation-seeking journalists, and foreign authors elevated it to a secret society of immense power in western Sicily. In the United States, the concept was transformed into the "Mafia," a highly structured organization found in Italian communities in American cities before World War I.

Spirit of Vengeance

1

Bloody Tangipahoa

The land that became Tangipahoa Parish[1] offered rolling hills with virgin pines in the north. The southern terrain, mosquito-infested marshes with moss-draped cypress and gum trees, bordered two large lakes that led into the Gulf of Mexico. There were ample opportunities for lumbering, agriculture, hunting, and fishing, which attracted many European settlers during the French and Spanish periods of Louisiana history. After the Louisiana Purchase, Americans moved into the territory that later became a part of the short-lived West Florida Republic (1810). By the early 1860s, there were finally enough residents along a railroad, later called the Illinois Central, to justify the creation of a new parish. This seemingly serene setting was to become the scene of ever-increasing acts of violence—some racial, some ethnic, some political, some random.

Carved from four neighboring parishes in 1869, Tangipahoa Parish from its inception was turbulent. Created during the Reconstruction period, the parish—like the rest of the state and the South in general—was often disrupted as conservative whites resorted to force in order to regain their lost authority. During this era the local chapter of the Knights of the White Camellia, led by Thomas C. W. Ellis, a state judge, resisted Radical Republican rule. After Reconstruction, Tangipahoa's conservatism and deep-seated belief in white supremacy often left the area's blacks vulnerable to the white majority. For example, in the late 1880s the Phantom Riders were able to set upon blacks with impunity, because some of the parish's leading whites belonged to the group. In July, 1889, two blacks were lynched in the town of Tangipahoa for unknown reasons. Six years later, several residents of Hammond lynched a black suspected of murder, and during 1897—

---

1. A parish in Louisiana is comparable to a county.

I

1898, Amite City, the parish seat, also witnessed the lynching of three blacks who were thought to be murderers. Elsewhere in the parish, blacks were lynched on three separate occasions between 1900 and 1905.[2]

Although blacks were generally the victims in the parish, the white Anglo-Saxon population also suffered. The intensity of violence reached such proportions in the 1890s that a "reign of terror" was said to exist, and the parish earned the infamous title "Bloody Tangipahoa." Murders in Tickfaw, Amite City, and other communities alarmed both state and local officials because most of the violence was a result of Tangipahoa's politics and Klan-like groups known as the White Caps. During this lawless period, Judge Robert R. Reid, a local political titan and an adversary of Judge Ellis, was often guarded to prevent assassination attempts by various feuding factions. Although the judge thwarted all attempts on his life, his brother was fatally wounded outside the courthouse in a neighboring parish. Reid's brother was only one of several noted parish figures murdered during the late 1890s, and charges abounded that the area courts were too lax and that the administration of justice was ineffective. Disturbed by the continuing mayhem, Governor Murphy J. Foster conducted in April, 1898, a personal investigation into Tangipahoa's penchant for violence.[3]

Years later, an Amite resident recalled the reign of terror and the White Caps. "Their object was to regulate the niggers," he explained. "After a while they fell out among themselves, and members of one faction would run the niggers off the other side's farms.

2. Ernest Russ Williams, Jr., "The Florida Parish Ellises and Louisiana Politics, 1820–1918" (Ph.D. dissertation, University of Southern Mississippi, 1969), 90, 271; New Orleans *Daily Picayune*, June 21, 1881; William Ivy Hair, *Bourbonism and Agrarian Protest: Louisiana Politics, 1877–1900* (Baton Rouge, 1969), 189–90; National Association for the Advancement of Colored People, *Thirty Years of Lynching in the United States, 1889–1918* (New York, 1969), 68–72; Hammond *Leader* quoted in Baton Rouge *Daily Advocate*, February 5, 1890; New York *Times*, September 22, 1900; Kentwood *Commercial*, September 22, 29, 1900, February 9, 1901; Amite City *Advocate*, November 30, 1905.

3. Newspaper clipping, *World*, April 7, 1898, in Vertical File, "Crime and Criminals," Rare Book Room, Troy H. Middleton Library, Louisiana State University, Baton Rouge; New Orleans *Times-Picayune*, January 15, 1923; Hammond *Daily Star*, May 3, 1981; Amite City *News-Digest*, June 24, 1960; Williams, "The Florida Parish Ellises," 269.

Then they started killing—not promiscuously, you understand, for the victims were always spotted." In an effort to keep these acts of violence quiet, the editor of the Hammond *Leader* explained that his paper never officially reported all shootings and murders. "You see we weren't publishing much of the bloody part then because we were out for immigrants. The I. C. railroad took 200 copies every week and distributed them through the North. The officials thought such things ought to be left out. If I'd kept track of everything like that that happened, the paper would have been full of it."[4]

Despite the reign of terror in the 1890s, Tangipahoa still managed to attract settlers and to expand economically. Encouraged by the Illinois Central Railroad, farm families from the Midwest settled the area, especially around the town of Hammond. And in 1890 an American strawberry farmer in the village of Independence recruited the first Italian immigrant families as laborers. During the 1890s, other Italians settled the Independence area as laborers and as strawberry farmers, and by 1900, 205 Sicilians lived there. Throughout the early 1900s, hundreds of Sicilians settled in the area. By 1909, there were between 1,100 and 1,400 immigrants, making it the parish's largest Italian settlement. There were others in towns such as Hammond, Natalbany, Tickfaw, Amite City, Roseland, Arcola, and Kentwood. But it was Independence, with a railroad-station sign that read "10,070 miles to Italy," that witnessed its native residents moving out and selling to Italians.[5]

Although the influx of Italians greatly stimulated the economy of the parish, the relationship between the Sicilian strawberry farmers and the native settlers was far from cordial. According to a

4. New Orleans *Item*, April 15, 1922.
5. John V. Baiamonte, Jr., "Immigrants in Rural America: A Study of the Italians of Tangipahoa Parish, Louisiana" (Ph.D. dissertation, Mississippi State University, 1972), 31–58; *Senate Documents*, 61st Cong., 2nd Sess., Vol. 84, pp. 267–68, 271; Fara Forni, "Gli' italiani nel distretto consolare di Nuova Orleans," *Bollettino Emigrazione*, No. 17 (N.p., 1905), 4; Giacomo Moroni, "La Louisiana e l'immigrazione italiana," *Bollettino Emigrazione*, No. 5 (N.p., 1913), 48; Hammond *Daily Herald*, 1907, quoted in Hammond *Daily Courier*, August 23, 1932; New Orleans *Times-Picayune*, May 2, 1920; New Orleans *Daily States*, December 23, 1888; New Orleans *Daily City Item*, October 28, 1891, February 27, 1893; New Orleans *Times-Democrat*, May 19, 30, 1892.

1909–1910 federal study, the Dillingham Commission, the Italians "fought their way inch by inch through unreasoning hostility and prejudice to almost unqualified respect or even admiration." The commission further stated that "at first there was considerable prejudice against the Italians, due largely to the fact that they were foreigners." In addition, Mafia and Black Hand disturbances in New Orleans and two local anti-Italian incidents created an unfavorable impression of the Sicilian immigrants.[6]

The so-called Mafia incident was the murder of David C. Hennessey,[7] chief of police for the city of New Orleans. In October, 1890, Hennessey was fatally wounded in a barrage of gunfire near his home. Before his death, he reputedly said, "The Dagoes did it." However, he did not identify his assailants or state that the Mafia was involved. Because of Hennessey's statement and the rumor that he was about to testify on behalf of Joseph and Peter Provenzano, who were being retried on charges of shooting members of Charles Matranga's rival gang of Italian stevedores, city officials began an immediate investigation. As a result, nineteen Italian immigrants or descendants of immigrants were indicted for the murder of Hennessey.[8]

After the conviction of the Provenzanos, the *Times-Democrat* had concluded that the "Mafia methods have lost their grip in this community," but after Hennessey's death the New Orleans press again warned its readers that the "Mafia . . . cannot be tolerated" in the city. Mayor Joseph A. Shakspeare, who firmly believed that the Mafia was planning to seize control of the city and was responsible for Hennessey's death, released a list of ninety-four murders supposedly committed by Italians. A recent study notes,

6. *Senate Documents*, 61st Cong., 2nd Sess., Vol. 84, pp. 242, 282.
7. Although the name of the chief of police was variously spelled in contemporary sources, it was most often given as "Hennessey."
8. John E. Coxe, "The New Orleans Mafia Incident," *Louisiana Historical Quarterly*, XX (October, 1937), 1068; Barbara Botein, "The Hennessy Case: An Episode in American Nativism, 1890" (Ph.D. dissertation, New York University, 1975), 84; Humbert S. Nelli, *The Business of Crime: Italians and Syndicate Crime in the United States* (Chicago, 1976), 47–49, 51; Richard L. Carroll, "The Impact of David C. Hennessey on New Orleans Society and the Consequences of the Assassination of Hennessey" (M.A. thesis, Notre Dame Seminary [New Orleans], 1957), 13–20; John S. Kendall, "Who Killa de Chief?" *Louisiana Historical Quarterly*, XXII (April, 1939), 510–11, 513, 515; New Orleans *Daily States*, October 16, 1890.

however, that the mayor failed to mention that the list included Spanish and French names that sounded Italian. Nor did Chief of Police D. G. Gaster, Hennessey's successor, inform the public that the murderer in these incidents was often unknown to the police. These errors and distortions served to "blacken the reputation of New Orleans Italians."[9]

Shortly after Hennessey's murder, Mayor Shakspeare also appointed prominent citizens, several of whom were members of the Anti-Lottery League, to the Committee of Fifty to help bring the chief's assassins to justice. The Anti-Lottery League, organized in February, 1890, to fight the charter renewal of the Louisiana State Lottery Company, was especially concerned that the lottery was an attraction for the large number of Italian immigrants arriving in New Orleans. Although Tangipahoa residents were not members of the committee, they were prominent in the league. Judge Tom Ellis, for example, was a member of the league's executive committee and maintained a professional and business relationship with two leaders of the league and the Committee of Fifty, W. S. Parkerson and John C. Wyckliffe. In addition, Ellis' son, Robert, a law student at Tulane, was on the staff of the league's newspaper, the *New Delta*, which was edited by Parkerson and Wyckliffe.[10]

When the Committee of Fifty decided to seek outside aid in convicting the Italians held in the Orleans Parish Prison, Tan-

---

9. New Orleans *Times-Democrat*, July 20, October 17, 1890; Botein, "The Hennessy Case," 41–42; Kendall, "Who Killa de Chief?" 513–14; Nelli, *The Business of Crime*, 32, 51.

10. The Louisiana State Lottery Company controlled the city waterworks, a large cemetery, cotton mills, and a sugar mill. Despite its alliances with several powerful state banks and political organizations, the Lottery Company was in political trouble because of charges of bribery and corruption. See Joy J. Jackson, *New Orleans in the Gilded Age: Politics and Urban Progress, 1880–1896* (Baton Rouge, 1969), 115, 120–21. For membership in the Anti-Lottery League and the Committee of Fifty, see Clarence C. Buel, "The Degradation of a State: Or the Charitable Career of the Louisiana Lottery," *Century Magazine*, XLIII (1892), 630; and Berthold C. Alwes, "The History of the Louisiana State Lottery Company," *Louisiana Historical Quarterly*, XXVII (October, 1944), 1054–57, 1063, 1091; Richard H. Wiggins, "The Louisiana Press and the Lottery," *Louisiana Historical Quarterly*, XXXI (July, 1948), 812; Williams, "The Florida Parish Ellises," 252; C. Harrison Parker to T. C. W. Ellis, December 4, 1891, and Notebook (1891), in E. John Ellis and Thomas C. W. Ellis Papers, Department of Archives, Troy H. Middleton Library, Louisiana State University.

gipahoa Parish residents became involved in the Hennessey affair. In early January, 1891, William Pinkerton, who had been a personal friend of Hennessey's, offered the services of his detective agency to stage the arrest of Frank Dimaio, a Pinkerton detective, in Amite City. It is not known why Amite was chosen. Perhaps the Ellises and other Amite residents who were members of the Anti-Lottery League helped the committee in its plans. Nevertheless, the United States Secret Service, which was cooperating with the New Orleans officials and the Pinkertons, arrested Dimaio on counterfeiting charges at an Amite boardinghouse. Dimaio's arrest caused quite a stir in the small town. When he was taken to the depot to catch a train to New Orleans, Dimaio acted the part of an arrogant criminal so well that several Amite citizens attempted to lynch him. Fortunately for Dimaio, who was probably unaware of the notoriety of Bloody Tangipahoa, the Secret Service agent got him aboard safely.

Once inside the prison, Dimaio was assigned to a cell with one of the defendants accused of murdering Hennessey. Hoping to elicit evidence for the state, Dimaio tried unsuccessfully for two months to gather incriminating statements. When the undercover operation ended in late March of 1891, it was several Tangipahoa residents who signed a $5,000 bond to secure the detective's release.[11]

The state then prosecuted nine of the nineteen Italians charged with Hennessey's murder. After the testimony concluded, the jurors deliberated for one day and returned with a mistrial verdict for three of the defendants and a not-guilty decision for the remaining six. The courtroom spectators and the vast majority of New Orleanians were outraged. When the judge ordered all of the defendants back to prison because of a pending charge, several members of the Committee of Fifty called a mass meeting for the morning of March 14, 1891. A few of the leaders of the committee and the Anti-Lottery League, including W. S. Parkerson, John C.

---

11. Wiggins, "The Louisiana Press and the Lottery," 739; Alwes, "The History of the Louisiana State Lottery Company," 1061, 1105–1108; James D. Horan, *The Pinkertons: The Detective Dynasty That Made History* (New York, 1967), 422–37; New Orleans *Daily Picayune*, January 16, 1891; New Orleans *Times-Democrat*, March 30, 1891.

Wyckliffe, and John M. Parker, Jr., then led a crowd estimated at between twelve thousand and twenty thousand to the Orleans Parish Prison, where the mob went on a rampage that resulted in the deaths of eleven Italians originally held for Hennessey's death.[12]

For the most part, the public, New Orleans newspapers, and many subsequent writers on the subject believed that all or some of the defendants were guilty. Herbert Asbury in 1936 maintained that the evidence was as conclusive "today as it was when presented on the witness stand." A 1969 study concluded that "the case against all but two was strong." However, Humbert S. Nelli, who believes that most writers on the subject have been influenced by a local myth about the Mafia, argued in 1976 that "none of the writers . . . examined the evidence carefully" and that they failed "to point out that the state presented a weak case." Although there were witnesses who identified some of the defendants as Hennessey's assailants, the police later admitted that their "most material witness" failed to see the face of one of the defendants during the shooting. Another witness under cross-examination acknowledged that four of the defendants looked "pretty much like" the men he saw that night. Furthermore, the defense attorneys throughout the trial attacked obvious gaps and inconsistencies in the state's evidence and presented alibis, which went unrefuted by the state, for all of the accused.[13]

Nelli's basic conclusions are partially bolstered by U.S. Attorney William Grant's 1891 investigation of the Hennessey case. After examining over eight hundred typewritten pages of testimony, Grant concluded that the "evidence . . . as a whole and in detail . . . is exceedingly unsatisfactory, and is not . . . conclusive

12. R. L. Carroll, "The Impact of David C. Hennessey," 39–40; Botein, "The Hennessy Case," 86, 91, 93, 101, 103, 107–12; New Orleans *Times-Democrat,* March 15, 1891; New Orleans *Daily Picayune,* April 15, 22, 29, 1890, March 14, 1891; Nelli, *The Business of Crime,* 57; Buel, "The Degradation of a State," 631; Jackson, *New Orleans in the Gilded Age,* 126; Matthew James Schott, "John M. Parker of Louisiana and the Varieties of American Progressivism" (Ph.D. dissertation, Vanderbilt University, 1969), 36.

13. Nelli, *The Business of Crime,* 52–58; Jackson, *New Orleans in the Gilded Age,* 248; Joseph E. Persico, "Vendetta in New Orleans," *American Heritage,* XXIV (June, 1973), 68. For other critical assessments of the Hennessey episode, see R. L. Carroll, "The Impact of David C. Hennessey," 33–37; and Botein, "The Hennessy Case," 95–99.

one way or the other." Another issue Grant treated was the defendants' involvement with the Mafia. Although he admitted that "the existence of such a society has been known and believed in by the public generally for a great many years," he was "unable to obtain any direct evidence connecting . . . the defendants with the Mafia, or any other association of a similar character in the city." Additionally, Grant examined the list of ninety-four murders released by Shakspeare and did not conclude that "these crimes were all the work of the Mafia."

According to Nelli, during the late 1880s and early 1890s the Italian criminal gangs in New Orleans adopted many Sicilian *mafia* methods, such as kidnapping and practicing extortion on wealthy Italians. They were also involved with the local political organizations of the city, especially the Ring (Choctaw Club), and they attempted to control the unloading of ships on the riverfront. For example, in 1881 the *Daily Picayune* reported that "Italian Bandits" had organized to coerce importers into using their gang members to unload fruit. However, these criminal organizations did not adhere strictly to *omertà*, the code of silence, nor did they have the support of the Italian community. Consequently, Nelli maintained, it is not accurate to describe these earlier Sicilian criminals in New Orleans as *mafiosi*. And if any of the defendants had murdered Hennessey, Nelli concluded, "the killing was merely part of a vendetta involving two feuding factions and did not represent an effort to establish *mafia* control over the city."[14]

In the months following the attack on the prison, many New Orleanians and journalists still connected the Louisiana State Lottery Company with the Mafia. One prominent member of the clergy attacked the Lottery Company and compared it to the Mafia. Robert H. Marr, Jr., who became the Orleans Parish district attorney in the early 1920s, stated that the Mafia and the Lottery Company were definitely connected. And a year later, a reporter for *Century Magazine* said that "the various Mafias are on the side of the Lottery, which is the masterful vampire Mafia of them all."

14. *Correspondence in Relation to the Killing of Prisoners in New Orleans on March 14, 1891* (Washington, D.C., 1891), 52; Nelli, *The Business of Crime*, 37, 66, 69; New Orleans *Daily Picayune*, August 21, 1881.

Tangipahoa residents were probably concerned about these supposed connections because John A. Morris, a financial backer of the Lottery Company, had developed a hunting resort for his family and friends on a vast rural estate in the parish. Furthermore, the issue of rechartering the Lottery had divided Tangipahoa politicians. The anti-Lotteryites were led by Judge Tom Ellis, who considered it a "battle of Christianity—God-fearing agrarians against godless factory workers and Negroes."[15]

In the 1890s in other parts of Louisiana, still other Italians became victims of acts of violence. In Hahnville, a community just upriver from New Orleans, three Italians were lynched in 1896; in Tallulah, in north Louisiana, five Italians were lynched in 1899 because of a quarrel over a goat. There were no Mafia overtones, and these outbreaks appeared to be caused by the Italians' aggressive economic competitiveness. However, the New Orleans press in the 1890s often connected Italian crimes with the Mafia, even when the incident appeared to be the result of an argument or of a family disturbance. In July, 1895, for example, an Italian laborer on a sugar plantation killed his wife during a family squabble, but the *Daily Picayune* carried the headline "Mafia Takes More Lives." The following day a similar incident occurred on another plantation, and the *Daily Picayune*'s headline was "More Mafia Murder Done." Finally, after a series of murders involving Sicilians on three different plantations, the *Daily Picayune* concluded that "the Mafia is rife among the Italians in Louisiana." Such reporting was not uncommon after Hennessey's death. According to Humbert Nelli, the "New Orleans affair marked a complete turning point," and "the American press quickly labeled all crimes in the immigrant community Mafia acts."[16]

15. Robert H. Marr, Jr., "The New Orleans Mafia Case," *American Law Review*, XXV (May-June, 1891), 414–31; Williams, "The Florida Parish Ellises," 250; Jackson, *New Orleans in the Gilded Age*, 119; Schott, "John M. Parker," 48; Buel, "The Degradation of a State," 631; Alwes, "The History of the Louisiana State Lottery Company," 1061.

16. New Orleans *Daily Picayune*, July 22–25, 1895, December 30–31, 1899; New York *Times*, July 22, 1899; Humbert S. Nelli, "Italians and Crime in Chicago: The Formative Years, 1890–1920," *American Journal of Sociology*, LXXIV (January, 1969), 375–76; Hair, *Bourbonism and Agrarian Protest*, 188; John Higham, *Strangers in the Land: Patterns of American Nativism, 1860–1925* (New Brunswick, N.J., 1955), 169; Jean Scarpaci, "Italian Immigrants in Louisiana's Sugar Par-

After the turn of the century, Italian criminality entered the era of the Black Hand, which lasted until about 1920 in the Little Italy sections of many United States cities. The Black Hand (*Mano Nera*) activities, which included blackmail, kidnapping, bombings, assaults, and murder, were usually the work of a small group or of individuals. Although some of the gangs were organized, there was no evidence that the Black Hand leaders were tied directly to the Sicilian *mafiosi*. According to one study, the "Black Hand . . . was a cultural but not an organizational offshoot of the *Mafia* and was completely Italian in origin and character." [17]

In New Orleans, a Black Hand murder in June, 1902, caused a series of feuds that lasted until 1904. Giving extensive coverage to the episode, the *Times-Democrat* felt obliged to rehash the Provenzano-Matranga clash, which had no relationship to the current Black Hand outbreaks. The newspaper also brought up the Hennessey case and warned that "we will soon be where we were in 1891." [18]

Then in 1907, Walter Lamana, the ten-year-old son of a wealthy Italian resident of New Orleans, was kidnapped and murdered. Many citizens and the press believed that the Mafia was also responsible for the heinous crime, and the trial of the Italians charged with the murder attracted statewide and national attention. Tangipahoa residents followed the proceedings in the New Orleans press and the Hammond *Daily Herald*, which associated the crime with the Black Hand. Although there were no reported *Mano Nera* activities in the parish, the residents were probably concerned because hundreds of Sicilians commuted weekly by train from New Orleans to labor in the strawberry fields. [19]

ishes: Recruitment, Labor Conditions, and Community Relations, 1880–1910" (Ph.D. dissertation, Rutgers University, 1972), 248; Botein, "The Hennessy Case," 186.

17. Nelli, *The Business of Crime,* 76–79, 83, 86; Francis A. J. Ianni, "The Mafia and the Web of Kinship," in Luciano J. Iorizzo (ed.), *An Inquiry into Organized Crime* (New York, 1970), 13.

18. Nelli, *The Business of Crime,* 74–76; Ralph Edward Carroll, "The Mafia in New Orleans, 1900–1907" (M.A. thesis, Notre Dame Seminary [New Orleans], 1956), 18–24, 35, 42; New Orleans *Times-Democrat,* June 13, 1902, August 11–12, 1903.

19. Hammond *Daily Herald* quoted in the Hammond *Daily Courier,* June 29, 1932; R. E. Carroll, "The Mafia in New Orleans," 50–53, 58, 60–61; John S. Kendall, "Blood on the Banquette," *Louisiana Historical Quarterly,* XXII (July, 1939), 826–27, 830; Baiamonte, "Immigrants in Rural America," 37.

The Amite City *Advocate* continued to carry articles about Black Hand threats to wealthy Italian merchants, especially in the French Quarter, where extortion notes were attached to disemboweled mules as a warning. In 1908 the New Orleans Sicilian community began to resist the Black Hand activities, which the newspapers often referred to as Mafia affairs. Through the assistance of the Italian Vigilance Committee, which was created during the Lamana case, New Orleans police arrested one of the rising young Black Hand leaders, Vito Di Giorgio.[20]

Ultimately, Di Giorgio was released because of insufficient evidence. Later, in May, 1916, he and an Italian strawberry farmer from Tangipahoa Parish were seriously wounded in a shooting at Di Giorgio's grocery store. The police immediately branded the violence a Black Hand vendetta, and the superintendent of police called for an end to a series of unrelated shootings and murders in the city's Italian communities. Perhaps prompted by the *Times-Picayune*'s warning that one of the shootings was "the first alleged attempt of Italian assassins to murder a person not of their own nationality since the killing of . . . Hennessey," the superintendent pleaded with the Italians for help. With the assistance of several Sicilian leaders in New Orleans, the police quickly apprehended Di Giorgio's assailant, an Italian ice-cream vendor who was once a strawberry picker in Tangipahoa Parish.[21]

During the investigation into the shooting of Di Giorgio, the New Orleans Police Department found a young Italian teenager, Joseph Bocchio, living with the Di Giorgio family. The youngster, who spoke no English, had been in the United States only a short while. Since the police had no reason to charge Bocchio, he was ordered to leave New Orleans. However, he and Di Giorgio remained in the city, only to become involved in a crime in Tangipahoa Parish that would rival the notoriety of the Hennessey murder.[22]

It was in Bloody Tangipahoa that Louisianians witnessed the

20. R. E. Carroll, "The Mafia in New Orleans," 45–47; New Orleans *Daily Picayune*, December 6, 1907, June 12, 18, 1908; Amite City *Advocate*, May 10, 1906; New Orleans *Times-Picayune*, May 14, 1916; New Orleans *Times-Democrat*, August 11, 1903, July 14, 1910.

21. Kendall, "Blood on the Banquette," 852–53; New Orleans *Times-Picayune*, March 8, 22, 26, April 3, May 9, 13–14, 18, 1916, May 14, 1922.

22. New Orleans *Item*, May 13, 1922.

most serious anti-Italian outbreaks since the 1890s. In February, 1908, the lumber mills in Kentwood laid off scores of workers and cut the wages of the remaining employees, most of whom were Sicilians. In addition, the unemployed Sicilians quickly sought the jobs available in the Kentwood area, an action which also angered the native population. Furthermore, the companies explained that the immigrants were retained because they were often better and more loyal employees. Shortly afterward, between fifty and sixty men visited the town's Italian section to warn the immigrants that if they did not leave by Saturday night, their homes would be dynamited. Fearing violence, twenty families packed their belongings and left on a train for New Orleans. The Sicilians who remained in Kentwood were protected by sheriff's deputies and Louisiana National Guard troops. Arrests were made, and the troops were removed. But they would return in a few months to quell a similar disturbance.[23]

In July, 1908, local authorities sought two Italian brothers for killing an employee of a lumber company in Natalbany. When the capture of one brother led sheriff's deputies on a massive manhunt through the Italian settlements, the lawmen met resistance. Italian strawberry farmers were wounded and one Italian boy was killed.[24]

Understating the emotions of the residents, the *Daily Pica-yune* reported that an intense feeling existed against the "dagoes" in the area. The paper concluded that if the missing brother had been captured, he "would have undoubtedly been at once strung up." Threats and rumors persisted, and it was reported that two thousand Italians, armed with large supplies of ammunition, were prepared to destroy the town of Natalbany. These reports gained credence when townspeople found some Sicilians huddling around campfires on the edge of town, but the immigrants had gathered there for protection because they feared returning to their cabins.[25]

23. Higham, *Strangers in the Land*, 158; *Florida Parishes Times* (Amite City), February 27, 1908 (extant copies were located in the attic of the Amite City *News-Digest* in 1969); New Orleans *Daily Picayune*, February 29, March 1–2, 1908.

24. New Orleans *Times-Democrat*, July 22–30, 1908; New Orleans *Daily Picayune*, July 23, 27, 1908.

25. New Orleans *Daily Picayune*, July 23–24, 1908; Giacomo Moroni, "Gli' italiani in Tangipahoa (Louisiana)," *Bollettino Emigrazione*, No. 7 (N.p., 1910), 5; New Orleans *Times-Democrat*, July 24, 1908.

That same July night, their fears became a reality when an explosion destroyed a grocery store. The Italian owner had earlier run afoul of a lynch mob led by a local preacher, and a deputy had rescued him. Although the explosion caused no injuries or deaths, Governor J. Y. Sanders dispatched sixty national guardsmen to Tangipahoa. Following the events very closely, Judge Tom Ellis wrote in his diary: "Man named Jno. Simmons of Magnolia [Mississippi] killed by a Dago. State troops sent up to Hammond when a Dago house was dynamited."[26]

Although the shooting of the mill worker sparked the disturbance in Natalbany, one underlying cause of the unrest was the Sicilians' keen economic competition. The *Times-Democrat* reported that their prosperity in the midst of a nationwide financial panic had led to poor relations with the Americans. The natives also believed that the immigrants were keeping their money out of local circulation. The *Daily Picayune* stated that the ill-feeling toward the Sicilians was due largely to the belief that they worked for lower wages than Americans did, and the residents of Tangipahoa were convinced that the Italian mill workers were responsible for the wage reductions. However, the paper correctly pointed out that the lower wages at the Natalbany and Kentwood mills were the result of the drop in lumber prices during the preceding winter.[27]

According to the *Daily Picayune*, white residents were not partial to the blacks, but preferred them to the Italians. A well-known leader of Natalbany perhaps best summarized that attitude: "I don't understand them [the Italians], although I have tried my best. They don't understand us because they don't seem to want to. As a laborer give me a negro every time. I can handle him and get results out of him. But I can never tell what an Italian is going to do next. In dealing with him I always make a mental reservation. He can and does live on less than any human being I know, and as for spending money, they don't know what such a thing is."[28]

26. New Orleans *Times-Democrat*, July 25, 1908; T. C. W. Ellis Diary, in Ellis Papers.

27. New Orleans *Times-Democrat*, July 24–25, 1908; New Orleans *Daily Picayune*, July 26, 1908; Moroni, "Gli' italiani in Tangipahoa," 6.

28. New Orleans *Daily Picayune*, July 26, 1908; New Orleans *Times-Democrat*, July 24, 1908.

Those sentiments were not uncommon in Louisiana during the early 1900s. Sicilian immigrants sometimes did the same sort of menial work as did blacks on the sugar plantations and on small farms. Further, the Italians avoided luxuries, spent little money in the local community, and paid cash to avoid high interest rates. Stereotyped as dirty, violent, and often members of the Mafia, the Sicilians were also criticized for living in colonies and for retaining their Old World customs and language. Additionally, the methods of mob terrorism used against blacks were sometimes extended to the Italians, though never in the same magnitude. This occurred not only in the southern part of the state but also in north Louisiana—in July, 1909, for example, several Italians were nearly lynched near Shreveport for killing a local planter.

However, the hostility toward the Sicilians in Louisiana was by no means universal. The Dillingham Commission (1909–1910) noted that the Italians in Tangipahoa Parish had been recognized for their thrift, industry, integrity, and "peaceableness," which had "won somewhat reluctant admiration of those who originally assumed a hostile attitude." Also, Louisiana's powerful economic interests, especially the sugar planters, supported efforts to recruit Italian laborers because they were often considered "superior" to other workers. Louisiana Congressman Charles F. Buck also defended the Italian laborers and opposed most federal restrictions on immigration. Furthermore, the Sicilians were able, for the most part, to get along with blacks and Cajuns on the plantations. For example, local residents of the town of Franklin in 1907 often joined the Italians in celebrating their religious festivals.[29]

While some parts of Louisiana made the Italians feel welcome and some did not, many Tangipahoaians were still determined to find outlets for their volatile natures. Only nine months after the

29. Charles Shanabruch, "The Louisiana Immigration Movement, 1891–1907: An Analysis of Efforts, Attitudes, and Opportunities," *Louisiana History*, XVIII (Spring, 1977), 216–20, 222; Jean Ann Scarpaci, "Immigrants in the New South: Italians in Louisiana's Sugar Parishes, 1880–1910," *Labor History*, XVI (Spring, 1975), 172, 174, 176, 178, 181–82; George E. Cunningham, "The Italian: A Hindrance to White Solidarity in Louisiana, 1890–1898," *Journal of Negro History*, L (June, 1965), 25; *Senate Documents*, 61st Cong., 2nd Sess., Vol. 84, p. 242; New Orleans *Daily Picayune*, July 10, 1909.

Natalbany disturbance, national guardsmen were sent back to the parish. This time it was for the trial of Avery Blount, who was convicted of a feud-related murder of a Tickfaw family in April, 1909. So disturbed were many prominent residents that they organized the Law and Order League to rid the parish of the cognomen Bloody. Fearing a lynching or the rescue of Blount by friends or relatives, Judge Robert S. Ellis, the former employee of the anti-Lotteryite leaders who stormed the Orleans Parish Prison in 1891, declared a state of martial law around the Amite courthouse. Blount's was one of the most dramatic and sensational murder trials in the history of Tangipahoa Parish and Louisiana. When Blount was hanged in October, 1909, the troops again turned the courthouse into an impregnable fortress. According to old-timers, Blount's execution marked only the second time in the history of Bloody Tangipahoa that there was an official hanging. The first had been in 1879, when a black man was hanged for the murder of a white boy.[30]

Except for the Kentwood and Natalbany disturbances, there were no other reported anti-Italian episodes in Louisiana during the pre–World War I period. However, some feelings of nativism were still evident. In Tangipahoa the Italians continued to be a major force in strawberry farming, the parish's lifeblood. In 1908 the parish was reputedly the third-richest agricultural county in the United States, and the Dillingham Commission characterized the Italian colonies in 1909 as wealthy and prosperous. But Tangipahoa experienced the xenophobia that gripped the nation during the economic slump of 1914. In January of that year, the White Farmers Association, which excluded Italians and Asians, was organized at Ponchatoula. Also, in the summer of 1914 the White Farmers Co-operative Association at Ponchatoula accepted all Caucasians but not Italians, Sicilians, Asians, or blacks.[31]

30. New Orleans *Daily Picayune*, March 3, 5, 7, 23–28, 30–31, April 1–3, 6–8, October 14, 16, 1909; clippings of New Orleans *Times-Democrat*, 1909, in Vertical File, "Crime and Criminals," Rare Book Room, Troy H. Middleton Library, Louisiana State University; New Orleans *Times-Picayune*, June 15, 1921.

31. Indictments, Appearance Bonds, and Court Summons, 1908–1920, Tangipahoa Parish Clerk of Court Office, Amite City, La.; Higham, *Strangers in the Land*, 169, 174, 183; Baiamonte, "Immigrants in Rural America," 101, 105, 107, 109, 113–14, 122–23; Charter Book No. 1, pp. 81–93, 135–41, Tangipahoa Parish

During the post–World War I period, Americans, disillusioned by the peace treaty, faced higher consumer prices, a massive demobilization effort, and a highly publicized epidemic of strikes and bombings. They also began to fear radicalism and communism from Bolshevik Russia. With tensions heightened, many Americans concluded that the unrest at home was being fomented by the "un-American" elements in the nation. As a result, a nationwide crusade—the Red Scare—was launched against left-wingers and foreigners whose Americanism was suspect. Leaving a "bitter heritage of suspicion of aliens," this crusade did not bypass Louisiana or Tangipahoa Parish. The local dailies carried headlines about the Red Scare in other cities, and New Orleans was hit during 1919–1920 with a series of nonviolent strikes. The postwar unrest spread from New Orleans to the town of Bogalusa, only thirty miles from Tangipahoa. In November, 1919, five labor organizers were murdered by a mob described as the "best citizens of Bogalusa." Furthermore, in the spring of 1920 there were rumors of a major strike among the Italians and other strawberry farmers in Tangipahoa.[32]

The Ku Klux Klan was attractive during this period because of its potential as a law-enforcement agency, its campaign against Catholics and foreigners, and its being a fraternal organization. Ironically, the center for Klan activities in 1920 and early 1921 was not the rural areas like Tangipahoa. In April, 1921, the governor of Louisiana received a confidential report on the Klan, which was holding regular meetings and classes at the Monteleone Hotel in New Orleans. The report claimed that L. A. Toombs, adjutant general of the Louisiana National Guard, and Guy Molony, superintendent of the New Orleans Police Department, were among its members. According to one study, it was not unusual for the Klan to have community leaders among its membership. Tangipahoa Parish, for example, with its large Italian immigrant popula-

Clerk of Court Office; Hammond *Vindicator*, August 6, 1937; *Senate Documents*, 61st Cong., 2nd Sess., Vol. 84, p. 268.

32. Schott, "John M. Parker," 394, 396; Spencer Phillips, "Administration of Governor Parker" (M.A. thesis, Louisiana State University, 1933), 154; William E. Leuchtenburg, *The Perils of Prosperity, 1914–32* (Chicago, 1958), 81; New Orleans *States*, January 25, 1920; Amite City *Times*, April 16, 1920.

tion, had four Klan chapters reportedly dominated by prominent citizens.[33]

As crime seemed to increase in nearby cities and towns throughout the state, the problem hit closer to home. In the spring of 1921, Tangipahoa also experienced a series of robberies and burglaries believed to be the work of criminals from New Orleans. On the morning of March 23, the Amite City night marshal was found murdered at the scene of a drugstore burglary. Convinced that criminals from New Orleans were again responsible, Amite lawmen began a massive manhunt. As posses scoured the countryside in vain, the Ponchatoula *Enterprise* warned that "the law will not be allowed to take its course if the bandits are caught." A month later, an Amite mob nearly lynched a black prisoner who had escaped from the parish jail after knocking a guard unconscious. Although no black had been lynched since 1917, Tangipahoa authorities moved the prisoner to the Orleans Parish Prison.[34]

In the midst of its own crime wave, Tangipahoa Parish, with its history of violent acts, intolerance toward the economically powerful Sicilian immigrants, and the appearance of the Ku Klux Klan, was about to confront its most nativist outburst. Although previous events in Bloody Tangipahoa attracted statewide attention, this episode would capture a national and an international audience.

33. Kenneth Earl Harrell, "The Ku Klux Klan in Louisiana, 1920–1930" (Ph.D. dissertation, Louisiana State University, 1966), 118–20, 132, 138, 145, 159–60, 261, 300, 324, 375; AMW Reports, April 11, 1921, L. A. Toombs to "Sir Knight," May 24, 1921, [?] to John M. Parker, n.d., [?] to John M. Parker, January 4, 1923, W. C. Robertson to John M. Parker, January 8, 1923, all in John M. Parker Papers, Southwest Archives and Manuscripts Collection, Dupré Library, University of Southwestern Louisiana, Lafayette. All references are to this collection unless otherwise noted.

34. New Orleans *States*, March 23, June 26, 1921; Ponchatoula *Enterprise*, March 25, May 6, 1921; New Orleans *Item*, April 26, 1921; NAACP, *Thirty Years of Lynching*, 73.

2

An Easy Chance

On the afternoon of Friday, May 6, 1921, a black Hudson Super-Six rolled out of a Tulane Avenue repair shop in New Orleans. The occupants, six Italians, would later claim that they were going to Tangipahoa Parish for a christening. But there were pistols, rifles, dynamite, and nitroglycerin, as well as other paraphernalia hidden in various parts of the car. One of the men was the repair-shop owner, Natale Deamore, a large, heavyset man with no education. The thirty-six-year-old Italian national, who had resided in New Orleans for nearly fifteen years, claimed he was only "borrowing" the Hudson. But he had been arrested four months earlier on charges of car theft.[1]

Also in the car was Deamore's friend Joseph Bocchio, who was the driver. Bocchio, twenty-one years old, had been in the United States for five years, but he was not a United States citizen. He had a minor criminal record in Milwaukee and New Orleans, where he was once arrested and released while living with the Di Giorgio family. Bocchio had studied engineering at an Italian academy for a year. He also had several years of experience as a machinist, chauffeur, and taxi-cab driver for Toye Brothers in New Orleans, and a nine-month enlistment in the U.S. Army Air Service in 1919. Wearing gold-rimmed glasses, Bocchio, who had studied for the priesthood, had the appearance of a student, not a criminal.[2]

1. *State of Louisiana* v. *Joseph Rini et al.*, Transcript of Appeal, No. 24,914, pp. 411, 489, 744, 868, 784–87, State of Louisiana Supreme Court Archives, New Orleans, hereinafter cited as *State* v. *Rini*, TOA, No. 24,914 (pagination is consecutive throughout all four volumes); newspaper clipping, Dallas Calmes Scrapbook, in possession of Mrs. Betty Salter, Denham Springs, La.; New Orleans *Item*, April 3, 1924; New Orleans *States*, May 9, 16, 1924.
2. Clement G. Hearsey, *The Six Who Were Hanged* (N.p., n.d.), 13; Joseph Bocchio to John M. Parker, May 1, 1924, in Parker Papers; newspaper clippings, in

Bocchio was unmarried, but he had a fiancée in New Orleans. Hoping to visit his mother before the wedding, Bocchio went to see his friend of three years, Deamore, to ask for help in getting a job on a steamer going to Italy. However, Deamore offered him another proposition, which Bocchio would later describe as "an easy chance to make some money." The only thing he had to do was drive the Hudson to the Italian settlement in Independence.[3]

Another occupant of the car was Rosario "Roy" Leona, who was thirty years old and a resident of Brooklyn. Leona was a small, wiry man with fiery eyes and a large, black moustache. He had lived in the United States for nine years, but he was not a citizen. For over a year, the former grocery-store owner had had tuberculosis, and in 1920 he went to live in California for health reasons. However, his illegal activities forced him to use at least two aliases to keep from being arrested. Roy Leona had recently arrived in New Orleans from Chicago with his friend Joseph Giglio, who was thirty years old and a naturalized citizen. Giglio, the fourth man in the car, did not look like a Sicilian. He was very pale and slim and had soft gray eyes and an aquiline nose. The World War I army veteran had delicate mannerisms. Like Leona, he had left his wife and family in Brooklyn.[4]

Both men arrived in New Orleans in late April with intentions of making large sums of money in bootlegging. But they soon met Vito Di Giorgio, now one of the city's reputed Mafia leaders, who told them about fortunes easily available in Independence. Leona and Giglio then went to the home of Deamore, who was a cousin of a friend in Brooklyn, to see about moving into a nearby rooming house.[5]

Giglio and Leona had renewed their acquaintance with the

Dallas Calmes Scrapbook; New Orleans *States*, May 9–10, 1924; New Orleans *Item*, May 9, 1921.

3. Hearsey, *The Six Who Were Hanged*, 4; Bocchio to Parker, April 24, 1924, in Parker Papers; *State* v. *Rini*, TOA, No. 24,914, p. 867; New Orleans *Times-Picayune*, May 11, 1924.

4. New Orleans *Item*, April 3, 1924; New Orleans *Times-Picayune*, May 10, 1924; New Orleans *States*, May 9, 1924.

5. *State* v. *Rini*, TOA, No. 24,914, pp. 498–501, 503–506, 857–59; newspaper clipping, in Dallas Calmes Scrapbook; Hearsey, *The Six Who Were Hanged*, 3–4; Charlotte Crowell, "Stern Justice Took Six Lives for One," Baton Rouge *Sunday Advocate*, May 10, 1964, p. 1–E.

other two occupants of the car, Andrea Lamantia and Joseph Rini, only a few days earlier in a New Orleans restaurant. Lamantia, a twenty-one-year-old barber and a native of Italy, had known Giglio for at least seven years in Chicago, where his wife and three children resided. He recalled Leona from Brooklyn, where he had operated a barbershop. Rini, who worked with Lamantia, was twenty-two and born in New York City. A World War I veteran, he had held odd jobs in a printing shop and as a bartender. After Rini and Lamantia explained that they had just come from Chicago, Leona and Giglio took their old friends to meet Deamore. In the repair garage, Leona, Giglio, Lamantia, Rini, and Deamore discussed their plans for a trip to Independence.[6]

On May 6, 1921, Joseph Bocchio drove the Hudson out of New Orleans, heading west on the River Road. Deamore realized they were lost, and he finally suggested that they should obtain directions from Pietro Leotta, who lived near the small town of Hobart. When they arrived, Deamore explained to his old friend from Italy that they were trying to get to Independence. He begged Pietro to go with them, but the old farmer insisted that he could not leave his place. Finally after Deamore's repeated proddings, he agreed to go. His ten-year-old son was picking strawberries near Independence.[7]

A few miles outside of Hobart, the party crossed Coyell Bay around ten o'clock that night. The ferryman later recalled that although the night was warm, the car's windows and curtains were drawn tight. Leotta was also suspicious—the car was loaded with firearms and dynamite. Remaining in the car, he apparently did not want to be seen by the ferryman, who was a friend. The ferryman could not resist asking why they were on the road at such a late hour, and Lamantia replied that they were going to visit a dying relative.

Shortly after midnight, their luck began to run out. The car misfired, and although they stopped briefly to repair the carbu-

6. *State* v. *Rini*, TOA, No. 24,914, pp. 788–90, 810, 876–77, 886–87, 906–907; Hearsey, *The Six Who Were Hanged*, 4, 7; newspaper clipping, in Dallas Calmes Scrapbook; New Orleans *Item*, June 21, 27, 1921, April 3, 1924; New Orleans *States*, May 9, 1924.

7. *State* v. *Rini*, TOA, No. 24,914, pp. 512, 608, 610, 618–19, 633, 661, 791–93, 844–46; Bocchio to Parker, April 24, 1924, in Parker Papers.

retor, the car still ran poorly. The road conditions became worse, and at one point they had to push the Hudson out of a mudhole. Then they took a wrong turn and got lost in a swamp. Finally, they had a flat tire only a few miles outside of Independence. As they fixed it they must have thought that they would never reach Independence under the cover of darkness.

Rini was disgusted, for he thought that they would have to spend the remainder of the night on the road, but Leotta insisted that they drive a half mile farther to the home of a relative. They went to the farmhouse of his cousin, Natale Giamalva, who also knew Deamore from their childhood days in Sicily. When Leotta got out of the car, it was nearly 1:30 Saturday morning, but Deamore and the others still urged him to accompany them into Independence. Wanting no part of their plans, Pietro merely told them the way into town. The six men then drove off toward Independence, and Leotta went inside to tell his cousin what to expect if they returned. Officials would later speculate that they went to Independence to meet other co-conspirators. However, it was equally probable that they went to complete the get-rich scheme they had planned in Deamore's garage.[8]

An hour and a half later, one of Giamalva's neighbors was awakened by the sound of a large automobile traveling on the Robertson Road and then the dead-end lane leading to his farm. He and his wife noticed that the car's headlights were out. Another neighbor, who lived two miles west of Independence, was returning from a dance when he heard a large car coming up the Robertson Road toward Giamalva's place. He, too, thought it strange for an automobile to be on the road at that hour with no headlights. Just as the automobile approached the Giamalva farmhouse, it passed the home of a third neighbor, who was getting ready to round up his workers for the morning bean harvest. He later recalled that there was a "pretty good bunch" in the vehicle without headlights.[9]

At three o'clock Saturday morning, Leona and the others returned to Giamalva's farm, parked the Hudson in a shed, and went

8. *State* v. *Rini*, TOA, No. 24,914, pp. 553, 630–31, 635, 637–41, 653, 846–47, 796–97; New Orleans *Times-Picayune*, May 12, 1921.
9. *State* v. *Rini*, TOA, No. 24,914, pp. 917–21, 924–26, 927–31, 987.

inside. While they ate a hastily prepared meal, Deamore, the only one who knew Giamalva and Leotta, tried to persuade the reluctant pair to help. As they discussed the venture Leotta's ten-year-old son, Joseph, was listening intently from a bedroom. Pietro said he would not go with them, because he feared that there would be bloodshed. The forty-three-year-old Giamalva also wanted no part of their scheme, but Deamore continued to plead for their assistance. Finally, Leotta decided that he would show them the way back to his farm in Hobart, once they were ready to leave Independence, but he again refused to accompany them into town.[10]

After breakfast on Saturday, May 7, the men kept trying to repair the car. Deamore asked Giamalva for his mule and wagon so he could go get oil and gasoline, but Natale refused, saying his mule was too tired. However, soon after lunch, Giamalva used the animal to haul more timber. Apparently, he did not wish to have the men seen in town with his mule and wagon.

After lunch Giamalva's unwanted guests rested, and Deamore visited Frank Pisciotta, a thirty-six-year-old berry farmer who lived across the road. He agreed to loan Deamore his horse and wagon after four o'clock that afternoon. When Deamore returned, Pisciotta insisted that Christmas Giamalva, Natale's thirteen-year-old cousin, go along. Having no choice, Deamore joined Christmas, who drove the wagon by the shed to pick up Rini and Leona. When they arrived in Independence, the small town was bustling with berry farmers selling their crops and cashing their checks at the banks. After purchasing some groceries and the fuel for the Hudson, they stood quietly on a street corner, observing the layout of the town so that they would be familiar with it at night.[11]

They returned to Giamalva's in time for supper, and later that night, Bocchio and Rini went to the shed to finish repairing the car. Using a lantern, Bocchio worked diligently on the carburetor, and by 9:30 he had the Hudson in running order. While they worked, the others milled around the shed, the yard, and the pas-

10. *Ibid.*, 610–12, 619–20, 645–47, 650, 962; New Orleans *Times-Picayune*, May 12, 1921; New Orleans *Item*, May 15, 1921.
11. *State* v. *Rini*, TOA, No. 24,914, pp. 628, 645–49, 668, 848–50, 654, 675–76, 683–88, 694, 800–801, 850–51; Crowell, "Stern Justice Took Six Lives for One," 1–E.

ture, avoiding the house because there was a large gathering of Giamalva's relatives and neighbors.[12]

Just as Bocchio finished with the Hudson, Dallas Calmes, an Independence merchant, closed his restaurant after a busy day. The 1921 season, with a $3.5 million crop, was considered the largest in the parish's berry farming history, and the Calmes family had served numerous customers at their café and at their rambling old hotel two blocks away. The fifty-year-old Calmes was well known and respected throughout the parish. He was especially popular with the Italians in Independence. Calmes and his wife Bessie had three children, and the family lived in the hotel. However, on Saturday night, May 7, the Calmeses were too tired to go home, and they decided to sleep in a back room partitioned off from the dining room. Getting into bed, Mrs. Calmes noticed that the inside lights of the Farmers and Merchants Bank were on, which was the normal custom.[13]

As the Calmeses retired for the night, Deamore and his cohorts prepared to leave for Independence. As they drove out, Giamalva eagerly opened the gate for them, but they stopped for a moment to remind him that they would return to pick up Pietro and Joe Leotta. They then left for Independence. Giamalva's neighbor, who the night before had seen a large car without headlights, was putting his horse and buggy in the barn. Thinking that he heard the same car, he stopped and looked toward the road. He saw a large automobile with no headlights stop five hundred yards east of Giamalva's farm. For five or ten minutes the car remained parked on the road, equidistant from Giamalva's and Pisciotta's. The neighbor watched with suspicion, but he later recalled seeing no one leave or enter the vehicle. Then the automobile sped off toward town.

An hour and a half later, a large automobile with no headlights entered Independence and proceeded down Fifth Street. Within one block of the railroad, the driver turned and parked the car so it was facing west. The occupants of the vehicle did not get out im-

12. *State* v. *Rini*, TOA, No. 24,914, pp. 649–50, 662, 669, 676–77, 803, 851–52.
13. *Ibid.*, 252, 287, 696; New Orleans *Times-Picayune*, May 9, June 15, 1921; New Orleans *Item*, May 9, 1921, May 4, 1924; Hammond *Vindicator*, May 14, 1943; newspaper clippings, in Dallas Calmes Scrapbook; Baiamonte, "Immigrants in Rural America," 128; interview with Dallas Calmes, Jr., April 7, 1980.

mediately. They waited patiently for the opportune moment to put their plans into action.[14] It was nearly 12:30 A.M. Sunday, May 8, and Independence was quiet. Nothing appeared to be unusual, except that the lights in the Farmers and Merchants Bank were now off. A block south of the bank, the large automobile was still parked.

Next to the bank, the Calmeses were asleep in the back of their restaurant. But Mrs. Calmes was awakened by the sound of a plank being pulled from the fence in the alley. She tried to make herself believe that she had imagined the sound. However, a short while later, she heard the same noise. Then she saw a man enter the alley quickly, pass the center of the yard, and go past the bank. Through the window, Mrs. Calmes saw a man creeping around their chicken coop. Finally, she shook her husband, but she steadfastly kept her eyes on the intruder.

Having had recent problems with chicken thieves, Dallas took out his .32 Colt automatic. He paused at the locked screen door and peered into the dark alley. Calmes then ran out into the yard. As Mrs. Calmes reached the door she heard her husband shout, "Halt there! Halt there!" His commands were lost in the sounds of gunfire.

The shooting was so fierce that smoke filled the yard and alley, and Bessie was barely able to see her husband as she ran to his side. "Oh, darling, I'm shot," said Dallas, as he fell to his knees. He fired two more rounds and dropped the Colt. He wanted her to take him back inside the restaurant, but she could not move him. She screamed for help.[15]

Hearing the gunshots, Lem Hoggatt, the town's night watchman, thought they meant that there was a fire on the back streets of Independence. When he got there, what he saw with the aid of a streetlight was a man running from the alley. Rather than pursue him, Hoggatt went to Mrs. Calmes.

As neighbors arrived at the restaurant other Independence resi-

14. *State* v. *Rini*, TOA, No. 24,914, pp. 621–23, 647–48, 664–67, 670–72, 689–92, 720, 735–37, 950–59; Bocchio to Parker, April 24, 1924, in Parker Papers.
15. *State* v. *Rini*, TOA, No. 24,914, pp. 265, 268, 271–72, 274, 287–89, 735–37; newspaper clipping, in Dallas Calmes Scrapbook; New Orleans *Times-Picayune*, May 9, 1922, May 8, 1924; Bocchio to Parker, April 24, 1924, in Parker Papers.

dents saw two men fleeing from the scene. An Italian teenager later recalled that a man, wearing a dark suit, a white shirt, and a cap, ran west past his home. The town's night telephone operator also saw two men running from the alley. Elsewhere down Fifth Street, a resident saw a man, wearing a dark suit and hat, running down the banquette. Behind the man was a car, traveling very fast with no headlights. As the car passed, the driver turned the lights on to locate the man. Less than fifty yards farther west down Fifth Street, the car slowed down and the man ran alongside it. He jumped inside, and the car sped off without headlights toward the Robertson Road. The whole sequence took less than three minutes. Despite all the eyewitnesses, no one would later be able to make a positive identification of the men seen that night.[16]

While residents witnessed the escape, Dr. Anthony J. Strange arrived and gave Calmes a quick examination and an injection, though he knew that there was little chance of survival. At 12 : 55 A.M., Dallas Calmes died. A coroner's inquest later that morning revealed that Calmes was struck by two bullets. One hit the inside of the right leg, traveled up through the muscles, and exited through the right buttock. The second bullet, which caused the death, entered the abdomen, penetrated the liver, and exited from the lower part of the back.[17]

When Dallas Calmes, Jr., reached the scene, his mother was hysterical. She kept repeating how she had seen a man shoot her husband. Leo "Roy" Calmes, the twenty-eight-year-old nephew of Dallas, later recalled that he asked his aunt who shot his uncle, but she replied that she didn't know. Roy Calmes then went outside to search for clues. As he combed the area, two local residents made their way through the crowd toward him. One said that they had seen a man jump in a car going west out of town. When the car was described as large and high-powered, Roy decided to borrow the "specially-equipped" Ford owned by Tom "Big Foot" Candiotta. Having gathered an unofficial posse, Roy and Big Foot sped off down the Robertson Road. Candiotta, an expert driver, adroitly

16. *State* v. *Rini*, TOA, No. 24,914, pp. 259–62, 268–71, 288–90, 292, 295–96, 298–310, 324–30, 717–19, 732–34.
17. *Ibid.*, 53, 246–51, 256.

maneuvered the Ford over rough spots in the road while the others looked ahead for the large automobile. Then they saw some tire tracks that went south toward the town of Albany.

It was nearly 2:30 Sunday morning when they finally spotted a car in Livingston Parish twelve miles from Independence. They gained on the vehicle, and then the driver pulled over and parked. Candiotta negotiated a curve in the road, and he and the others could see the car perfectly. As they rode past they saw the driver, an average-sized man wearing a sweater and a cap. Driving his Ford about a quarter of a mile farther, Candiotta crossed a bridge to the top of a small hill and stopped.

The posse walked back down the road. They listened for conversations from the vehicle, but they heard nothing at first. Then the stillness was broken by three loud blasts of a car horn. Calmes whispered that he thought it was a signal for the suspects to return to the car. The quietness of the dark countryside returned momentarily. Then there was a whistle, followed shortly by the slamming of car doors. Candiotta ordered the posse to push a big log across the road. But as they tried they saw the headlights. Big Foot shouted for them to hurry because it would take the car only an instant to cross the bridge.

"Halt!" demanded Calmes, stepping into the path of the automobile. The driver did not attempt to stop, and three men inside shot at Calmes from both sides of the vehicle. Blinded by the lights, Roy dropped to the roadside unharmed and fired twice at the car. He shot three more rounds wildly, but then his gun was empty. Another posse member fired a round of buckshot into the car, but that did not stop the vehicle either.

As the car passed, the driver lowered his head to dodge the shots. When he hit the brakes to avoid the log, the car pulled sharply to the right, and the front wheels went into the ditch. Four men, firing their weapons continuously, immediately jumped out of the right side of the car, and two ran across a pasture. They dropped their empty weapons and ran into the woods. Another suspect, carrying a valise, was also seen escaping. Since the headlights of both vehicles had remained on during the shoot-out, the posse saw a fourth man escaping over a barbed-wire fence. When the suspect became entangled, a posse member fired his shotgun. But the man managed to run into the darkness of the woods.

Silence again prevailed over the countryside north of Albany. As the posse approached the car Calmes saw another man in the back seat. Since they were without ammunition, Calmes warned, they were in danger. The posse moved back into the shadows of the woods and listened to someone in the car talking in Italian.[18]

As Calmes and his party sat at the side of the road near Albany, Tangipahoa Sheriff Lem Bowden conducted his initial investigation of the murder of Dallas Calmes. The thirty-nine-year-old sheriff, who had been in office since June, 1920, arrived at the murder scene around 2:15 Sunday morning. Searching the alley and the yard, he paid particular attention to the bullet holes in the kitchen wall, in the wheelbarrow, and in an oil tank near the fence beyond the back door. Bowden was especially interested in the seemingly different directions of the numerous bullet holes.[19]

While Bowden was at work, Roy Calmes and some members of the posse obtained arms and ammunition from the Albany postmaster. Calmes then called Bowden, who ordered Roy to leave someone in Albany to show him exactly where the suspects' car was.

At daybreak, Harvey Stewart, a local farmer, approached the vehicle cautiously. He heard three men and a little boy speaking in Italian, and he continued toward the car. Two of the men walked away quickly, and Stewart saw their small revolvers. He began to talk about the shoot-out with an older man and a little boy, whom he later identified in court as Pietro and Joseph Leotta.[20]

Shortly after Stewart left, Calmes returned. He now heard someone thrashing about inside the car. Thinking an armed man was in the vehicle, the posse walked nervously toward it. Then the Leottas got out of the car. When Roy showed his gun, Pietro quickly raised his hands. The posse searched the car thoroughly but found

18. *Ibid.*, 282–84, 334–39, 341–42, 346–50, 537–46, 572–77, 612–16, 719–26, 747–52, 759; New Orleans *Times-Picayune*, May 11, 1922, May 4–6, 1924; Dallas L. Calmes, Jr., to John M. Parker, n.d., Bocchio to Parker, April 24, 1924, both in Parker Papers; Ponchatoula *Enterprise*, May 13, 1921.
19. *State* v. *Rini*, TOA, No. 24,914, pp. 251, 257, 262, 264, 267, 278, 281, 623.
20. *Ibid.*, 537–46, 575–77; New Orleans *Item*, June 12, 1921.

no one else. In the immediate area, however, they found dynamite fuses and caps, nitroglycerine, something that looked like soap, and a ball of cotton hidden in a culvert. The posse concentrated on questioning Pietro, who was terrified. Calmes grabbed him by the collar and demanded to know who else had been in the car, insisting that Pietro was one of the "Dagoes" they were tracking. But Candiotta was quick to reply that he was positive that Leotta was not one of the murderers. Pietro continued to act as if he were not comprehending the conversation, and Roy, finally losing his patience, hit Pietro several times with the palm of his hand. Leotta said only that he and his son had been near Independence picking strawberries. Roy decided that "stronger medicine" was necessary. He picked up an oak limb and struck Pietro's head. But Leotta still refused to answer. Calmes gave him a much harder blow with the limb and was about to hit him again, when Pietro finally identified himself. Candiotta asked Leotta who else was in the car, but Pietro claimed that he did not know them. Seeing about eight or ten carloads of men arrive with the sheriff, Candiotta announced that he was sure that Leotta would now cooperate.[21]

After being told what was going on, Sheriff Bowden said that he would indeed "encourage" Leotta to talk. The sheriff grabbed Pietro, laid him across a log, and placed his foot on Pietro's throat. Two other men beat him savagely. Thinking that the sheriff's posse was about to murder his father, Joe shouted that he would answer their questions if they stopped beating his father. Lem Hoggatt took the boy aside to question him. As Joe told what he knew, Hoggatt feverishly wrote down the account, especially the names of those riding in the car.

Despite Joe's cooperation, Bowden's men continued to beat Pietro for at least five minutes. When he did speak, hardly anyone understood him because he was speaking in Italian and English. Finally, Leotta admitted that there were six men, himself, and his son in the car. Pietro told Bowden that although he rode with them from his home in Hobart to Independence, he did not know their names. Waiting a short while, Bowden returned to question

---

21. *State* v. *Rini*, TOA, No. 24,914, pp. 340, 347, 624–26, 722, 728–29, 753–55; New Orleans *Times-Picayune*, May 6, 7, 1924.

Leotta, but Pietro still refused to give the names. Pietro again was punched and kicked senseless. The second beating did not last long, because Leotta finally shouted that he now recalled some of the names. Since Leotta's English was poor, an Italian from Independence acted as interpreter. Admitting that he knew only one of the six men, Natale Deamore, Pietro said he knew the others by first names only. Without any more intimidation, Leotta related what had happened at Giamalva's farm. When Bowden again pressured Leotta for the full names of all six men, Pietro told him to ask Natale Giamalva and Frank Pisciotta. Believing that Leotta was now probably telling the truth, Bowden issued an order for his deputies in Tangipahoa to arrest the two men.

Some of the posse searched the Hudson and the surrounding woods and pastures and found numerous rounds of ammunition, four new revolvers of various calibers, a .30-.30 rifle, and a sawed-off shotgun. Furthermore, inside the car were several items that could be used to make duplicate keys and some tempered-steel drills. In the glove compartment was a paper which showed that the car belonged to Leon Prestia of New Orleans, and Bowden immediately ordered a deputy to phone the New Orleans Police Department with a request that they arrest Prestia.[22]

While Bowden interrogated Leotta, a Livingston Parish sheriff's deputy, on his way back to the scene of the shoot-out early that morning, saw a stranger walking along the Albany Road. Offering him a ride, the lawman continued toward Albany. As they neared the small town, the hitchhiker said that his name was Natale Deamore. The officer saw that his passenger had one pistol in his inside coat pocket and another one stuffed partially under his clothing. The deputy immediately took both weapons without a struggle. Since there had been trouble nearby, he said, he would have to deliver Deamore to the sheriff.

When they reached Albany, the deputy handcuffed Deamore and tied his feet with rope. As they waited for Sheriff Bowden, a crowd gathered about Deamore. A short while later, Lem Hoggatt

---

22. *State* v. *Rini*, TOA, No. 24,914, pp. 343–46, 350–58, 368–70, 624–26, 705–706, 754–57, 770–73; Calmes to Parker, n.d., in Parker Papers; New Orleans *States*, June 25, 1921, May 1, 1924; New Orleans *Times-Picayune*, May 6–7, 1924; New Orleans *Item*, May 11, 1921.

arrived and questioned Deamore about the Calmes murder. Natale insisted that he knew nothing. Deamore later testified that during Hoggatt's questioning, members of the crowd threatened to hang him and to shoot him.

Not satisfied with Deamore's answers, Hoggatt decided that Sheriff Bowden should question him. So he ordered Deamore to get in a nearby car. Having difficulty because of his bound feet, Natale became angry, turned, faced Hoggatt, and said, "God damn, son of a bitch." A deputy punched Natale's head, and Hoggatt struck Deamore across the forehead with his revolver. With blood pouring down his face and onto his clothing, Natale got in the back seat and screamed out in pain. He repeatedly said that they had the "wrong man."

Hoggatt then ordered Natale to hold his head outside the car so that no blood would fall on the seats. Deamore did as he was told because Hoggatt threatened to strike him again. He rode that way for the next couple of miles, and Natale's profuse bleeding covered the car door. As they drove away from Albany, Deamore feared for his life. Three months later he would testify that the occupants of the car repeatedly threatened to stop and hang him from the nearest tree.

Three and a half miles north of Albany, Hoggatt joined Bowden's party and continued toward Amite. A short while later the entourage, believing that they had spotted the other suspects in the woods, stopped to search the area. Charles Pulliam, a member of the posse, left the woods after a few minutes to question Deamore. Blood oozing from the wound over his left eye, Natale became excited. "You see what they got me into, the dirty crooks," he said. "I hope you all catch them. You ought to go see where they killed a man, the dirty son of a bitches."

Bowden, who was standing nearby, finally walked over to question Natale for the first time, but Deamore was still excited. When the sheriff asked a question, Natale spoke rapidly and tried to give Bowden lots of details. The sheriff finally requested only yes or no, but Deamore continued to give long, complicated statements. Losing his temper, Bowden struck Deamore's face with an open hand and repeated his questions. When Natale again did not comply, Bowden struck his face repeatedly. Finally, Deamore told

Bowden that Giglio and Leona's address was 1601 Tulane Avenue in New Orleans. At Bowden's order, a deputy telephoned the New Orleans Police Department, asking that several officers be dispatched to the address. After Bowden finished questioning Deamore, he decided to take him and the Leottas to the Amite jail, where Giamalva and Pisciotta had been since their arrest earlier that morning.[23]

As Bowden traveled toward Amite, residents of Ponchatoula spotted three men, later identified as Bocchio, Leona, and Giglio, north of the train station around noon. Just as the trio approached Ponchatoula, Ed Tucker, the town's chief of police, received a phone call from the sheriff's office about the murder in Independence. Having a hunch that the suspects might be in the area, Tucker immediately got in his car and drove around Ponchatoula. When he reached the railroad tracks, he spotted Bocchio walking alone and ordered him to raise his hands. Tucker asked Bocchio where he was going, and Joe replied that he was on the way to visit a cousin south of the depot. But the police chief responded that there were "no Dagoes allowed down here." After Tucker put him in his car, Bocchio said that he worked for a farmer three miles east of Hammond. But Tucker was skeptical, especially since Bocchio could not recall the man's name. After traveling a few miles toward Hammond, Bocchio admitted that he had not been employed by anyone in the area.

Tucker, who suspected that Bocchio had been lying before his admission, continued toward Hammond. However, just before he left Ponchatoula, the chief called Independence to report that he thought he had captured one of the murder suspects. Roy Calmes, who had returned home, took the phone call and realized that if Tucker brought a prisoner through Independence on the way to Amite, there might be a lynching. When Calmes returned to Independence just before noon, he found the streets filled with tense and angry men from nearby towns, parishes, and counties in Mississippi. Whenever there was a rumor that the captured suspects

23. *State* v. *Rini*, TOA, No. 24,914, pp. 371–73, 864–65, 362–66, 393–96, 400–406, 766–70, 854–56, 355–57, 376–91, 397–98, 491–97, 544, 398–99, 771–72, 868, 651, 677, 681, 527–36; New Orleans *States*, April 29, 1924; New Orleans *Times-Picayune*, May 7, 1924.

were in a certain section of town, the angry crowd surged in that direction with shouts of "Let's hang them, every one of them!"

Calmes decided to stop Tucker before he reached Independence. When he met the chief in Hammond, they agreed that the situation was volatile. Tucker brought Bocchio through the back roads of the parish to the Amite jail, where Bowden now had in custody Giamalva, the Leottas, Pisciotta, and Deamore, who continued to incriminate himself and the others by repeating how "those crooks" killed a man.

When local officials assured the mob that several of the suspects were now safely in the Amite jail, the angry crowds dissipated. Although the likelihood of a lynching had lessened, Bowden and his deputies knew that their work was not nearly complete because other suspects remained at large.[24]

24. New Orleans *Times-Picayune*, May 7–8, 1924; *State* v. *Rini*, TOA, No. 24,914, pp. 342–43, 527–32, 866.

3

Please, Oh Please, Mister

Two patrolmen, Jacob Uhle and Joseph Horton, arrived at 1601 Tulane Avenue around 7:30 P.M. Sunday, May 8. When they found that Giglio and Leona were not in their room, they waited outside on the street. Just before 11:00, they saw a car occupied by three men stop at Deamore's garage, several houses down from where they were parked, and one of the men spoke to Mrs. Deamore. As the car drove off, the patrolmen wrote down the license number.

A short while later, two men approached the rooming house at 1601 Tulane Avenue. When they reached their room, Horton and Uhle rushed the pair and grabbed them. Neither man resisted—both appeared to be exhausted. They were dressed in overalls and caps and were covered with mud.

As they walked to the First Precinct Station, six blocks away, the two men identified themselves as Joseph Giglio and Roy Leona. During questioning, Giglio and Leona told the policemen only that they had been hunting in St. Bernard Parish at a friend's farm, but neither man could give an exact location.[1]

At the precinct station, the patrolmen gave Assistant District Attorney Thomas Craven a letter found in Giglio's pockets. It was addressed to Giglio at 903 St. Maurice Street. Craven, who was in charge of the Calmes investigation, was looking into Leona's and Giglio's background at Sheriff Bowden's request. He decided to search the premises. When Craven and the officers arrived there early Monday morning, they learned that Giglio and several other men had mail delivered to the address but that all mail was picked up by Mrs. Leonardo Cipolla of 843 Tupelo Street.

Since Tupelo was only a few blocks away, Craven decided to

1. New Orleans *Times-Picayune*, May 10, 15, 1921; New Orleans *Item*, May 9, 15, 1921; New Orleans *States*, May 15, 1921; *State* v. *Rini*, TOA, No. 24,914, pp. 506–507, 510–12, 570–72, 580–83.

question the woman. As they approached the home, Craven and the officers saw two men sitting in a Ford parked in front. The license number was, a patrolman said, the same one they had seen near Deamore's garage. Walking up to the car, an officer shoved the man sitting behind the wheel, and he fell onto the dashboard. The other man did not respond. The men had been killed by shotgun blasts to the head. On one of the bodies were some cards bearing the name of Joseph Rini and a .32 Colt revolver. The right side of the vehicle was riddled with buckshot and bullet holes, as was the Cipolla home.

Inside the house, there was clothing all over the floor and hanging out of the bureau and armoire drawers. The general disarray suggested that Leonardo Cipolla and his wife had recently left in some haste. The police also found four stolen license plates. And in a shed were fourteen barrels of homemade wine, several gallons of whiskey, and a number of tires.[2]

Making no connection at first between the Tangipahoa case and this double murder in New Orleans, Craven returned to headquarters to question Giglio and Leona. Giglio later testified that during his interrogation, he was beaten unconscious with a blackjack. Leona testified that Craven held him by the throat while patrolmen Uhle and Horton beat him.

Rini and Lamantia were still at large in Livingston Parish, where local authorities were assisting Tangipahoa lawmen. Walking in circles, Rini and Lamantia had spent all day Sunday trying to find their way back to New Orleans. Early Monday morning they attempted to get a drink of water at a farmhouse, but they were shot at by a suspicious farmer. Within a few minutes, Sheriff Bowden and several deputies with bloodhounds were chasing them through a swamp near Albany. Rini and Lamantia were finally discovered huddled in a brier patch. The deputies searched Lamantia and found a telegram addressed to him in care of the St. Maurice Street address.

Then a member of the posse pulled off some of Rini's clothing and cut strips to tie him up. By this time a large crowd had gath-

2. New Orleans *Times-Picayune*, May 10, 1921; New Orleans *Item*, May 9, 15, 1921.

ered from the nearby communities, and the situation was becoming serious. Apparently the crowd interpreted the deputies' actions as an invitation to abuse the prisoners. Someone in the crowd drew a knife and cut off Lamantia's clothes. Another person struck Rini and Lamantia with a double-barreled shotgun, and someone else hit them in the ribs. Somebody yelled, "Let's shoot the Dagoes right here!" A state prison official finally demanded that the two not be harmed. It was the opinion of most at the scene that had the officer not spoken when he did, there would have been a lynching. Of course, had the suspects been black they would have probably been hanged, even if the lawmen had interceded on their behalf.

Bowden realized that it was safer to take Rini and Lamantia to New Orleans via the state capital than through Tangipahoa Parish. So they were taken back to Albany to wait for the next train to Baton Rouge.[3]

While Rini and Lamantia were on the train Monday morning, the New Orleans police returned to Cipolla's home. Leonardo Cipolla, reputedly the New Orleans Mafia chieftain, was thirty-eight and a native of Palermo. Having lived in Brooklyn, Cipolla had moved to New Orleans in 1917 and become a "dealer and peddler" in Italian produce. Now there was a citywide search for him and his wife. Although Cipolla's house yielded no clues to his whereabouts, Craven did find some clothing, which Giglio later identified as his, a trunk belonging to Giglio, several more business cards with Rini's name written in pencil, and stolen car plates. Craven thought that he had conclusively linked Giglio to the city's Mafia leader and the New Orleans double murder.[4]

Later that Monday morning, while Joe Leotta remained in protective custody in Amite, Deamore, Pietro Leotta, Giamalva, Bocchio, and Pisciotta finally arrived at police headquarters in New Orleans. On Sunday afternoon, because of the mobs in Tangi-

3. *State* v. *Rini*, TOA, No. 24,914, pp. 422–24, 441, 518–604, 806–808, 822–23, 825, 884, 945; New Orleans *Times-Picayune*, May 10–11, 1921, May 7, 1924; New Orleans *States*, May 10, 1921; New Orleans *Item*, May 4, 9, 1921.

4. *State* v. *Rini*, TOA, No. 24,914, pp. 935–37, 939, 944; newspaper clipping, in Dallas Calmes Scrapbook; New Orleans *Item*, May 15, 1921; New Orleans *Times-Picayune*, May 10, 1924.

pahoa Parish, prominent citizens and a district court judge had urged that the men be moved to a safer jail. The deputies and Brittain B. Purser, an Amite attorney, had escorted the prisoners to a train. They rode to Jackson, Mississippi, then back to Baton Rouge, and into New Orleans.

Craven was especially happy to see Deamore—an informant had said that Deamore, one of the intended victims of the double murder, had information about the killings. By this time, the dead men had been identified as Joseph Gaeto, a twenty-seven-year-old former garage mechanic employed by Deamore, and Dominick DiGiovanni, a twenty-six-year-old stevedore. Craven decided to focus his investigation on Natale Deamore. For a short while, though, he left Deamore alone.[5]

Craven tried to determine what the other suspects knew about the double murder. Taking Leona to the morgue to identify the bodies of Gaeto and DiGiovanni, Craven, according to Leona's testimony, said: "I am going to take you to see two men that I shot last night, Sunday. Maybe I'm going to do you just the same." Craven asked Leona whether he could provide the victims' names, and Leona replied that he only knew one of the men. Craven allegedly grabbed Roy by the back of the neck and shoved his face into the face of one of the dead men. Leona later testified that he was taken back to headquarters, where Craven and New Orleans police officers beat him on the chest with a blackjack.

Craven tried desperately to connect the Calmes killing and the Gaeto-DiGiovanni murders. For the rest of Monday morning, he paraded Deamore, Giglio, and Bocchio to the morgue. When Deamore arrived, the coroner was performing an autopsy on DiGiovanni. Natale nevertheless identified the bodies—Gaeto, his former mechanic, and DiGiovanni, a friend. Deamore later testified that after the trip to the morgue, Craven threatened to kill him if he did not tell the truth about his part in the three slayings. In addition, he recalled that while he was being transferred to

5. *State* v. *Rini*, TOA, No. 24,914, pp. 416–19, 435–36, 461, 610, 652–53; New Orleans *Times-Picayune*, May 9, 10, 1921, May 7, 1924; Ponchatoula *Enterprise*, May 13, 1921; newspaper clipping, in Dallas Calmes Scrapbook; New Orleans *Item*, May 15, 1921.

a solitary cell in an uptown precinct, the police threatened him again with hanging if he did not cooperate with Craven.

Giglio also charged the assistant district attorney with brutality. He claimed that after his visit to the morgue, Craven grabbed him by the neck and punched him senseless during questioning. And when he failed to give satisfactory answers, Giglio said, Uhle, Horton, and Craven took turns knocking him unconscious. Giglio's recollection was that one officer told him to start praying, because they were going to hang him.

When Rini and Lamantia, who Craven later believed were hired gunmen from Chicago, arrived at police headquarters at 9:00 P.M. Monday, May 9, the assistant district attorney began questioning the pair right away.

"Andrea Lamantia, 22 [*sic*], of 26 Wabash Avenue, Chicago," said Lamantia, who was still handcuffed. He said he arrived in New Orleans at 11:00 P.M. on Saturday from Chicago, and he steadfastly denied knowing Leonardo Cipolla. When questioned about the Independence murder, Andrea protested, "I never killed a man. I never rob a bank. I don't know nothin' 'bout it. If they hang me, they hang an honest man."

Craven took Lamantia from the interrogation room, which was filled with reporters, into a nearby detective's office to question him privately. Andrea later claimed that Craven, Uhle, and Horton choked and punched him into unconsciousness. The reporters heard Lamantia proclaim his innocence and saw him in tears as he was led to his cell.

Then Craven called for Joseph Rini. When Rini arrived in the room, he was calm but sullen. Craven asked for his name and address. The response was "Joseph Rini, 1150 Milton Avenue, Chicago." Asked about his recent travels, Rini, too, lied about how he arrived in New Orleans.

"Do you know Leonardo Cipolla?" asked Craven.

"Never heard the name before."

"And you never heard of Leonardo Cipolla?" insisted Craven, who was trying to connect Rini with the city's reputed Mafia leader.

"No. I told you I never heard that name," said Rini.

"Then explain this," Craven said as he handed Rini the card found at Cipolla's. "That card I found myself in Cipolla's house in front of which the two men were murdered. And yet you say you never heard of Cipolla?"

"No," replied Rini, nervously twisting his cap. "I never heard of him before. I don't know him."[6]

Just as Rini left the office, the telephone rang. The message was that Cipolla could be found in a barn on an old plantation in St. Bernard Parish. The New Orleans police went there and found instead a stolen car and license plates that belonged to Vito Di Giorgio, the former Black Hander and reputed *mafioso* who was thought to be in California. Craven was convinced that he had uncovered another branch of the Mafia controlled by Cipolla and now specializing in bootlegging and car theft. His investigation became a nationwide search. Craven also believed that if Cipolla was not captured, there would be further bloodshed. On Tuesday morning, May 10, the New Orleans *Times-Picayune* carried the headline "Vendetta Feared." Both the *Times-Picayune* and *States* explained that officials were afraid of more assassinations in connection with the Gaeto-DiGiovanni murders and the killing of Dallas Calmes.[7]

Later Tuesday afternoon, Craven decided to question Lamantia again, but Andrea refused to talk. He later claimed that during the questioning, Craven held him by the throat and choked him every time he refused to answer a question.

Unable to obtain information from Lamantia, Leona, Giglio, Rini, and Bocchio, Craven believed that his only hope was Deamore. Natale would surely talk if he believed that Gaeto and DiGiovanni were murdered as a result of betrayal by the five men who accompanied him to Independence.

Shortly before four o'clock on Tuesday afternoon, Natale sent a message that he wanted to speak to the assistant district attorney. After nearly two days of solitary confinement in a dark cell, Dea-

6. *State* v. *Rini*, TOA, No. 24,914, pp. 416–17, 425, 438–39, 441, 444, 457–59, 465–70, 473–74, 903, 992–94; New Orleans *States*, May 10, 13, 1921; New Orleans *Times-Picayune*, May 10, 1921; New Orleans *Item*, May 10, 15, 1921.

7. New Orleans *States* and New Orleans *Item*, May 10, 1921; New Orleans *Times-Picayune*, May 10–11, 1921; newspaper clipping, in Dallas Calmes Scrapbook.

more was ready to talk. When Natale arrived at police headquarters, he appeared to be so frightened that his face seemed greenish gray. Natale was a large man with an olive complexion, brown eyes, and a heavy shock of black hair. His nails were black and broken from his work as a mechanic.

"Please, oh please, mister, don't let anybody know I tell you," said Natale to Craven. "Don't let the newspapers know. I fear for my life. If I tell, they get me."

Craven then granted his request for a private meeting. The assistant district attorney assured Natale that he would keep his conversation out of the papers, but Craven had no intention of keeping his promise.

Deamore explained that the "five crooks" asked him to accompany them to Independence on Friday, May 6, because they needed a mechanic. Craven was immediately suspicious—he thought that Giglio was also a capable mechanic. Deamore again lost credibility when he denied knowing who owned the Hudson; Craven already had evidence that the car belonged to one of Natale's customers. According to Deamore, two of the "five crooks," whom he did not identify, threatened his life on Saturday if he did not keep quiet about their plans. He admitted going into Independence on Saturday evening but claimed that he was forced out of the car because they knew he was an honest man. Finally, Deamore related how he was arrested in Albany as he wandered in the woods, hoping to come out near a train station. When Craven asked whether he could identify the "five crooks," Deamore said yes, but he would be afraid.

Since Bocchio was in the hospital suffering from appendicitis, he was not brought to police headquarters to be identified by Deamore. Although Giglio, Leotta, Rini, Lamantia, Leona, Pisciotta, and Giamalva were sent to the superintendent's office, Craven was mainly interested in the four who accompanied Deamore to Independence. When he asked them privately whether they knew Natale, they all denied everything.

Craven brought Deamore into the superintendent's office. The prosecutor wanted to be sure that Natale would not change his mind, so he repeated in gruesome detail the murder of his two friends, Gaeto and DiGiovanni. Craven immediately achieved the

39

result he wanted. Deamore, pointing a trembling finger at each man, identified Leona, Giglio, Rini, and Lamantia as the men he accompanied to Giamalva's and Independence.

As Deamore spoke, Giglio interrupted and claimed that Natale was only trying to get out of trouble himself. Twitching his eyebrows and glaring, Rini tried to signal a message to one of his friends. Rini said nothing, but Leona started to cry. "He is trying to get us in it," he said, "and get himself out of it."

When Deamore pointed to Lamantia, Andrea became pale with anger. "You louse! Oh you goddamn louse!" Lamantia leaped at Deamore's throat. Shouting murderously in Italian, he was restrained by two detectives. "Where you know me? Where you see me? What's my name?" yelled Andrea. "What's my name? You lousy son-of-a-bitch! I'll get you. You want to ruin me. I got a wife and two [*sic*] children in [Brooklyn]."

Craven then turned Deamore's attention to Rini, who was still quiet. "Did you ever see this man before?" Craven asked Rini.

"I never saw him," Rini said softly.

"What you tell a lie for?" shouted Deamore.

"You try to do me harm," Rini replied angrily, and muttered Italian curses. Rini's manacled hands shook.

"I try to do all you people harm," said Deamore. "You get me in bad. I try to get you in bad. You was in the automobile, and you go in the wagon for gasoline."

At this point Rini rushed toward Deamore, but he was stopped by a detective. "He's a liar," Rini shouted, "the lousy bastard! I never saw him before!" Detectives struggled to lead him from the room. "You louse!" he shouted. "You try to get me, huh? I'll—" Rini swore in Italian and then yelled, "I don't know you, you bastard. You know I don't know you. I never saw you."

"What you want to lie to me for?" retorted Deamore. "You know me. You know me goddamn well. You know me! You try to get me, huh? I'm gonna get you and get all you nasty people."

The actions of Rini, Lamantia, Giglio, and Leona undoubtedly confirmed Deamore's suspicions that they had betrayed him and had probably killed Gaeto and DiGiovanni. Obviously pleased that his ploy had worked, Craven listened to Natale as he gave more evidence on the "five crooks." Speaking freely, Deamore finally identified Anthony Prestia and his son Leon as the owners of the Hudson and Bocchio as the driver. He now claimed that they went to Independence to buy some grapes and land, but he said he had gone to Independence on Saturday afternoon with Leona and Rini solely to survey the town and bank building that they were to rob.

After Deamore finished his version, Craven allowed him to confront Leotta, Pisciotta, and Giamalva, who were probably ready to help in the prosecution of the case. Deamore identified Leotta and Giamalva as the farmers in Independence in whose house they stayed overnight. Both men began to shout that they did not know about the plans to rob the bank. Calling Deamore several derogatory names in English and Italian, Giamalva protested his innocence vigorously. Pisciotta added that he knew nothing about the attempted bank robbery or the murder of Calmes. Finally, Leotta insisted that Deamore was the gang's leader.[8]

Craven had had a successful day. He had skillfully created suspicion and doubt between Deamore and the "five crooks" and between Deamore and Giamalva, Pisciotta, and Leotta. Craven probably knew that the dissension between the former group would not last. Therefore, he began to concentrate on building his case around the possibility of Giamalva and the others as state witnesses.

8. *State* v. *Rini*, TOA, No. 24,914, pp. 408–13, 422, 429–30, 433–34, 469–70, 478–82, 552–53; New Orleans *Item*, New Orleans *Times-Picayune*, and New Orleans *States*, May 11, 1921; newspaper clipping, in Dallas Calmes Scrapbook.

4

You Make Mistake

On Wednesday, May 11, officers at the First Precinct Station began the day quietly. However, while sandwiches and coffee were being served to the prisoners, there was an attempt to establish communication with friends on the outside through the owners of the Hudson, Anthony Prestia and his son, Leon, who were in a nearby cell.

Giglio asked the jailer to take his sandwich to Anthony Prestia. The jailer instead took it out to the clerk's office. The note inside requested a lawyer and assistance from Giglio's uncle in Brooklyn. After finding the message, the police searched all cells. Under Giglio's blanket, they discovered another note, this one on a piece of cardboard, which asked for aid from George Gulotta, a New Orleans attorney.

When Sheriff Bowden was informed about the incident, he requested that the Orleans authorities keep the prisoners apart so that they could not collaborate on a defense. The New Orleans police placed them in three separate precinct stations for the remainder of the week.[1]

Later that Wednesday morning, Sheriff Bowden and District Attorney Matt J. Allen of Tangipahoa arrived in New Orleans with Joe Leotta, Pietro's son. Hoping that Joe would identify the six men who had picked up his father in Hobart, Tangipahoa authorities ushered the boy into the superintendent's office. He was a small child and was dressed in baggy blue overalls. Sitting in a large chair, Joe laughed and joked with the detectives, other officials, and reporters. Appearing to be conscious of his major role in

1. New Orleans *Times-Picayune*, May 11, 12, 1921; New Orleans *Item*, May 11, 13, 1921; New Orleans *States*, May 11, 13, June 23, 1921; newspaper clippings, in Dallas Calmes Scrapbook; *State* v. *Rini et al.*, Original Brief, p. 95, in TOA, No. 24,914.

the investigation, Joe replied succinctly and often in good English. But he unwittingly revealed a presumption of his father's implication in the attempted robbery, though not an actual participation. Joe told how Lamantia and the others tried to force his father and Giamalva to go with them to rob the bank in Independence. Although he said that his father refused, Joe also stated that his father and Giamalva agreed to explain the route to Independence and the exact location of the bank.

When the suspects were brought in, Joe could not identify Giglio, who breathed a sigh of relief. However, when Lamantia entered the room, Joe shouted, "Oh! That's George." Lamantia frowned and looked concerned, but he said nothing. The police were aware that Joe knew one of the men as George. It was this man who supposedly urged Joe's father and Giamalva to rob the bank.

When Deamore, Leona, and Rini entered the room, Joe Leotta identified them as the other members of the gang. Law-enforcement officials were impressed by the boy's emphatic identifications. Joe appeared not to be intimidated, and his performance Wednesday morning convinced Bowden and the others that he would make an excellent material witness. The officials were so appreciative, they stuffed his pockets with change and bought him ice cream and cake.[2]

Then Tangipahoa and Orleans officials decided to proceed on Craven's hunch that the boy's father and Natale Giamalva were ready to cooperate. Lamantia, Giglio, Rini, and Deamore were brought from the Third Precinct Station shortly after noon. When Pietro Leotta saw Giglio, he jumped from his chair and shouted excitedly, "That's one of them! I'll tell the truth if they kill me." He continued to mutter, "I know he's one of them. I know he will kill me." Leotta raised his fist and shook it in Giglio's face. Cursing him vehemently, Leotta suddenly started crying.

"Peter, do you know these men in this room?" asked Allen, who seemed unfazed by the display of emotion.

"Yes, I know them," insisted Leotta.

2. *State* v. *Rini*, TOA, No. 24,914, pp. 550–52, 762–65; New Orleans *Item* and New Orleans *States*, May 11, 1921; New Orleans *Times-Picayune*, May 12, 1921; newspaper clipping, in Dallas Calmes Scrapbook.

"Were they in the automobile the night of the bank robbery?" Bowden asked.

"Yes, every man in this room was in the automobile," Pietro said.

"They arranged with me when they returned to show them the way back to New Orleans. It was about 2 A.M. when they returned. I and my son got up and got in the automobile with them. The whole six men were in the machine with me and my son. We started riding down towards the city," he explained. "Soon some shots were fired at us. Then the other men started to run. They jumped out of the automobile and ran in all directions. They scattered everywhere. The shots continued. Me and my son remained in the automobile until the people came up."

When Bowden brought Pietro Leotta and Giamalva before Deamore for a positive identification, both men said Deamore was the cause of all their present troubles. They insisted that he was a member of the gang, but Natale continued to proclaim his innocence. As he explained his version Leotta and Giamalva leaped toward him with outstretched hands. Policemen were able to restrain them. Cursing Deamore vigorously in Italian, they promised to kill him. After the confrontation with Deamore, the officials brought Leotta into a detective's office where he also identified Leona.[3]

The only one not identified by the Leottas was Bocchio, who was still in the hospital. When they arrived at Charity Hospital, Bocchio saw Bowden enter the ward, and he pulled the covers over his face. The sheriff, obviously tiring of the prisoners' theatrics, yanked the covers off. Joe Leotta identified Bocchio as the driver.

The boy left the ward, and the police escorted his father in. Bowden asked whether he recognized the man lying in the hospital bed.

"Yes, he's one of them," replied Pietro. "He's the man who drove the car."

"Yes, I drove the car," said Bocchio, to everyone's astonishment. "But I did not drive it all the way to Independence. I had carbu-

3. *State* v. *Rini*, TOA, No. 24,914, pp. 662–63; New Orleans *States* and New Orleans *Times-Picayune*, May 11, 1921; newspaper clippings, in Dallas Calmes Scrapbook.

retor trouble near Independence, and the others got out and walked.

"They came back to the car afterwards," he added, "and told me to drive quickly. I did."

Bocchio, who had not shaved in the last several days, did not look well. He was nervous throughout the questioning, and it is not known whether he understood that he had added to the state's ever-increasing circumstantial evidence.

With Bocchio's identification on Wednesday afternoon, District Attorney Allen told the press that Tangipahoa Parish was ready to prosecute the Calmes murder case. When asked whether a change of venue would be necessary, he replied that he and other officials would fight any such attempt. The defendants could get justice in Tangipahoa, he said, but at the same time he boasted that all the lawyers in the parish had volunteered to help him.[4]

Although Allen was satisfied with the progress of the investigation, Craven was still eager to capture Cipolla, who he thought had masterminded the murders in Independence and New Orleans. Late Wednesday afternoon, Craven ordered the police to watch Cipolla's cousin, Giacomo Bucaro, and the office of George Gulotta, Cipolla's attorney. Later that evening, the police also questioned an Italian minister and a reputed Black Hander from New York about where Cipolla might be.

Craven decided to check Bucaro's residence. Cipolla was found upstairs, lying on the floor with a pistol next to him. The police quickly jumped on him and pinned his arms to the floor. The room was tiny, tightly shuttered, unlit, and filthy. On the floor were remnants of coarse bread, a half-eaten cucumber, a plate of untouched spaghetti, and a milk bottle partially filled with water. The reputed Mafia leader, who had apparently been hiding in the room for the last few days, had a bristly black beard.[5]

An obviously exhausted Cipolla gave no resistance, and the police quickly took him to the Seventh Precinct Station. But it was nearly 10:30 Wednesday night before Craven and the police questioned him. Craven was elated—he could now question the area's alleged *capo mafioso*.

---

4. *State* v. *Rini*, TOA, No. 24,914, pp. 548–51, 570–73; New Orleans *States*, May 11, 1921; New Orleans *Times-Picayune*, May 12, 1921.

5. New Orleans *Times-Picayune* and New Orleans *Item*, May 12–13, 1921.

"Leonardo Cipolla, 38, married, no children. Born in Palermo, Italy. Came to America when I was 21, lived in Brooklyn until I came to New Orleans almost four years ago."

"Were you with DiGiovanni and Gaeto the night they were murdered in front of your house?" asked Craven.

"Yes."

"What were you doing?"

"They took me and my wife for a ride around the city."

"Did you stop in front of Deamore's garage at 1561 Tulane Avenue?"

"No."

"Bring Detectives Horton and Uhle in here," ordered Craven. When the two officers arrived, they identified Cipolla as the man they saw in a car with DiGiovanni in front of Deamore's place.

"You make mistake," Cipolla replied to the two officers.

"That clinches it," said Horton. "He's the same man, and he speaks the same broken English. There isn't any mistake."

"I don' wanna talk wit'out my lawyer," Cipolla insisted, but Craven ignored his request.

"What were you doing in front of Deamore's place Sunday night—the night after they tried to rob the Independence bank and killed Dallas Calmes?"

"I ainta dere. Mista' you gotta me wrong."

Craven returned to the double murder in front of Cipolla's house, and Leonardo freely admitted that he and his wife were there.

"How could you be in that car that's full of buckshot holes and not be wounded?"

"No, I wasna in da car. When those shots fire, I lay down in the grass."

"Where was your wife?"

"She standa there by me."

"What did you do?"

"I crawla through da grass, jump da back fence, go over da garden, climb that Burgundy Street fence and I run."

What became of your wife?"

"I dunno."

Cipolla usually answered sarcastically or shrugged his shoulders and frowned. Showing signs of nervousness, he twisted his white handkerchief.

Craven tried to determine what Cipolla knew about the men held for the murder of Calmes. "Why did Lamantia and Giglio get their mail at your house?"

"I dunno. They do. Thass all I know. It come there. I give it to 'em when they come."

"You just let 'em get their mail at your house and you don't know anything about it?"

"How canna I help ifa da people send mail to me," asked Cipolla with an arrogant sneer.

"They didn't send it to you. They sent it to Tony Carrolla's store, and you called for it and kept it for them, like that telegram to Lamantia we found at your house. How do you explain that?"

"I dunno."

Craven asked about the large number of tires and the barrels of wine and whiskey found at his house, but again Leonardo was evasive.

"What did you have all that wine for—about 10 barrels of it? Sell any?"

"No, that's for my personal use."

"What did you have all those cognac labels and bottle caps and cognac flavor for?"

"I don't want that. It ain't mine. That's Giglio's."

"It was in your house and that trunk of Giglio's."

"Uh, huh."

"What were you doing with that ten-gallon whiskey still in your house?"

"Still?"

"Yes, still. You heard me," insisted Craven.

"What still?"

"Oh, hell," said Craven impatiently. "You know what still. The ten-gallon copper whiskey still we found hidden in the china closet in your front room."

"Oh, that still?" Cipolla said with a serene smile. "I maka leetle whiskey for myself in that still in casa da seekness. I guess every man do that, huh? Thass no crime. You getta every man what maka da wine and da whiskey, you getta everybody."

Not responding to Cipolla's goading, Craven tried to return the questioning to the Calmes case. "Why did Giglio and Leona leave all their clothes in your house?"

"I dunno. They jus' leave 'em there."

Craven questioned Cipolla until three o'clock Thursday morning, but Leonardo offered to sell him obviously stolen tires and cases of sardines. As he smiled and sneered at Craven, Cipolla was also brazen enough to admit he carried a concealed .32 revolver.

"You say you are innocent of any connection with that murder?" Craven was referring to the deaths of Gaeto and DiGiovanni.

"Sure I'm innocent."

"Why were you hiding, then?"

"I wasn't hidin'. I walk out on the street. I wasa gonna surrend' when my lawyer Gulotta tell me to."

"No, it looks as if you weren't afraid," snapped Craven, "locked up in that hole with a gun and food and water. If you're innocent, why not call the police. Why have a lawyer and try to make a deal about your bond through him?"

"I dunno."

Amid laughter and general disgust, Craven ordered the officers to take Cipolla to a cell. Despite an interrogation that lasted nearly five continuous hours in a cramped room, Craven had gathered little evidence to connect Leonardo to the double murder and the Independence slaying. Nevertheless, the Orleans prosecutor was still adamant in his belief that Cipolla was the area's Mafia leader and the mastermind of both crimes.[6]

The next day, Craven received news that bolstered his theory that the New Orleans–based Mafia was involved in a series of major crimes in other Louisiana parishes and Mississippi. The William J. Burns Detective Agency, hired by the Farmers and Merchants Bank of Independence, reported that Leona and Giglio fit the descriptions of suspects involved in a bank robbery in Marthaville, Louisiana, and that witnesses from a score of other robberies were to arrive in New Orleans to identify the pair. The robberies of the banks, many of which were clients of Burns, did fit

6. New Orleans *Times-Picayune*, New Orleans *States*, and New Orleans *Item*, May 12, 1921.

the general pattern—nearly all were at night, and there was substantial evidence that nitroglycerin and blasting caps were used.

The police suspected that Giglio and Leona, as members of the gang, had stolen approximately $50,000 over the last few months. Law-enforcement officials and the Burns Agency also stated that the gang's headquarters was New Orleans, and there were branches along the Mississippi Gulf Coast, in Jackson and Hattiesburg, Mississippi, and in Shreveport, Louisiana. These theories, however, offered no evidence that the New Orleans Mafia was powerful enough to have such branches. Furthermore, the only description of one robbery suspect did not fit Leona, Giglio, or any of the other four. The Burns Agency reported that one suspect was forty-five to fifty years old, weighed 175 pounds, and had gold-filled lower teeth. The other description was so general that it could apply to the majority of younger white males in the area.[7]

On Thursday afternoon, Craven decided to resume his questioning of Lamantia. But when Andrea repeated his answers, Craven resorted to violence. Officers Uhle and Horton stood on each side while Craven held his throat. When Andrea refused to talk, the officers took turns kicking his shins, his sides, and his solar plexus, making it virtually impossible for him to breathe. Despite denials by Craven, Uhle, and Horton in courtroom testimony, Andrea's beating required the attention of the prison druggist, who later testified that he treated Lamantia's shins for bruises, fresh wounds, and abrasions.[8]

Thursday night, the New Orleans police received reports that Cipolla's gang was going to attempt to rescue him from the Tenth Precinct Station, which was quickly surrounded by guards. Later that night, George Gulotta arrived at Craven's office to see his client, but the prosecutor did not want his prime suspect to have access to an attorney at this time. Gulotta insisted, and Craven, at first seeing no way to avoid their meeting, told Gulotta that he could see Cipolla. But Craven had Cipolla moved from the Tenth Precinct Station to the St. Bernard Parish jail. Craven later de-

7. New Orleans *States*, February 1–2, 1921; New Orleans *Item*, May 12–13, 1921.
8. *State* v. *Rini*, TOA, No. 24,914, pp. 423, 442, 469–70, 774–77, 908.

fended his action, saying that St. Bernard officials wanted Cipolla on car-theft charges, but the real reason was that he wanted to prevent Gulotta from speaking to Cipolla.[9]

Two events probably embedded further in the minds of many the possible connection of the Calmes case and the Gaeto-DiGiovanni murders with the Mafia. On Thursday, Sheriff Bowden took Joe Leotta from New Orleans under unusually heavy guard to the Tangipahoa Parish jail. Bowden said he intended to protect his star grand-jury witness from the city's Mafia. Bowden frankly admitted that he feared Joe Leotta would be kidnapped and murdered. He mentioned Walter Lamana, the ten-year-old boy who was brutally slain in 1907.

On Friday, May 13, writs of habeas corpus were denied for Leon Prestia and a suspected Black Hander from New York. The proceedings were held before Judge Joshua G. Baker, who presided over the Hennessey trial and other supposed Mafia and Black Hand cases during the early 1900s.[10]

Bowden also had Pietro Leotta, Natale Giamalva, and Frank Pisciotta moved to Amite City, but not to avoid Mafia retaliation. The Tangipahoa Parish Grand Jury was in session, and the three men were scheduled to appear on Friday. During the week the grand jurors heard testimony from Roy Calmes and several others involved in the Albany capture. But Joe Leotta was the state's star witness. The session lasted into late evening, and the grand jury issued an indictment of first-degree murder and conspiracy to commit robbery against Joseph Rini, Roy Leona, Joseph Bocchio, Andrea Lamantia, Joseph Giglio, Natale Deamore, Pietro Leotta, Natale Giamalva, and Frank Pisciotta. The rumors were, however, that the latter three were ready to become state witnesses. Also, it was reported that the grand jury might reconvene on Saturday or Monday to investigate charges against Leonardo Cipolla and the Prestias.[11]

Craven brought the grand jury's verdict to Deamore, who

9. New Orleans *States*, May 12, 1921; New Orleans *Times-Picayune* and New Orleans *Item*, May 13, 1921.

10. New Orleans *Times-Picayune*, May 13–14, 1921; New Orleans *Item*, May 12–14, July 24, 1921; New Orleans *States*, May 12–13, 1921.

11. New Orleans *Item* and New Orleans *Times-Picayune*, May 14, 1921; New Orleans *States*, May 13–14, 1921; *State v. Rini*, TOA, No. 24,914, pp. 2, 4, 49.

trembled at the news that he had to return to Tangipahoa for a trial. Seeing that Natale was depressed, Craven allowed him to see his wife, who had visited him daily at the Tenth Precinct. Determined to show her support and her belief in his innocence, Mrs. Deamore brought meals to her husband and tried desperately to comfort him throughout his ordeal.[12]

Craven publicly stated that the Calmes case and Gaeto-DiGiovanni murders were connected. As the chief investigator for both cases, he had convinced Tangipahoa Parish authorities that Cipolla had masterminded both the bank robbery and double murder. But Craven was admitting privately that the evidence of Cipolla's involvement in the double slaying was getting weaker each day. Nevertheless, he believed that the Mafia was so powerful in New Orleans that he retained a squad of policemen to guard the Tenth Precinct Station, even though Cipolla was in a St. Bernard Parish jail cell.[13]

According to Craven, the men arrested for the Calmes and Gaeto-DiGiovanni murders were part of a larger criminal organization with connections in the North and the Midwest. He released information that possibly linked Rini to a murder in Ohio. For several days, the major dailies carried stories that Rini, as Scratch Ryan, was wanted for the 1920 murder of a young man at a resort. The police also reported that they had evidence that Rini came to New Orleans via Houston, not Chicago, because he was trying to escape Toledo authorities. Although the killer was later captured, this episode probably added to the ever-growing belief that the two crimes were part of a wider conspiracy involving the mysterious Mafia.[14]

Fearing more Mafia murders in retaliation for Sunday's double slaying, the New Orleans police sent plainclothes officers and detectives into the Italian sections of the city. The police department also acknowledged that hired assassins might be arriving from other cities. Consequently, the police were ordered to arrest

12. New Orleans *States*, May 15, 1921.
13. *Ibid.*, May 13–14, 1921; New Orleans *Item*, May 14, 1921.
14. *State* v. *Rini*, TOA, No. 24,914, p. 827; New Orleans *Times-Picayune*, May 14, 1921; New Orleans *Item*, May 13–15, 1921; New Orleans *States*, May 13–14, 1921.

all suspicious Italians who appeared to be strangers and who could not give legitimate reasons for being in the city.[15]

The New Orleans press, especially the *States*, continued to add to the Mafia mystique. Andrew J. Ojeda, who was covering the recent murders in Tangipahoa and New Orleans, warned that New York City and New Orleans were the centers for feuding factions of the Mafia—a claim for which he offered no proof. Ojeda was correct, however, in his observation that a younger generation of Italians was now engaged in car thefts and bootlegging in the New Orleans area. He also noted that both the "old organization," the earlier Mafia leaders, and the "new blood," the younger, rising Italian criminals, still adhered to the old Sicilian *mafia* code: "If I die I'll forgive you. If I live I'll kill you!" The *States* reporter further warned that these Italians were "linked together in a brotherhood." Adding to the mystique of this "brotherhood," Ojeda wrote that "the Italian feuds in this city may be traced back thirty years when two factions—the Provenzanos and Matrangas—fought each other bitterly. . . . That incident marked the beginning of one of the bloodiest feuds in the history of this city and culminated in the assassination of Dave Hennessey."

Ojeda then recounted Black Hand incidents in New Orleans over the past fifteen years, and he highlighted the gory details of the earlier "Axe Murders," which many residents believed were the Mafia's work. The reporter also rehashed the 1916 shooting of Black Hand leader Vito Di Giorgio and reminded his readers that the attempted assassin was an Italian strawberry picker from Tangipahoa Parish.[16]

According to historian John Kendall, one of the police theories was that the Calmes and Gaeto-DiGiovanni murders marked a new era in the development of the city's Mafia. Illegal liquor and car theft had replaced the Black Hand's extortion and blackmail. The police also believed, as did Ojeda, that 1921 marked the beginning of a younger generation of Italians taking over the leadership of the Mafia. Historian Humbert Nelli also concluded that this "Americanization" process, whereby the younger immigrants

15. New Orleans *States*, May 15, 1921.
16. *Ibid.*

and the second-generation Italians purged the old-time Mafia leaders, did not occur in New Orleans until the late 1930s or early 1940s. However, the Independence incident and the Gaeto-DiGiovanni murders revealed that this process was probably begun as early as 1921 by the Italian-American criminal gangs in New Orleans.[17]

Furthermore, sociologist Francis Ianni maintains that except for Al Capone in Chicago, the 1920s represented "a transitional period in the rise to dominance of major ethnic groups in organized crime. The Jews were replacing the Irish in the early Twenties and their ascendancy was not threatened by the Italians until the end of the decade." Nelli also noted that the manpower for the criminal syndicates of the Prohibition era "came from a number of sources: some 'graduated' from Black Hand and Italian-colony 'Mafia' groups; others had served as whorehouse proprietors, gambling-house operators, labor goons, counterfeiters, narcotics dealers, and a wide range of petty crooks and thieves."[18] Rini and his comrades were, therefore, excellent examples of the transitional Italian-American criminals. Two of the main characters, Di Giorgio and Leona, were thought to be former Black Handers. Cipolla was reputedly the leader of the Mafia gangs in New Orleans, and the others certainly fit the description "petty crooks and thieves."

In accordance with the official police theory, Leonardo Cipolla was the Mafia *capo* over all areas of New Orleans and the southern section of the United States, but the police offered no evidence to substantiate that charge. Although the police did not believe that Deamore and the others held for the Calmes slaying were directly responsible for the Gaeto-DiGiovanni murders, they were convinced that both crimes were committed by two separate Mafia gangs under Cipolla's control.

The scenario created by Craven and the police had Cipolla in full knowledge of both crimes, which developed independently in the city. Probably in late April, two of Cipolla's men brought a

17. Kendall, "Blood on the Banquette," 853–54; Nelli, *The Business of Crime,* 101, 134, 179–80, 256.

18. Ianni, "The Mafia and the Web of Kinship," 13–15; Nelli, *The Business of Crime,* 101, 256–57.

stolen car to Deamore and Gaeto for repairs. Natale, who supposedly operated Cipolla's clearinghouse for stolen vehicles, decided to sell the car and keep the money. Several days later, Cipolla's men returned, but Deamore said that the New Orleans police had confiscated the automobile. Unfortunately for Deamore, the two men discovered that was not true. Several of Cipolla's men threatened Deamore with death, but Natale stood by his story. As a result, Gaeto and Deamore were marked for death.

In the meantime, Leona and Deamore had developed with Vito Di Giorgio a scheme to rob a bank in Independence. This part of the scenario implied that Di Giorgio recruited outside Mafia men, such as Rini, Lamantia, Giglio, and Leona, to execute the robbery. Then on Sunday night, Cipolla, who was fully aware of the Independence plans, borrowed DiGiovanni's car. Planning to avenge Deamore and Gaeto's betrayal, he wanted to lure Gaeto into the car for a ride to Deamore's. Once both men were in the car, he was to take them to a prearranged spot to murder them. The only thing Cipolla did not count on was DiGiovanni's insistence on riding along.

When Cipolla arrived at the garage, he did not find Deamore at home. Leonardo was in a predicament. He feared taking Gaeto and DiGiovanni to his house, where the killing was to occur. However, if he did not, the city's other *mafiosi* would believe that he had betrayed them. Feeling that he had no choice, Leonardo ordered DiGiovanni to take them to his home. There in a barrage of gunfire, Gaeto and DiGiovanni, rather than Deamore, were murdered by Cipolla's men.[19]

In addition to the lack of evidence to support the theory, there were major flaws in regard to the role of Cipolla. If Cipolla was truly the *capo mafioso*, he would have commanded DiGiovanni not to accompany him that night. Furthermore, it was highly unlikely that Cipolla planned to murder two members of the Mafia in front of his own home. Nor would Cipolla have put into action

---

19. New Orleans *States*, May 9, 13, 15–17, 1921; New Orleans *Times-Picayune*, May 10–11, 13, 15–17, 1921; New Orleans *Item*, May 9–10, 14–17, 1921; newspaper clippings, in Dallas Calmes Scrapbook; Hearsey, *The Six Who Were Hanged*, 6; State v. Rini, TOA, No. 24,914, p. 666.

a scheme that would have endangered his wife. Finally, it was only supposition that linked Cipolla to the murder in Independence.

According to Nelli, there were Mafia gangs in the nation's major cities, "but these were pale imitations of the New York groups, which themselves were not the omnipotent organizations that journalists and gang members pictured them to be."[20] However, the New Orleans police and the district attorney forged a motley group of Italian hoodlums into a broader concept of the Mafia. Although there were Italian Mafia gangs in New Orleans, the first two years of Prohibition were hardly enough time for them to form a multistate organization with headquarters in the city and branches on the Mississippi Gulf Coast and in neighboring states, and with the ability to call upon other gangsters from northern and midwestern states. Interpreting the Italians' mobility and social relationships as evidence of a multistate criminal organization, New Orleans officials helped foster a modern concept of the Mafia and its somewhat exaggerated powers. This would affect the case of *State of Louisiana* v. *Joseph Rini et al.* and color the nation's perception of the Italian criminal syndicates.

20. Nelli, *The Business of Crime*, 134.

5

To Maintain Law and Order

Early Monday morning, May 16, Sheriff Bowden and three heavily
armed deputies took Rini and the others from the Orleans Parish
Prison for their arraignment in Amite City. Giamalva, Leotta, and
Pisciotta, who were said to have become state witnesses, remained in New Orleans. During the train ride, only Bocchio
showed fear of returning to Tangipahoa Parish. His continuing
problems with appendicitis probably added to his uneasiness.

At 9:00 A.M. the train arrived at the Amite City station. The
streets were filled with residents of Amite and Independence.
Hands and legs in shackles, the prisoners moved slowly from the
train to the platform. There, six more deputies armed with pistols,
shotguns, and rifles surrounded them. As they walked to the parish courthouse two blocks away, the crowd followed closely. Although no one showed any animosity toward them, the prisoners
were visibly shaken.

When they entered the crowded courtroom, nearly three hundred grim-faced spectators stared at them. Although there was absolute silence, everyone felt the tenseness of the situation. There
were only three Italians there to witness the proceedings, one of
whom was Mayor Charles Anzalone of Independence.

During arraignments, only one judge usually presides. That
Monday, however, Judges Robert S. Ellis and Columbus Reid, two
of the parish's leading political rivals, conducted the proceedings.
Ellis asked the prisoners whether they had attorneys. Bocchio,
Rini, and Leona said yes, but they were in New Orleans. The other
three defendants said no, but they would obtain counsel when
they got back to the city. District Attorney Matt Allen requested
that they be arraigned anyway, and the judges agreed.

After Ellis read the indictment charging them with murder, the
defendants pled not guilty. Ellis then ordered the case assigned for

56

trial on June 13. The arraignment lasted only a half hour, but Bowden and his deputies were anxious to usher the prisoners out of the courtroom and up to a third-floor jury room. For security reasons, they remained there until the one o'clock train to New Orleans was to leave.

As Rini and the others rode back to the city, Cipolla and two of his men were formally booked by the New Orleans police for the murders of Gaeto and DiGiovanni. Later that afternoon, Matt Allen announced that the Tangipahoa Parish Grand Jury would convene May 23 to continue its investigation of Cipolla and the Prestias on charges of conspiracy to commit robbery.[1]

The unfounded rumor that New Orleans Police Superintendent Guy Molony had been shot while investigating "Italian gangs," and the wave of crimes attributed to the Italians and the Mafia, probably affected the deliberations of the Bill of Rights Committee of the Louisiana Constitutional Convention of 1921. The chairman of the committee was former judge Robert R. Reid of Tangipahoa Parish, and a committee member was Thomas Craven. For at least two weeks, the committee had debated the use of the "third degree" in extracting confessions. Craven vigorously objected to any law that would regulate police methods. Because of the controversy, the committee recommended that everything dealing with the examining of suspected criminals be omitted. As a result, the bill of rights of the new constitution simply stated that no person charged with a crime shall be compelled to be a witness against himself.[2]

Two days after the arraignment in Amite, the New Orleans *States* commented on the "third degree" issue. "The recent crimes of a band of Italian banditti," argued the *States* in an editorial, "should suggest to it [constitutional convention] the wisdom of modifying its Third Degree article." Then, in a total distortion of the known facts, the *States* claimed that the suspects had murdered a respected citizen of Tangipahoa and returned to the city to kill two "of [their] own nationality." Even Craven had admitted

1. *State* v. *Rini*, TOA, No. 24,914, p. 5; New Orleans *States*, May 16, 1921; New Orleans *Item* and New Orleans *States*, May 16–17, 1921; New Orleans *Times-Picayune*, May 13, 16–17, 1921.
2. New Orleans *Item*, May 17, 1921; *State* v. *Rini*, TOA, No. 24,914, p. 430.

privately that it was physically impossible for anyone involved in the *Rini et al.* case to have murdered Gaeto and DiGiovanni. Finally, the *States* recommended that the convention reopen the "third degree" question and "let it prohibit physical torture of prisoners under any circumstances. But let it strike out the provision which puts the interests of the criminal above those of society."[3]

The Ponchatoula *Enterprise* castigated the New Orleans paper for its stand. The *Enterprise* was certainly no friend of the parish's Italian community. When Ed Tucker arrested Bocchio, the paper stated that "it was easy for the chief to spot the wop." Nevertheless, the *Enterprise* charged that the *States* lamented the passing of certain police methods. "If the police of New Orleans cannot 'dee-tect' without torture," the *Enterprise* concluded, "they had better resign."[4]

There was also a conflict between New Orleans' Italian-language weekly newspapers. On the morning of the arraignment, Cono Puglisi, editor of *L'Italo-Americano*, urged Italians not to be silent and not to fear revenge. He recommended a mass meeting at which they would form a committee to cooperate with local officials. After Puglisi's statement received wide attention in New Orleans, Frank Cabibi wrote a letter to the *States*. Cabibi, the owner of *La Voce Coloniale* and one of the city's leading Italians, argued that a mass meeting was unnecessary. Furthermore, the editor noted, there was no evidence that a band of criminals had invaded the city and the state. The following day, Puglisi accused Cabibi of wearing "the garb of a clown." Puglisi denied that he wrote that Italian criminals were invading New Orleans, and he continued to urge the mass meeting.[5]

While the Italian editors traded barbs, Tangipahoa and New Orleans officials gathered more evidence in New Orleans on the Calmes case. On Thursday, May 19, Bowden and Allen visited Giamalva, Pisciotta, and Leotta for a few hours. When the sheriff emerged from the prison, he announced that the three men had

3. New Orleans *States*, May 18, 1921.
4. Ponchatoula *Enterprise*, May 27, 1921.
5. New Orleans *States*, May 16, 18, 1921; New Orleans *Item*, May 16, 1921; New Orleans *Times-Picayune*, May 17, 1921.

finally agreed to be state witnesses. Although they were fully aware of the activities of Rini and the others, Bowden was convinced that they were not involved in the attempted robbery and the murder of Calmes.

The following day, Craven received word that Rini was ready to confess. Since the assistant district attorney considered Rini a hired Mafia gunman, he was eager to talk to him. Believing that Rini had information on the double murder, Craven announced to the press that he had a definite tip that would lead to the arrest of the Gaeto-DiGiovanni killers. However, the meeting never materialized because Rini changed his mind.[6]

Craven doggedly pursued his case against Cipolla. Since the evidence was not strong, a New Orleans judge released Cipolla on June 4 on a $10,000 bond obtained by Gulotta. Three days later, however, the Orleans Parish Grand Jury indicted Cipolla for the Gaeto-DiGiovanni murders. He was rearrested and held without bond. A few days later, he obtained a $10,000 bond through special arrangements with District Attorney Robert H. Marr, Jr. Once Cipolla obtained his freedom, he disappeared from New Orleans. A year later, it would be reported that he had been murdered in St. Louis.[7]

For all practical purposes, the Gaeto-DiGiovanni case ended with Cipolla's disappearance, and the New Orleans officials could devote more time and resources to help Tangipahoa authorities prosecute Rini and his confederates. On May 27 the defense attorneys filed an application for a change of venue. After hearing preliminary pleadings, the Twenty-fifth District Court granted a full hearing on June 1, which caused considerable comment in the parish. According to the editor of a weekly newspaper in Hammond, residents of Tangipahoa vigorously opposed any attempt to move the trial to another parish. The editor also asserted that even the Italians of the parish believed that "the accused should be punished to the extreme."[8]

6. New Orleans *Item*, May 20, 1921; New Orleans *Times-Picayune*, June 14, 1921; New Orleans *States*, May 19–20, 1921.
7. New Orleans *Item*, June 7, 1921; New Orleans *Times-Picayune*, May 14, 1922, May 10, 1924.
8. *State* v. *Rini*, TOA, No. 24,914, p. 6; George Campbell to John M. Parker, May 24, 29, 1921, both in Parker Papers.

Considering Tangipahoa's violent history and some past incidents of intolerance toward its minorities, George Gulotta, who was now the chief defense attorney, and his co-counsels were prepared to argue that their clients could not receive a fair and impartial trial in Amite. Gulotta, a thirty-three-year-old Louisiana State University Law School graduate, had chosen three local attorneys to aid in the defense. Brittain Purser, who had accompanied Deamore and the other prisoners to New Orleans, was a prominent forty-six-year-old Amite lawyer. After graduating from Tulane Law School in 1903, he engaged in a lucrative law practice with former judge Robert R. Reid, who was now one of the two special prosecutors helping District Attorney Allen. The other Amite attorney was forty-year-old William B. Kemp. A lifetime resident of Amite, Kemp graduated from Tulane Law School in 1904. Five years later, he was one of the defense attorneys in the Avery Blount case, which until 1921 was the parish's most notorious trial. The third defense attorney was Lewis L. Morgan of Covington. Morgan was a former district attorney for St. Tammany Parish and a former U.S. congressman.[9]

The prosecutors included fifty-year-old District Attorney Allen, also a graduate of Tulane Law School. Although the prosecutor had experience in handling major cases, two prominent Tangipahoa attorneys, Robert R. Reid and Amos L. Ponder, assisted him. Reid, who had been district judge for twelve years, retired from the bench in 1904. Having survived several assassination attempts in Bloody Tangipahoa, he returned to his law practice. In 1909, Reid had assisted the district attorney's office in prosecuting Blount. Two years later, he was an unsuccessful candidate for attorney general. With gray hair, a full white beard, and a patriarchal face, the sixty-six-year-old Reid was an imposing and distinguished figure who commanded statewide respect. Amos L. Ponder was another well-known Louisiana politician. Earlier in his career, Ponder had served as district attorney of the Twelfth Judicial District and was a member of the 1898 constitutional

9. New Orleans *States*, June 19, 1921; *Florida Parishes Times* (Amite City), 1909, reprinted in *Tangi Talk* (Amite City), March 26, 1969; New Orleans *Item*, June 20, 1921; New Orleans *Times-Picayune*, October 21, 1977; *State v. Rini*, TOA, No. 24,914, p. 795.

convention. He ran unsuccessfully for Congress and considered entering the 1920 gubernatorial race. Even though Ponder was helping the state, it was rumored that he had been offered $10,000 to aid the defense.[10]

On the morning of Wednesday, June 1, the defense was probably shocked to find that special prosecutor Reid would argue the change-of-venue issue before his son and Robert Ellis, who were sitting as a panel. This was unquestionably a conflict of interest. Nevertheless, the defense charged that the following conditions warranted a change of venue: the pretrial publicity was prejudicial to the defendants; mob violence was threatened if there were no conviction and hanging; there was a deep-seated prejudice toward Italians in the parish; and any jury would be intimidated by open threats.

As state and defense witnesses spoke Gulotta and the other defense attorneys realized that it would be useless to continue the session. Nearly everyone testified that it was possible to conduct a fair and impartial trial. Rather than prolong the hearing, the defense withdrew its petition for a change of venue.[11] What happened at the hearing was not clear. The defense apparently expected its witnesses to testify that there were grounds for moving the trial to another jurisdiction. Possibly conditions in the parish were such that no Tangipahoa resident felt safe to testify truthfully on the merits of a change of venue.

Tangipahoa Parish began to prepare for the trial. Deputies busily served witnesses and veniremen, who had been drawn a month earlier, and local officials had taken special steps to ensure a speedy trial. One reason for placing the case on the docket so rapidly was that a committee of non-Italian residents from Independence called upon Judge Ellis to insist on an immediate trial.

On the weekend before the opening of the trial, there was

10. New Orleans *Item*, May 14, 1921, June 29, 1923; Ponchatoula *Enterprise*, January 19, 1923; New Orleans *Times-Picayune*, February 3, 1920, January 3, 15, 1923, November 9, 1936; *Florida Parishes Times* (Amite City), 1909, reprinted in *Tangi Talk* (Amite City), March 26, 1969; newspaper clipping, in Dallas Calmes Scrapbook; New Orleans *States*, January 1, 1920.

11. New Orleans *States*, May 28, June 14, 1921; New Orleans *Item*, May 28, June 1, 1921; *Florida Parishes Times* (Amite City), January 7, 1922; *State* v. *Rini*, TOA, No. 24,914, pp. 7–8, 54–57.

hardly a hotel room or boardinghouse available for those wishing to attend the proceedings. All the major daily newspapers from New Orleans had sent reporters to cover it. The *Times-Picayune* and *States* planned to file their stories by Western Union or by telephone. The *Item* set up a direct telegraph wire between Amite and New Orleans and employed a special telegraph operator to assist the reporter.

On the eve of the trial, rumors persisted throughout Tangipahoa and New Orleans that mob action was imminent. "Those six Italians are going to hang up at Amite," said one New Orleanian. "If they're not hanged by legal sentence—well—they'll be hanged!" According to the *Item*, this was a common sentiment. But Sheriff Bowden promised that there would be "no jail delivery and no jail escape." He employed extra deputies and planned to search everyone entering the courthouse.

On Sunday, June 12, the Amite churches were packed, and the ministers incorporated the seriousness of the impending trial into their sermons. "I do not believe," said one preacher, "it is merely a policy with us to maintain law and order. It is more than that—it is a principle." At the Amite Baptist Church, the pastor added, "The good citizens are in the vast majority in the parish, and it is their duty to suppress crime and vice and maintain law and order."[12]

Also concerned with the threat of mob violence was Judge Ellis. He had visited Ku Klux Klan gatherings throughout the parish and, as the judge explained two years later, urged them not to resort to lynch parties or other lawless acts. Since Ellis was an avowed Klansman himself and was the presiding judge, the hooded order heeded his advice. Moreover, if reports reaching the governor's office were accurate, virtually the entire administration of the trial, with the exception of the defense attorneys, was in the hands of the Klan. According to secret documents, Judges Robert Ellis and Columbus Reid, District Attorney Allen, Sheriff Bowden, and the two special prosecutors, Reid and Ponder, were mem-

12. New Orleans *Times-Picayune*, June 13, 1921; New Orleans *States*, May 17–18, 1921; New Orleans *Item*, June 12, 1921; *State* v. *Rini*, TOA, No. 24,914, pp. 201, 209, 302.

bers of the Klan, which had been active in Kentwood, Amite, Hammond, and Ponchatoula before the Calmes murder.[13]

The Louisiana governor who was gathering information on the Klan was John M. Parker, Jr., one of the leaders of the 1891 mass meeting at the Orleans Parish Prison. The governor, who had been a personal friend of Calmes's for twenty years, was deeply interested in the case. Maintaining a special file of correspondence and newspaper articles, Parker noted each development. He also sent letters commending the actions of those who captured the six defendants. The state prison official who helped capture Rini and Lamantia was cited by the governor for "coolness and courage . . . in taking these armed men and then in protecting them from lynching." He later congratulated Sheriff Bowden on his "coolness and excellent judgement in preventing mob violence, at a time when passions ran high and public feeling was very bitter."

Approximately one week after the murder of Calmes, Parker wrote an interesting letter to Cono Puglisi, editor of *L'Italo-Americano*. "It is unfortunately the case," wrote Parker, "that whenever a number of men of a particular race commit an atrocious crime, a stigma attaches in the minds of unthinking people to the entire race. As you know, this is particularly true of the Italian race." Intolerant of Sicilians, the governor in 1911 regarded them as "just a little worse than the Negro, being if anything filthier in [their] habits, lawless, and treacherous." Furthermore, Parker never denied his part in the bloody 1891 incident, and he insisted that he had not used his gun. Moreover, throughout the latter part of the 1890s and the first two decades of the twentieth century, Parker was still a firm believer in the existence of the Mafia, which he thought the New Orleans police had failed to destroy.[14]

13. New Orleans *Times-Picayune*, March 27, April 8, 1923; Ku Klux Klan List of Amite City, n.d., in Parker Papers; Charter Members of the Ku Klux Klan at Amite, Louisiana, n.d., in W. D. Robinson Papers, Southern Historical Collection, Walter Royal Davis Library, University of North Carolina, Chapel Hill.

14. New Orleans *Item*, May 14, 28, 1921, May 21, 1939; John M. Parker to L. H. Bowden, May 16, 1921, John M. Parker to Cono Puglisi, May 17, 1921, John M. Parker to Rene Calmes, May 28, 1921, all in Parker Papers; Schott, "John M. Parker," 34–36, 154, 164–65, 334, 338.

After 1912, Parker was determined to destroy the Ring (Choctaw Club), the city's powerful political machine. In the 1916 Louisiana gubernatorial election, Parker ran as the Progressive party candidate, but he was soundly defeated. However, in 1920 he rejoined the Democratic party and again ran for governor on a reform platform. Parker assured the voters that he would end corrupt machine politics in the state and he denounced the Ring as a "band of crooks." After his election, he promised the business community that he would put a permanent end to the Ring's rule in New Orleans and the rest of the state. The New York *Tribune* noted that Parker had, in the recent gubernatorial election, defeated the Ring, which was supported by "the forces of the lower world." Although Parker did not specifically charge that the Ring was connected with the city's Mafia, he was certainly aware that since the 1890s the Sicilians had supported the Choctaw Club. Furthermore, by 1920 the Italians were so powerful in New Orleans that the Ring usually gave them special consideration when election slates were drawn up.[15]

Having won a great victory over the Ring, Parker now faced a resurgence of the Klan and the murder of Calmes, a major crime allegedly committed by the Mafia. In late May, 1921, Parker thought it best to notify Secretary of State Charles Evans Hughes that mob violence might occur during the upcoming trial. Governor Parker unabashedly displayed his anti-Italian sentiments: "A crime wave by Italians from your state and a number of other Northern states and a number of murders by this class of criminals has so inflamed a section of this state that I fear we might have another outbreak of mob violence. . . . I feel it is my duty to advise you that there is always a danger of an outbreak following a series of murder and robbery which is invariably performed by Italians from outside states brought in by local criminals in order to prove an alibi." After reading Parker's dispatch, Hughes thought the sit-

15. Perry H. Howard, *Political Tendencies in Louisiana* (Rev. ed.; Baton Rouge, 1971), 206–209, 215; Schott, "John M. Parker," 91–121, 226, 242–76, 347–48, 351; George Reynolds, *Machine Politics in New Orleans, 1897–1926* (New York, 1936), 13–14, 55, 74, 93, 116, 173, 178, 185; Allan P. Sindler, *Huey Long's Louisiana: State Politics, 1920–1952* (Baltimore, 1956), 22–26, 35, 40; "Louisiana 'Ring Rule' Smashed," *Literary Digest*, LXIV (February 7, 1920), 18; T. Harry Williams, *Huey Long* (New York, 1969), 136.

uation in Tangipahoa warranted the attention of Attorney General Harry M. Daugherty.

This was the first of many letters and telegrams between Parker and Hughes. Despite his anti-Italianism, Parker sincerely wanted to avoid any violent action in Tangipahoa that might precipitate an international incident, as had happened in 1891. If this were not enough, friends and foes alike would be reminding Parker about the New Orleans prison incident. For example, George Campbell, the Hammond *Vindicator* editor who kept Parker informed about events in Tangipahoa, warned the governor that it was imperative that "the entanglements observed in the days of thirty years ago down in New Orleans" be avoided.[16]

As the trial date approached, the defense attorneys were probably aware of the formidable forces surrounding *Rini et al.* The case was being tried in a parish with a history of anti-Italian incidents, and the administration of the judicial system was perhaps controlled by the Klan. If the six men were convicted, the only man who could commute their sentence or pardon them was a governor who believed that most Italian criminals were part of the Mafia and who had no remorse for his part in the death of eleven Italians in 1891.

16. John M. Parker to Charles Evans Hughes, May 25, 1921, Hughes to Parker, June 23, 1921, Campbell to Parker, May 24, 1921, all in Parker Papers.

Dallas Calmes
Courtesy of Miriam Calmes Cartwright

Left to right: Delmas, Dallas, Jr., Bessie,
and Natalie Calmes
Courtesy of Natalie C. Salter

Sheriff Lem Bowden
Courtesy the Tangipahoa Parish Sheriff's Office

Governor John M. Parker
Courtesy the Department of Archives and Manuscripts,
Louisiana State University, Baton Rouge

Brittain B. Purser
Courtesy John T. Purser

William B. Kemp
Courtesy of Ruth Kemp Dyson

George Gulotta
Courtesy of James C. Gulotta

The "Six Italians"

6

Deadline for Italians

When Sheriff Bowden arrived at the Orleans Parish Prison on Monday, June 13, to remove his prisoners for trial in Amite, it was nearly 2:00 A.M. As Rini and his comrades left their cells Bowden was stunned by their attire. According to the *Item*, they were "garbed in the latest of Canal Street's extremist fashion," with trousers that had "razor-edified creases." They also wore expensive boots and silk shirts and scarves. As they lumbered under the heavy chains they saw the waiting crowd of officials. Giglio, at the end of the procession, only glared at the newspapermen and muttered some obscene threats. Following behind them were the state witnesses, Giamalva, Leotta, and Pisciotta.

At Union Station, the reporters converged upon the entourage. As the cameras flashed, each prisoner tried to hide his face with his hat or by dropping his head. Also in the crowd were Katherine Rini, Joseph's cousin, and Patrina Fanucci, Bocchio's fiancée.[1]

Surrounded by heavily armed guards, the prisoners took their seats on the train quietly. Waiting for the train to depart, they joked among themselves and smoked cigarettes. Several ate some fruit from the baskets brought by the two young women, who were also allowed to stay on the train. Just as the train was leaving, Rini leaned out of an open window and in a falsetto voice said, "Good-bye, sweetie" to one of the Orleans Parish deputies on the platform. They all laughed good-naturedly. Seemingly without a care in the world, each told a story or sang a song in Italian. Despite their joviality, Rini and the others were self-conscious about their handcuffs, which they covered with handkerchiefs.

In Ponchatoula the prisoners continued their chatter and laugh-

1. Patrina Fanucci is a fictitious name supplied by the author. The newspapers erroneously identified this woman as Mrs. Joseph Bocchio. She was actually Bocchio's fiancée. All attempts to determine her real name proved fruitless.

ter as they looked through the train's wide windows at the town's twinkling lights. Without warning, a car door slammed shut nearby. Fearing an attack, Bowden ordered the windows closed and the curtains pulled down. For a few strained moments, there was total silence. As the train gathered speed, the prisoners resumed their joking. But at each stop in Tangipahoa, Bowden ordered the same precautions until they reached Amite.

When they arrived at the Amite depot at four o'clock Monday morning, Bowden examined the railroad platform carefully before ordering everyone out. The heavily armed deputies surrounded the prisoners as they walked down Oak Street toward the jail. No one else was on the streets. The pale lights of the jail were easily discernible, but there was no one inside. They had not been expected to arrive until 9:00 A.M., and Bowden's deputies were not on duty. While someone went to open the jail doors, the others sat on the steps and waited. Patrina sat next to Bocchio and patted his hand.

"All right, boys, the hotel's ready," Bowden said.

"Ready to have your picture taken now?" asked a newspaper photographer.

"Nothin' doin'," answered Giglio with a smile. "After we get outa this we may run for governor or mayor or somepin'. Then we'll pose all day."

The others smiled approvingly and started the short walk into the jail. "Hep-hep, hep-hep, one, two, three, four," chanted Giglio, who continued to joke. His comrades only grinned slightly.

The women were escorted across the street to the home of a friend. Deputies led the nine men up a narrow steel stairway to their cells. The prisoners were startled to see the open trap and the beams of the gallows through the windows. Bowden said, "Only one man has been hanged on these gallows. He was Avery Blount, who was convicted of murder in 1909." No one responded, and they entered their cells quietly.[2]

Bowden sent deputies to rope off the courthouse grounds in anticipation of the crowds. The yellow-brick courthouse, built in

2. New Orleans *Item* and New Orleans *States*, June 13, 1921; New Orleans *Times-Picayune*, June 14, 1921.

1908, was separate from the jail, but both were located in the center of Amite's main square. The setting was pleasant—the attractive structure surrounded by trees and an expanse of green lawn. But on the morning of June 13, ropes, barricades, and armed deputies marred its serenity.

Under a blazing sun the first cars and wagons arrived at eight o'clock, and the nine o'clock train brought many people from the southern part of the parish and New Orleans. As the crowd milled around the courthouse, the curious spectators stared at the massive jail walls. Before they entered the building, they usually asked the guards whether the prisoners were in the jail. Among the first to arrive were Rene Calmes, Dallas' brother, and Roy Calmes. Both men spoke to the press—they wanted to see orderly proceedings and no violence during the trial.

To ensure the prisoners' safety, Bowden had employed fourteen special deputies to guard the jail and courthouse. They were heavily armed and were not to allow anyone to enter the courthouse without an official permit from Bowden. In addition, the deputies searched all spectators, especially those from Independence.[3]

At 9:20 A.M. a court official rang the second-floor-gallery bronze bell. As the prisoners entered the courtroom Rene Calmes tensed. They were smiling and well dressed. He watched them intently as they took seats next to their attorneys.

As soon as Deamore sat down, his wife greeted him with a kiss. Mrs. Deamore then took a seat between Patrina and Katherine. The two young women, who were both well dressed and attractive, were the center of attention. Patrina, who always smiled and laughed, sat directly behind Bocchio and kissed him tenderly at every opportunity. Katherine spent most of her time talking to Rini, but she also offered words of encouragement to the others.[4]

During the first ten minutes, the defense filed a motion to quash the indictments because of allegedly faulty grand-jury proceedings. William B. Kemp charged that the clerk of court had

3. New Orleans *Item*, June 13–14, 1921; New Orleans *States*, June 13, 17, 1921, May 7, 1924; New Orleans *Times-Picayune*, June 13–14, 1921, May 10, 1924.
4. New Orleans *Item*, June 13–14, 1921; New Orleans *Times-Picayune*, June 14–15, 1921; New Orleans *States*, June 13–14, 19, 1921.

failed to take his oath of office, and his participation in drawing the grand jurors made the indictment therefore invalid. Moreover, a jury commissioner held two public offices, which also invalidated the indictment. The clerk produced his notarized oath of office, but the state had difficulties with the allegations against the jury commissioner. After a lengthy recess, court reconvened that afternoon. More than three hundred spectators jammed the courtroom and the courthouse square. When the commissioner finally took the stand, he admitted that he had never taken the oath of office as the town clerk of Kentwood. That meant, Judge Ellis said, the commissioner had failed to qualify legally as town clerk, so he held only one office. Ellis overruled the motion.[5]

The defense's next technical move was to request a delay because a defense witness could not be located, but that also failed. Jury selection finally began late Monday afternoon. No jurors were chosen, and the process continued on the following morning in the sweltering courtroom. Observers noted that the defense challenged talesmen who were married and had children. Their conclusion was that the defense attorneys wanted no family men in the jury box, because Dallas Calmes had been married and had three children. Although this was probably a defense strategy, it did not work, because the second juror chosen was married and had four children.[6]

Jury selection proved to be extremely difficult. First of all, Judge Ellis ordered the clerk of court to exclude all possible jurors from Independence because of fear of prejudice. Additionally, jurors were excused in large numbers for holding fixed opinions, opposing the death penalty, or not being able to convict the defendants on circumstantial evidence. Seeing that a few hundred talesmen would have to be called, court officials estimated that the jury selection alone would cost the parish five hundred dollars per day. Each talesman received four dollars per day and ten cents per mile.[7]

5. New Orleans *Item* and New Orleans *States*, June 13, 1921; New Orleans *Times-Picayune*, June 14, 1921; *State* v. *Rini*, TOA, No. 24,914, pp. 85–86, 90, 97.

6. New Orleans *Times-Picayune*, June 13–15, 1921; *State* v. *Rini*, TOA, No. 24,914, pp. 14–19, 124–25, 832; New Orleans *Item*, June 14–15, 1921; New Orleans *States*, June 14, 1921.

7. New Orleans *Item* and New Orleans *States*, June 14, 1921.

On Tuesday afternoon, June 14, the crowd increased. Also in court were three "portly Italians, garbed in clothes of metropolitan cut." Reports were rampant around Amite that these men were friends of the defendants. Because they carried large, expensive bags with unknown contents, they were objects of considerable attention.

The reputedly sizable defense fund was also an issue among the spectators and reporters. Vigorously denying rumors that between $10,000 and $15,000 had been raised, the defense asserted that the defendants' families and friends had given only a few thousand dollars. Although the Mafia was not specifically mentioned, Gulotta and his colleagues denied that any associations or organizations were involved in the collection of the fund. "Their apparent lavish expenditure of money," stated the *Times-Picayune*, "had only made the citizens more determined to see that the law is carried out. It was pointed out that the six men as a whole have appeared in court better clothed than judge, attorneys, and court attachés, and this display of finery has only served to anger many persons."[8]

On Wednesday, June 15, the defendants were as "foppish as ever." The *Item* also noted that Patrina Fanucci wore her third new hat and that Katherine Rini was well dressed. The crowd was not large, and it was especially noted that W. G. McMichael, the father of Mrs. Dallas Calmes, was in the courtroom. He was provided a special seat directly in front of the line of chairs used by the six defendants. McMichael stared at the men accused of killing his son-in-law. Occasionally, he turned and tooked at the talesmen seated in the courtroom, but he said nothing.

The tedious jury selection continued Wednesday morning in the depressingly hot and fly-infested courtroom. The defendants watched Lewis Morgan with keen interest. He asked several jurors: "Have you any feeling of enmity against the Italian race—men called 'Dagoes' in the common parlance of the street?" The state did not object to this frequent question, but the courtroom dialogue became heated when Purser persisted in asking, "If the

8. New Orleans *States*, June 14, 1921; New Orleans *Item*, June 13–16, 1921; New Orleans *Times-Picayune*, June 20, 1921.

state bases its case on circumstantial evidence in part, will you require the state to prove their guilt by a chain of circumstances so connected and positive as to be incapable of explanation of any other theory than the guilt of the accused?" Reid quickly objected that the question was hypothetical, irrelevant, and confusing. Ellis upheld the objection, to which Purser filed a bill of exception.

The line of questioning Wednesday morning revealed to many observers part of the defense's strategy. Gulotta and his colleagues, now including Morgan's partner C. Sidney Fredericks, were apparently going to insist that the state specifically identify who killed Dallas Calmes. Further, the defense would likely rely upon the state's inability to produce an eyewitness to the shooting and its difficulty in presenting an unbroken chain of circumstantial evidence.

Just before the noon recess, seventy-four talesmen were examined, but only three more jurors were selected, which surprised Judge Ellis, the state, and the defense attorneys. Most lawyers, observing the morning session, predicted that the difficulty in selecting a jury would help in an appeal. The defense could show that they had to accept a particular juror when all peremptory challenges had been exhausted.

Courthouse spectators noticed that the same three Italians had again slipped quietly into the courthouse. When they took their seats in the last row of the gallery, Patrina whispered to Bocchio, who looked over his shoulder and caught their eyes. At noon they joined Patrina for lunch. During the meal, a curious *Item* reporter walked over to their table and asked them whether they were in town for the trial. "What the hell is it to you?" was their surly response. Although the reporter decided not to antagonize the burly trio, several townsmen kept them under surveillance throughout the afternoon. If the opportunity presented itself, they planned to pay the three mystery men a "courteous" visit.

During the afternoon session, no jurors were chosen, but the defense revealed another line of strategy through Purser's repeated question: "Will you let the case the state attempts to make against each defendant stand on its own . . . or will you throw them all in the same basket?" Most lawyers in the courtroom believed that the defense planned to argue that each of the defendants who allegedly attempted to rob the bank did not shoot Calmes. Therefore, all of the defendants were not equally guilty of murder.

When the courthouse bell rang at 5:30 that Wednesday evening, there was relief on everyone's face. Most people went home, but Bowden and his deputies jumped into their cars to serve papers on another one hundred talesmen for Thursday morning. Other deputies took the next Illinois Central train to the farthest part of the parish. If they left before dinnertime, the deputies chose jurors from the northern end of Tangipahoa; and if they could not leave until after dinner, most of the prospective jurors were from the southern end. Since these deputies had to walk miles into the piney woods, the majority of the talesmen selected lived in wards that bordered the railroad or were close to it. While Bowden and his deputies scurried about the parish serving papers, the prosecution and defense attorneys sent out their own investigators each evening to "get a line" on the qualifications of prospective jurors.[9]

On Thursday morning, the defendants, except for Deamore, entered the courtroom in a jovial mood. There was an air of excitement—one of the six, it was rumored, had offered to confess if he were granted life in prison, and supposedly Deamore was the man. Although Natale did look pale and appeared to have spent a restless night, he was in fact ill. He was so tired during the morning session, he often fell asleep.

"That rumor is absolutely without foundation," insisted Morgan when questioned about the supposed confession. "It is absolutely groundless." Despite the continuing rumors of plea bargaining, District Attorney Allen would not comment. It was also reported that Allen had refused to compromise.

Despite the persistent rumors, there was no confession, and only one juror was selected that morning. In the afternoon session, two more jurors were chosen. The case had probably now set a record in Louisiana for jury summons—the large number of pe-

9. New Orleans *Item*, June 15–16, 1921, April 4, 1922; New Orleans *States*, June 15, 19, 1921; New Orleans *Times-Picayune*, June 15–16, 1921; *State* v. *Rini*, TOA, No. 24,914, pp. 21, 207–208; *State of Louisiana* v. *Joseph Rini et al.*, Transcript of Appeal, No. 25,583, pp. 245–46, State of Louisiana Supreme Court Archives, New Orleans, hereinafter cited as *State* v. *Rini*, TOA, No. 25,583.

remptory challenges continued to plague the process. By Thursday afternoon, the defense had used fifty-five of its seventy-two peremptory challenges, and the state had used eleven of its thirty-six.

In the midst of the day's excitement, the three suspicious Italians reappeared in Amite. Shortly thereafter, a vigilante committee of townspeople decided to question them. The conversation was reportedly "polite," and by late afternoon Amite residents were assured that the three Italians had left town by train. When questioned about the trio, Gulotta said the whole episode was "nothing but newspaper talk." Allen and Ponder were also interviewed about the incident. Although they said they knew nothing officially, they smiled cryptically at the reporters.[10]

On Friday morning, June 17, a report circulated that one or more of the defendants would plead guilty, with life imprisonment as punishment. But according to the *Item*, Allen was still refusing to compromise. On the other hand, Morgan denied emphatically that the defense had attempted to plea-bargain.

Friday's morning session began, not with a confession, but with Allen's attempt to prove that Kemp had tried to bribe a prospective juror. After hearing the testimony, which proved that there was no attempt at jury tampering, Ellis, rather than dismiss the charges, announced that he would render a judgment after the end of the trial. Hoping that the clash between the state and the defense was over, Ellis attempted to get on with jury selection. But Morgan demanded a mistrial because, he argued, the whole proceeding had been "highly prejudicial to the defendants." When Reid and Allen countered that the defense should have filed its objections prior to the hearing, Ellis denied the motion for a mistrial. The defense filed another bill of exception.

After the jury-tampering hearing, the rest of the day was devoted to completing the jury. Again there were reports that the three Italians were lurking around the courthouse, asking questions about the physical layout of the building. Many people were

10. New Orleans *Item*, June 16, 1921; New Orleans *Times-Picayune*, June 17, 1921; New Orleans *States*, June 16, 1921, January 2, 1922; *State* v. *Rini*, TOA, No. 24,914, p. 22.

now convinced that the Italians had been sent from Chicago, Brooklyn, and St. Louis to help the defendants escape. Although Bowden found no evidence to support this theory, he ordered his deputies and the New Orleans police assigned to his office to search the town that afternoon. In addition, the sheriff instructed his men "to shoot to kill" if anyone attempted to rescue the six defendants.

Friday's session ended at six o'clock, and only two more jurors, farmers from northern Tangipahoa, had joined the panel. Opposition to the death penalty, the inability to convict someone on circumstantial evidence, and fixed opinions were still the main reasons that jurors were excused for cause. By the end of the day, the defense had used sixty-nine of its seventy-two peremptory challenges, and the state had used twenty-one of its thirty-six.[11]

Expecting that testimony might begin that Saturday, June 18, the crowds jammed the small courtroom at midmorning. The first two talesmen were excused because of fixed opinions, but shortly after ten o'clock, Purser announced that he would use his last peremptory challenge. The spectators' sigh of relief was audible.

When a Ponchatoula talesman took the stand, he stated that it was common knowledge in the parish that a creek above Ponchatoula was the "deadline for Italians," beyond which the immigrants and their children did not venture without an explanation. For unknown reasons, the state challenged the prospective juror successfully. Just when it appeared that another day would be necessary for completing the jury, a Spring Creek resident was chosen as the twelfth juror at 10:30 A.M. Two hundred ninety talesmen had been called; 230 examined. With one exception, they lived in the northern part of the parish. There were no Italians on the jury—Ellis had excluded all talesmen who lived in the Sixth Ward, the center of the Italian settlements.

The judge ordered three deputies to take charge of the jurors, and after the instructions to the deputies, Ellis accepted Joseph Graziano, the president of a farmers' association, as the trial interpreter. The judge also announced that he was ready to resume the

11. New Orleans *Item*, June 16–18, 1921; New Orleans *Times-Picayune* and New Orleans *States*, June 17–18, 1921; *State* v. *Rini*, TOA, No. 24,914, pp. 162–85.

contempt hearing against Kemp. After adjourning court until 9:00 A.M. Monday, Ellis ordered the jury out of the courtroom. Reid rehashed the state's evidence, and Ellis found that the testimony exonerated Kemp. Since Kemp's alleged co-conspirator was not in the courtroom, Ellis deferred the decision on him until Monday morning.[12]

With the prisoners securely in the parish jail, Bowden and his forces continued to investigate a plot allegedly devised by the three Italians. At noon on Saturday, a formal report from the New Orleans police officers in the parish confirmed that the three were staying in Tickfaw at the home of one of Frank Pisciotta's cousins. Further, the three Italians were overheard talking about a bomb in the Hudson. Bowden had been using the car on official business, and he had a mechanic inspect it for explosive wiring that afternoon. Although nothing was found, Bowden ordered guards around the car on a twenty-four-hour basis until the end of the trial.

The three suspicious Italians were not the only strangers in town. On Friday afternoon, the Illinois Central brought scores of curiosity seekers to Amite. Hotel and boardinghouse rooms were at a premium by Saturday. So numerous were the spectators that many veteran observers compared them to the crowds at the Avery Blount trial in 1909.[13]

The tedious week of selecting the jury had been enlivened by rumors of a confession by one of the defendants, alleged plots by three suspicious visitors, and a jury-tampering hearing. Tangipahoa residents had witnessed other notorious legal proceedings, but this trial, which would contain other surprises and more intrigue, would capture a huge audience.

12. New Orleans *Item,* June 18–20, 1921; New Orleans *Times-Picayune,* June 19, 1921; New Orleans *States,* June 18–19, 1921; *State* v. *Rini,* TOA, No. 24,914, pp. 25, 189, 247–48, 264, 781.

13. New Orleans *Item,* June 19, 20, 1921; New Orleans *States,* June 17, 1921; *State* v. *Rini,* TOA, No. 25,583, p. 207.

7

Applauding of the Spectators

The crowd for the opening day of testimony on Monday, June 20, was estimated at between eight hundred and one thousand. The courthouse floor and gallery were filled to capacity, and spectators gathered outside each window. At 8:45 the six defendants arrived in the courtroom. They were well dressed and appeared cheerful. When they took their seats, they stared straight ahead. Fanning themselves with palm-leaf fans, they hardly looked at the crowd.

Before the proceedings began, the prosecutors were granted a two-hour recess, and Allen, Reid, and Ponder joined Sheriff Bowden in the district attorney's office. Bowden showed them a letter received that morning. Poorly written on brown wrapping paper and postmarked Hammond, the letter offered the jailer $20,000 to allow the defendants to escape and was signed "Friends of the Italians."

Bowden said that he had been expecting such a letter. Moreover, he and Allen had learned Sunday evening that Lynn Evans had attempted to bribe two prospective jurors, Fenner Tynes and Tyrell Bennett of Kentwood, on Friday. The state attorneys thought it best to hear from Bennett and Tynes. Their statements essentially agreed with Bowden's account, and the state decided to arrest Evans immediately.

"I have filed . . . [a bill of] information against Lynn Evans charging that he has tried to bribe two prospective jurors," Allen said to the press and nearby spectators during the prolonged recess. "Those two talesmen are Fenner Tynes and Tyrell Bennett, both of Kentwood. It was on Friday in Amite, while Tynes and Bennett were in the city [as] talesmen summoned for examination as prospective jurors, that I charge Evans approached them.

"Our evidence shows," Allen continued as the crowd increased, "that he offered Fenner Tynes first $400, then $800, and at last raised his offer to $1,500, on the condition that Tynes 'hang' the jury. He also offered to bribe Bennett to vote for acquittal or hang the jury, and offered to go fifty-fifty with him on the money to be split."

Allen's announcement caused a furor on the courthouse grounds. Although the Mafia was not specifically mentioned, several men charged that "sinister agencies" were disrupting the trial, and many expressed fear that a mistrial would be declared.

Disturbed over the latest events, Rene Calmes asked Governor Parker to help avoid a possible lynching. Since L. A. Toombs, the adjutant general of the Louisiana National Guard, was already at the trial, the governor ordered him to assure the spectators that there was no need to resort to violence. Parker also had a company of national guard troops ready to go to Amite at a moment's notice to assist the federal marshals.

Also concerned with the bribery charges was defense attorney Lewis Morgan, who argued heatedly with his associates during the recess. Perhaps Morgan suspected that his colleagues were involved in the alleged bribery, but rumors persisted throughout the day that he was threatening to withdraw from the case.

The first action of the afternoon session was a defense motion for a mistrial on the grounds that the alleged jury-tampering incidents were prejudicial to the defendants. Ellis denied the motion, and he ordered the state to call its first witness.

For the rest of Monday afternoon, the prosecution tried to establish one main point—that the attempted bank robbery and the murder of Dallas Calmes were committed by more than one man. The prosecution also emphasized the fact that the lights in the bank were out that night. The implication was that someone other than the defendants had turned out the lights to make detection of anyone in the bank more difficult. Through photographs and witnesses, the state tried to establish that the physical evidence behind the restaurant proved that at least two gunmen fired at Calmes. Although bullet holes at the murder scene appeared to indicate that shots were fired from more than one direction, the defense, unfortunately, failed to challenge the state's evidence, particularly in regard to the oil tank and the wheelbarrow. Either object could have been moved inadvertently by someone in the crowds that night, thus causing the appearance of different angles of fire.[1]

After Monday's developments, Bowden enlisted the services of several more special deputies in order to increase security for Tuesday morning, which also brought more rumors of a bribe attempt. According to the courthouse gossip, certain defendants offered Giamalva, Leotta, and Pisciotta large sums of money to say that a seventh man went to Independence that Saturday night and escaped. Although Monday's report of bribes deeply affected the crowd, Tuesday's rumors caused little or no disturbance. The spectators were apparently more anxious to hear the evidence against the defendants.

The first major witness Tuesday morning, June 21, was Mrs. Calmes, who rose slowly when her name was called. With assistance from relatives, she entered the witness stand and sat down. After taking her oath, she turned and looked directly at the jury. There was a slight rustling among the spectators, who were trying to hear her every word.

"I could hardly see him," Mrs. Calmes stated as she described the man who shot her husband. "The man I saw running through the yard was a medium-built man, not overly heavy nor overly thin."

Recalling going to aid her husband, she said, "I couldn't get him inside, so I screamed." Mrs. Calmes was now visibly distraught. She raised a handkerchief nervously to wipe her tears. While she regained her composure the courtroom remained silent.

Several spectators also cried, as did Deamore and Leona. When Deamore showed no signs of stopping, Lamantia kicked Natale's ankle and whispered, "Buck up. Be a man."

"Were there any shots coming from behind the pile of barrels there?" Reid asked.

"Yes," she answered. "They were shooting at him."

Reid did not ask her to specify whether more than one man was shooting at her husband.

1. New Orleans *States,* June 20, 26, 1921; New Orleans *Item,* June 20, 30, 1921; New Orleans *Times-Picayune,* June 21, 1921; Ponchatoula *Enterprise,* June 24, 1921; *State* v. *Rini,* TOA, No. 25,583, p. 212; *State* v. *Rini,* TOA, No. 24,914, pp. 27–28, 30, 263, 266; Parker to Hughes, May 19, 1922, in Parker Papers.

Then the prosecution asked the only eyewitness to the shooting whether she saw any shots fired from another point behind the restaurant. "I was looking too intently at those men," she replied, "to notice whether shots were being fired from elsewhere."

The defense declined to cross-examine Mrs. Calmes, and her statements about the exact number of men she saw in the alley went unchallenged. On being recalled by the state later Tuesday afternoon, Mrs. Calmes stated that the man she saw shooting at her husband wore a hat. Her testimony, however, had references to "both pistols," "men," and "they." But when the state asked whether more than one man shot at her husband, she said she could not recall. The defense again declined to question the witness, to dispel the notion that more than one man fired at Dallas Calmes.

Moreover, the defense attorneys failed to challenge the parish coroner and Dr. Anthony J. Strange, whose testimony implied that at least two men shot at Calmes. Both doctors testified that the wound through the abdomen took a downward path while the other went upward. The different bullet tracks were possibly caused by Calmes's moving when he was fired upon or by the erratic movement of the murderer as he ran through the alley. Nevertheless, the defense's failure to challenge the doctors' testimony left the impression that more than one gunman fired at Calmes.

Part of Tuesday's testimony was concerned with the introduction of the state's chain of circumstantial evidence and the alleged confessions by the defendants. Through Sheriff Bowden and other witnesses, the prosecution presented evidence to prove that the tire markings of the car captured outside of Albany matched those left near the murder scene. In addition, Roy Calmes testified that Bocchio was the driver of the Hudson in Albany.[2]

On Tuesday afternoon, the jury was retired, and the state presented its case on the admissibility of Deamore's alleged confession in Albany. Morgan, however, attempted through cross-examination to prove that Deamore's statements were involuntary, the result of a beating administered by deputies. The following

2. Ponchatoula *Enterprise*, June 24, 1921; New Orleans *States* and New Orleans *Item*, June 21, 1921; New Orleans *Times-Picayune*, June 21–22, 1921; *State v. Rini*, TOA, No. 24,914, pp. 248–49, 252, 290–91, 322, 341.

morning, Deamore, under both direct and cross-examination, insisted that the Albany posse had placed a rope around his neck and threatened to hang him. He also charged that he was pistol-whipped, kicked, and punched before he spoke to Charles Pulliam. Then Pulliam testified that he had initiated a conversation with Deamore, who was "in pretty bad shape—bleeding from that cut." He spoke to Deamore in a friendly manner and saw no one threaten him, but Pulliam admitted under cross-examination that hanging threats may have occurred before his arrival.

The state countered with witnesses who stated that Pulliam's conversation with Deamore occurred an hour and a half after the beating. Implying that sufficient time had passed for Deamore not to fear for his life, the state also offered testimony that Deamore appeared eager to talk. However, under redirect examination, Lem Hoggatt, who had struck Deamore with his revolver, admitted that Bowden had also slapped Deamore vigorously during questioning, but this occurred after the Pulliam-Deamore conversation.

When Ellis ruled that Natale had voluntarily spoken to Pulliam, the defense objected and filed one of its numerous bills of exception. After a short recess, Thomas Craven took the stand to testify about the circumstances of his conversation with Deamore in New Orleans. A few moments later Morgan objected to Craven's testimony on the grounds that he had been in constant attendance throughout the trial. When Ellis ruled that he had been excused from the normal procedures, Morgan filed another bill of exception.

Craven stated that Deamore had voluntarily requested a private meeting with him and that he had not been threatened. During cross-examination, Purser asked, "Did you not at that time, in my presence, . . . have a conversation with Deamore and with Bocchio?"

Craven responded, "I said to Deamore that I had known that we would catch him for a long time, because I had a tip on him—that he was the leader of a gang of thieves. . . . I did not want to ask him if he was in it, because I knew he would lie to me."

The packed courtroom broke into applause. They laughed and stamped their feet. For nearly one minute, Judge Ellis rapped for order and instructed the deputies to silence the spectators.

After Ellis admonished the audience, Purser asked Craven whether he threatened to shoot Natale if he did not "tell everything he knew about the Independence murder." But Craven was steadfast in his denial. When Craven answered Purser's questions, he often sneered and laughed at the Amite attorney. In answer to one question, Craven, appearing to search his memory, answered, "Well, as I remember . . ."

"Answer my question," snapped Purser, "yes or no."

"The witness has the right to make a statement if he wants to," objected Reid.

"I think that Mr. Craven is a lawyer," Purser said sarcastically, "and competent to answer questions as a witness the way they should be answered."

"I think that Mr. Craven is a gentleman," countered Reid, "and is conducting himself as such at this trial and is entitled to gentlemanly treatment."

The partisan spectators again responded with loud applause for Reid's defense of Craven. Ellis was able to maintain order, but he failed to discipline anyone.

Purser asked about Craven's position on the "third degree" issue. Although Craven said that he was against the "third degree," he later stated that he had "advocated against corporal punishment upon prisoners as far as possible." He left the impression that some form of physical abuse of suspects was permissible. Purser charged that Craven, Horton, and Uhle had repeatedly used blackjacks on Giglio, beating him unconscious.

"No-no," answered Craven wearily. In answer to numerous other questions, he denied that he and the New Orleans police had severely beaten Lamantia, Leona, and Rini. After more than one hour of cross-examination, Craven was no longer laughing and sneering at Purser. The Amite defense attorney's relentless questioning had left Craven grim-faced and belligerent.

When two New Orleans police officers also denied participating in or witnessing any physical abuse of the defendants, the defense placed four of the accused on the stand. Deamore testified that Craven warned him at the morgue to tell the truth—or Craven would kill him as he had shot Gaeto and DiGiovanni. Natale also recalled that on several occasions police officers urged him to speak to Craven or he would be hanged. Under cross-examination, however, Deamore's memory appeared to fail him repeatedly. A frequent answer to Reid's questions was "Maybe I did. Maybe I didn't. I don't remember."

Leona also recounted how he was beaten with a blackjack by Craven and the New Orleans police. Then Lamantia showed his wounds, to prove that Craven and some policemen had kicked him during an interrogation. Finally, Giglio told about the hanging threats and beatings. Ellis listened to the defense's objections to admitting the Pulliam and Craven statements. The judge ruled that their testimony would go to the jury. Morgan undoubtedly recognized that the defense had suffered a major defeat, and he filed another bill of exception.

On Wednesday afternoon, the jury returned to the courtroom to hear Craven's testimony. He said that in a private interview Deamore, who often referred to the other defendants as those "five crooks," identified everyone except Bocchio as members of the gang that forced him to go to Independence that Saturday night. According to Craven, several defendants stated that Deamore was trying to implicate them and to exonerate himself. Under cross-examination, Craven denied having threatened Deamore at the morgue or physically abusing him to obtain statements.

Then the jury for the first time heard the damaging testimony about Deamore's conversations in Albany. Robert Thompson and Charles Pulliam both testified that they heard Natale frequently repeat: "'You ought to go up there and see where they killed a man.'" According to the two witnesses, Deamore also referred to the other defendants as "dirty crooks."[3]

At six o'clock, Judge Ellis recessed the trial. Virtually the whole day had been spent arguing over the admissibility of testimony before a packed courtroom. And spectators cheered and applauded the evidence against the defendants. Although the observers did not applaud Ellis' allowing the introduction of Deamore's state-

3. Ponchatoula *Enterprise*, June 24, 1921; New Orleans *States*, June 22, 1921; New Orleans *Item* and New Orleans *Times-Picayune*, June 22–23, 1921; newspaper clippings, in Dallas Calmes Scrapbook; *State* v. *Rini*, TOA, No. 24,914, pp. 202, 222–28, 376–88, 393–448, 457–97.

ments to Pulliam and Craven, the ruling was a fatal blow to the defense.

On Thursday morning, June 23, a heavy downpour caused low attendance in the courtroom. Bowden nevertheless increased security—there were reports of possible Italian demonstrations in the parish. The sheriff had heard that "two swarthy men" had attempted to purchase buckshot shells at a hardware store.

To everyone's surprise, the state presented three witnesses to prove that Deamore and Lamantia had been seen around Independence and Tickfaw on the Thursday prior to the shooting of Calmes. Although the witnesses stated that Deamore had gone to Independence to deliver a steamship ticket to his cousin's wife, the implication was that Deamore and Lamantia were in Tangipahoa to plan the bank robbery.

Following this revelation, a Livingston Parish farmer stated that he saw Giglio and Leona leave the Hudson that Sunday morning after the shoot-out. Other witnesses testified that Bocchio, Leona, and Giglio were seen Sunday morning in Ponchatoula. The prosecution then recalled Sheriff Bowden, who stated that Bocchio had admitted that he drove the Hudson to Independence on Saturday night, May 7, and that he ran from the car when it was fired upon in Albany.

The last witness called on Thursday afternoon was Pietro Leotta, who was the first to testify that the defendants dropped him off at Natale Giamalva's early Saturday morning. Implying that the defendants went to Independence to complete their plans to rob the bank, the prosecution also left the distinct impression that the defendants met with another party or parties in that conspiracy. Leotta also explained that the six defendants left for Independence at 10:00 P.M. Saturday and did not return to Giamalva's until 3:00 A.M. Sunday. Since the time of the shooting was 12:30 or 1:00 A.M. Sunday, it was apparent to nearly everyone that there were two hours between Calmes's being shot and the defendants' return to the farmhouse. Finally, under direct examination, Leotta stated that the defendants were in the car from which guns were fired at Roy Calmes's posse in Albany.

When Morgan cross-examined Leotta, he tried to establish that a seventh man, George Brocata, was at Leotta's home and joined them for the ride to Independence. But Pietro insisted that the only other person there was his wife. When Leotta left the witness stand, most observers agreed that his testimony was the most damaging against the defendants that day.[4]

On the following day, Friday, June 24, Natale Giamalva finally took the stand. Speaking with an Italian accent and in an animated manner, Giamalva testified that the defendants left his home for Independence around 10:00 P.M. Saturday and returned around 2:00 A.M. He also verified that when Leotta arrived early Saturday morning, Deamore and the other defendants went on into Independence. Posing a question which attempted to imply that Giamalva had prior knowledge of the murder and was the first to awaken and tell the defendants about the shooting, Purser startled the spectators and Giamalva, who appeared not to understand it. According to one newspaper, Giamalva replied in a shrill voice: "A-a-a-aw, you maka da mistake. I tella you da truth. I tella you da truth. Ha! you maka mistake. I tella you da truth."

Giamalva's accent, gestures, and intonations caused the spectators to laugh uproariously and some cheered. The jurors were especially amused, and even Judge Ellis struggled to hide his laughter. When it appeared that the outburst would not end quickly, Purser jumped to his feet.

"We'll have to ask you to clear the courthouse or keep these folks quiet," he demanded.

"I can't do either," replied Ellis, who was still smiling, "but I'll do the best I can."

"Then," Purser stated, "we ask that this jury be discharged because of listening to this outburst of applause prejudicial to the defendants."

Reid objected to Purser's motion because there was no applause, only laughter at Giamalva's manner and gestures. The courtroom was now totally silent—the spectators recognized the seriousness of the situation. Ellis looked at the crowd and again admonished the spectators.

"The defendants, and each of them, on account of the outburst of applause, ask that a statement of the facts be dictated to the

4. New Orleans *States*, June 23–24, 30, 1921; New Orleans *Item*, June 23, 1921; New Orleans *Times-Picayune*, June 24, 27, 1921; *State* v. *Rini*, TOA, No. 24,914, pp. 514–63, 570–74, 607–29.

stenographer by the Judge and the jury discharged," Purser repeated. After stating that there was no burst of applause, Ellis sustained Reid's objection, to which Purser filed a bill of exception.

The morning session was somewhat humorous, but the afternoon testimony proved to be both interesting and volatile. When Allen called one of the prosecution's star witnesses, Joe Leotta, to the stand, he walked nervously through the packed courtroom. Appearing bewildered by the crowd, he blinked his eyes continuously, looked around rapidly, and fidgeted in the chair. After Ellis determined that Joe was a competent witness, Allen asked some general questions. The district attorney then asked Joe to identify the men who accompanied his father to Independence. Joe pointed to the defendants and then left the witness stand to touch each one of them.

When Allen concluded his questions, Purser cross-examined the boy. "Just before you came up here this gentleman right here, Mr. Allen, and this one right over here standing up, the sheriff, and some others were up there in the jail with you and were talking to you, were they not, son?"

"Yes, sir."

"When you went in there which one of the men asked you about the man who drove the car?"

"That short one at this end."

"Go show him to us, Joe. Look at all of them, Joe. Show me the one you told Mr. Allen was the man that drove the car."

Joe left the stand again, went over to the defendants, and placed his hand on Rini.

"Now," Purser asked, "when you told the sheriff that was the man that drove the car, what did he say to you?"

"Nothing."

"Did he not say this to you: 'No, little boy. Let's get this right. Why don't you say what I have been telling you all the time.'"

"Yes, sir."

Joe's answer caused a swift intake of breath among the spectators. Everyone's attention was on the little boy.

Purser asked, "Which gentleman said that to you? This one here or the one back there? I mean the one standing up by the door there."

"I don't understand what you say."

8

No Fair Trial

That Friday night, June 24, Sheriff Bowden brooded over the implication that he and others had tampered with Joe Leotta's testimony. Still upset on Saturday morning, Bowden sent a mutual friend of his and Purser's to seek a retraction. When Purser refused, Bowden decided to confront him outside the courthouse before the trial reconvened. Bowden demanded a public retraction and an apology, but Purser hesitated. The sheriff's response was a slap to Purser's face. Seeing that the sheriff was armed, Purser decided not to strike Bowden, and the sheriff landed two more hard blows. Before he could strike Purser again, several deputies rushed over to separate the two.

After that confrontation, court convened; and Allen immediately announced that the state had closed its case. The defense attorneys requested a short recess and, after speaking to several of their witnesses, returned, ready to proceed. As part of his opening tactic, Purser questioned several witnesses about the events surrounding Deamore's statements in Albany. Robert Wilson testified that several men warned Deamore that he would hang if found guilty, but he insisted that the crowd did not threaten to hang Deamore from a nearby tree. Lem Hoggatt admitted striking the handcuffed Deamore with a revolver because he hesitated getting into the car. However, Hoggatt denied that anyone else abused or threatened Deamore prior to his conversation with Pulliam.[1]

Ellis adjourned court at noon on Saturday, June 25, for the weekend. The New Orleans *States* reported that "in its entire history, perhaps, Amite has never felt such a feverish interest in a trial like in the present case." The "feverish interest" turned into

---

1. New Orleans *Times-Picayune*, June 25–26, 1921; New Orleans *States* and New Orleans *Item*, June 25, 1921; *State* v. *Rini*, TOA, No. 24,914, pp. 35, 90–91, 215, 738–61, 766–70; interview with John Purser, May 14, 1984.

strong rumors of mob violence—should there be a hung jury or a not-guilty verdict, the prisoners would be lynched. Bowden doubled the guards around the courthouse and at the second-floor courthouse windows, which overlooked the jail. In addition, the sheriff wanted all reports of suspicious characters sent directly to him, and every train passing through Amite was to be watched closely.

When Governor Parker heard about the same rumors, he ordered Adjutant General Toombs to Baton Rouge for a conference. Agreeing that conditions were serious in Tangipahoa, Parker and Toombs decided upon a contingency plan. The state officials were not the only ones concerned about possible violence. Since four of the defendants were Italian subjects, Victor Loisel, the United States marshal in New Orleans, decided that he and several more deputy marshals should be in Amite when court reconvened.[2]

On Monday morning, June 27, speculation was rife that the defendants would take the stand and blame the murder on Deamore. According to newspaper reporters, their sources were the defense attorneys. Similar rumors had surfaced earlier in the trial, but many officials were still skeptical.

When testimony resumed, Purser offered, not a confession, but the first witness who could prove that New Orleans officials had beaten at least one of the defendants. The prison druggist stated that he had treated Lamantia for abrasions on his shins. In addition, Purser instructed Lamantia to reveal the scars to the jury.

He then introduced testimony to establish the reason for the defendants' being in Tangipahoa. Deamore's cousin stated that he had asked Natale to be his child's godfather, and the christening was scheduled for Sunday, May 8. But under cross-examination, the witness admitted that he had not made arrangements for the church ceremony.

Purser then placed Joseph Rini on the stand. The voice of the twenty-two-year-old navy veteran carried well. As he related his account of the trip to Independence, Rini insisted that a seventh man, George Brocata, and Pietro Leotta joined them in Hobart and continued with them to the Giamalva farm. Early Saturday morn-

2. New Orleans *Item*, June 30, 1921; New Orleans *Times-Picayune*, June 27, 1921; New Orleans *States*, June 26–27, 1921.

ing was the last time he saw Brocata. Rini stated that Giamalva insisted that they spend the night again and leave early Sunday morning for the christening. Rini's recollection was that Giamalva woke them up at 1:30 A.M. Sunday and told them to leave because there had been a shooting at Independence. They went into the yard and found that their car was gone. After Giamalva refused to let them back inside and would not tell them where the car was, Rini and the others left. He concluded his account of the events with his capture.

"Look at the jury there and tell these gentlemen if you shot Dallas Calmes," said Purser.

Rini looked at the jury, smiled, and said, "No, sir, I never did."

"Were you where you could see Mr. Calmes when he was being shot?"

"No, sir."

"Were you where you could hear any shooting when he was shot?"

"No, sir."

"Do you know anything about the killing of Mr. Calmes?"

"No, sir."

Then Deamore took the stand and testified that George Brocata joined them at Leotta's house. Thereafter, Deamore's story was identical to Rini's and to his own testimony the previous week. When asked why he was in Independence on Thursday, Natale stated that he had gone to see his cousin about postponing the christening because his own baby was ill. Deamore admitted that he, Rini, and Leona were in Independence on Saturday afternoon, but he denied going there early Saturday morning or later that night.

"Were you in town when Mr. Calmes was shot?" Purser asked.

"No," replied Natale.

"Do you know who shot him?"

"No."

"Did you shoot him?"

"No, sir."

Under Ponder's cross-examination, Deamore responded to questions about his conversation with Pulliam: "Maybe I say that, because they was killing me. They tried to kill me, hang me. I could say anything on account of that." Throughout, Deamore suffered from lapses of memory. As he squirmed about in the witness chair he perspired copiously, especially when questioned about George Brocata.

"Don't you know that there's no such man as George Brocata?" Ponder asked in a strident voice.

"I don't know myself," Natale answered, twisting his hands.

After the state concluded its cross-examination of Deamore, Lamantia was the next witness. The testimony of the twenty-one-year-old barber was virtually identical to Rini's and Deamore's. He, too, denied shooting Calmes. Andrea again showed the marks on his shins to the jury as evidence of brutality by New Orleans officials. Under Reid's cross-examination, Lamantia had great difficulty explaining how eight men could ride comfortably in the Hudson between Leotta's house and Independence. Nevertheless, he insisted that it was possible if one man placed his legs out the door. Reid then asked Lamantia hard questions about statements he made at his capture and in New Orleans. Perspiring profusely, he often answered, "I don't remember."

When Reid concluded his cross-examination, the court adjourned at its usual hour. Later that Monday evening, Adjutant General Toombs arrived in Amite with instructions from Governor Parker. He pledged his support to Bowden for the remainder of the trial and then outlined his contingency plan. There were two national guard units ready in New Orleans and one in Bogalusa, each fully armed with riot gear and weapons. Eight men had Browning automatic rifles, and the New Orleans company had machine guns. In order to expedite troop transport, Toombs said, he had arranged for the railroad to clear all tracks. The first troops could be in Amite within two hours.[3]

When court convened on Tuesday morning, Purser, attempting to bolster Deamore's claim that he was in Independence on Thursday to cancel the christening, offered one witness to prove that Deamore's baby had been ill. The defense counsels then announced that they had concluded their case. The spectators, as well as the

3. New Orleans *Times-Picayune*, June 28, 30, 1921; New Orleans *Item*, June 27–28, 30, 1921; New Orleans *States*, June 27, 1921; *State* v. *Rini*, TOA, No. 24,914, pp. 774–77, 781–83, 788–909.

Deamore, who was sitting on the edge of his bunk with his head in his hands, nodded a silent approval. Lamantia and Leona, standing nearby, also agreed.

"They lied like hell about us, those state witnesses," Giglio shouted through a small opening in the cell door. "They talk about those guns and that soup [nitroglycerine]. What the hell. Are we the only people in the world can have guns? We don' know nothin' about 'em.

"That witness . . . for the state," he continued. "He says he's out picking beans at three o'clock in the morning. Is a guy gonna know whether he's picking green things or ripe things that time in the dark?"

"Sure," added Rini, "they all lied about us. That Mrs. Giamalva, she testifies that we left her house for Independence that Saturday night we was sleeping there. Course she ain't gonna testify against what her husband says. But she lies too. They all lie."

"Look at Lamantia," Giglio said, enraged again. "They say those scars on his shins is mosquito bites and bullet holes. He was the one the New Orleans police kicked on the shins in Mr. Craven's office. You think mosquito bites gonna last that long? You think bullet wounds gonna get well that quick? I seen him when his shin was all swollen up and cut from them kicks. But they take the stand and lie about us and they lie some more."

"Then you think the verdict is going against you?" Frost asked.

"It's a frame up," Giglio went on. "There's that man Evans. He sit in the court all through the trial and then he get up and the judge let him testify that he saw the tracks of our automobile past his house. I tell you what he saw, the lousy son-of-a-bitch, goddamn bastard.

"Sorry I used the bad words," he said apologetically, "but I got sore. It's a frame up."

"They don't give us a square deal," added Bocchio. "We ain't got no fair trial."

"You bet we don't," Rini responded quickly. "It's a frame up from the minute they pinch us."

"I tell you this," said Giglio, "we gonna get a fair trial somewhere. We don't get it here, we get it in another court."

Lamantia, Deamore, and Leona, who had remained silent throughout the interview, again nodded their approval.

"That's right," said Bocchio. "Everybody been against us. They hang us. I tell you somebody got murder on their conscience. They talk about we have guns. That Giamalva have a half dozen guns in his house when we're there."

"Are you accusing Giamalva or Leotta or Pisciotta of trying to break into the bank?" asked Frost.

"We ain't saying anybody did it," Giglio answered.

As they began to dress for court Giglio turned suddenly and said, "You think we bring the guns and the dynamite up here for a christening?" But before Frost could answer, Giglio said disgustedly, "Aw, hell."

On Wednesday, June 29, the expected high was 93 degrees, but the hot, muggy weather did not stop the spectators from attending court. As early as six o'clock that morning, the first spectators began to arrive to find good seats. A holiday spirit prevailed, and it appeared that nearly every farmer in Tangipahoa and Livingston parishes and in the nearby counties of Mississippi was there. By nine o'clock, parish officials were sure that a new trial-attendance record had been set. Some spectators looked through the windows; others jammed the corridors. Outside the courthouse, hundreds more, expecting to be able to hear the conclusion of the closing arguments, sat on the grounds. All around the courthouse square, there were at least two hundred cars, saddled horses, buggies, and mule wagons—nearly all of the side streets were blocked.

Among the huge crowd were Victor Loisel and his deputy marshals, as well as several federal agents, probably from the Justice Department and the State Department. Four of the defendants were Italian citizens, and Loisel said the federal government remembered all too well the Hennessey case and its diplomatic repercussions.

Inside the courtroom, Reid reminded the jury not to be frightened because the lives of six men were at stake. "The responsibility is not all yours," he said. "I tell you that I believe that the six men before you are guilty of the murder of Dallas Calmes, and I am willing to assume full measure of moral responsibility for a verdict of guilty as charged." Reid said that the jurors, the trial judge, and the governor were all equally responsible for any execution.

Speaking for one solid hour, the former judge assailed the defense's case. He admitted that he could not say whether Leotta, Giamalva, Pisciotta, and the others had prior knowledge of the crime. But, argued Reid, if it were true that they did know, he would be back in court to assist Allen in their prosecution. Finally, Reid took great delight in ridiculing the defense's mystery man, George Brocata.

During the closing arguments, which lasted nearly all day, the defendants sat waving palm-leaf fans and anxiously watching the jury's reaction. As the attorneys spoke Rini nervously wiped his face with a soaked handkerchief, and Lamantia's head twitched sporadically. Giglio displayed no emotions. His gray eyes partially closed, he fanned himself and watched the proceedings carefully.

Kemp stressed that there was enough reasonable doubt for the jury not to convict the defendants. He argued that he "wouldn't hang a sheep-killing dog on the evidence the state has presented in this trial." Speaking for twenty-five minutes, Kemp recalled two criminal cases in which men condemned to hang were proved innocent just prior to their execution date. He emphasized the danger of hanging men as a result of circumstantial evidence.

After Kemp's arguments, George Gulotta spoke. "Eliminate the testimony of Giamalva, Leotta and Pisciotta," he said, "and the state has no case. Self-preservation is the motive of their testimony." Then for several minutes he addressed the jury on the unfairness of hanging all six defendants for the murder of one man.

"This is not only circumstantial evidence on which the state asks you to convict these six men," he argued, "but it is conflicting circumstantial evidence." After pointing out several inconsistencies in the testimony, Gulotta concluded his arguments.

Amos Ponder then resumed the state's closing statements. "There are just the essentials for you as jurors to consider," he began. "Was Dallas L. Calmes murdered? Did that murder take place in the Parish of Tangipahoa? Has the state proved beyond reasonable doubt that the six men on trial today are responsible for that murder?

"Calmes is murdered," Ponder continued. "There sits his widow," he said, pointing. "He was murdered in the Parish of Tangipahoa, and the state has shown you by a chain of evidence beyond reasonable doubt that there sit his murderers.

"George Brocata—that mythical character introduced by the defense—that flower so rare that he could not bear the light," Ponder said mockingly. "Brocata was the physical and spiritual birth of the fertile mind of the six defendants and their learned counsel."

He methodically attacked the defense's evidence and bolstered the state's testimony. At the end, he insisted that the only reasonable action for the jury was a verdict of guilty as charged for all six defendants. "The hanging of these men," Ponder argued, "is as important to any city or section of the country as it is to the Parish of Tangipahoa. It will help destroy gangs of bandits and assassins who go about the country stealing what others have earned and shooting down men who attempt to stop them."

When Ponder concluded at 12:30 P.M., Ellis recessed court until 2:00 P.M. In the afternoon session, Reid, Ponder, and Allen continued to assail the defense arguments, which were, according to the state, insults to the jurors' intelligence. The prosecutors asked for a capital verdict.

After the closing arguments, Ellis charged the jury. At the request of the defense, he included ten special charges. But when Ellis was finished, Purser stood up to make the defense's most important objection since the trial began.

PURSER: If the Court please, the defendants except to the charge, on the ground that it is partly written and partly oral. . . .

ELLIS: Mr. Lefevre [court reporter], you take this down before we send the jury out: The Court had its charge prepared—its general charge prepared. It also had the Sections of the textbooks, which I read from, marked; and in addition to that, the defendants brought the stenographer in and sat him down under leave of the Court, and had the charge taken down by him. Do you get it all, Mr. Lefevre?

STENOGRAPHER: Yes, sir.

PURSER: To which ruling of the Court, the defendants, and each of them, except and reserve a formal bill of exceptions. . . .

ELLIS: Mr. Sheriff, show the jury to their room.

The jurors went to a deliberating room at 4:24 P.M. on Wednesday, June 29. Relatives stood behind the defendants and talked quietly. As Bocchio waited impatiently for the jury to return he was still confident of a favorable verdict.

After deliberating only twenty-two minutes, the jurors returned to the packed courtroom. The clerk of court ordered the defendants and the jurors to face each other. As the defendants gazed straight ahead, they smiled at the jurors.

"We find the defendants guilty as charged," read the clerk of court. Rini, Deamore, and Bocchio quickly lost their smiles, but they continued to stare at the jurors. Leona flashed a nervous smile, but Giglio remained smiling as he turned to his attorneys.

The verdict brought a small ripple of applause from the audience, but Rene Calmes, who was standing beside Judge Ellis, raised his arms to demand silence. The applause ended quickly. Twenty heavily armed deputies positioned themselves to protect the defendants. The verdict was whispered from one spectator to another along the back wall to hundreds of others in the corridor, on the stairways, and on the grounds.

The defense attorneys immediately asked the court to poll the jurors. "Is this your verdict?" asked the clerk. As the jurors answered affirmatively, the defendants tried to smile, but they couldn't. They calmly fanned themselves. Lamantia, trying to appear unconcerned, plucked at his fingernails.

When it appeared that the sheriff was ready to remove the defendants, Katherine approached them and began to talk quietly to Rini and Leona. She told them a joke in Italian, and they laughed heartily. She tried to force a smile, but she was fighting back tears.

Patrina spoke softly to Bocchio, but she expressed no emotion. When Bowden announced he had to return the men to their cells, Sal Rini shook hands nervously with his son. Katherine finally managed a smile as she bade her cousin farewell. Patrina and Mrs. Deamore threw their arms about their loved ones and kissed them repeatedly. With tears welling in their eyes, the two women turned away and left the courtroom.

While the defendants were consoled by family and friends, Mrs. Calmes shook the hand of each juror. As she was personally introduced by Sheriff Bowden, she said, "Thank you.

"I wanted to see justice done," she said. "You've done it. Oh, if it would only bring my Dallas back to me again." Mrs. Calmes broke into sobs, and relatives escorted her from the courthouse.

After the deputies handcuffed and shackled the defendants in pairs for the first time since the trial started, reporters gathered around to question them. The defense attorneys and relatives refused to comment, but some of the defendants were eager to talk.

"We did not get a fair trial," one said snappishly.

"Everything was against us," added Giglio, "and some of the state's witnesses were allowed to stay in the courtroom, which was unjust."

Deamore said that he still had hope.

When the reporters finished their interviews, Bowden ordered the defendants to proceed toward the jail. Surrounded by twenty deputies carrying double-barreled shotguns, the defendants walked down the narrow back stairs of the courthouse. Bowden, also carrying a shotgun, led the procession through nearly two thousand spectators. The crowd remained quiet until the deputies and the defendants disappeared behind the jail door. Their curiosity satisfied, people quickly dispersed.

The significance of the verdict was not lost on the officials and the press: "The conviction of six men for murder, all with capital punishment," wrote a *Times-Picayune* reporter, "is believed to set a new national record. Never in the history of the State of Louisiana or the United States, it is said, have six men been hanged for one offense.

"As the result of the assassination of Police Chief David Hennessey in New Orleans in 1890," continued the reporter, "eleven men were lynched by citizens after a mistrial had been entered by the jury." Both the New Orleans *States* and the Ponchatoula *Enterprise* mentioned the uniqueness of the verdict, and the two papers reminded their readers about the 1891 New Orleans prison incident, which took the lives of eleven Italians.[5]

The unprecedented verdict of *Rini et al.* was not unexpected.

5. *State* v. *Rini*, TOA, No. 24,914, pp. 38–39, 49, 58–83, 219–20, 229–32; New Orleans *Item*, June 29–30, 1921; Joseph Bocchio, "Last Days of a Condemned Man," ed. Herman Drezinski, in New Orleans *Item*, January 29, 1924 (this series of articles is Bocchio's diary of his three years in prison); New Orleans *States* and New Orleans *Times-Picayune*, June 29–30, 1921; Ponchatoula *Enterprise*, July 1, 1921; newspaper clippings, in Dallas Calmes Scrapbook; *State* v. *Rini*, TOA, No. 25,563, p. 183.

Robert R. Reid
Courtesy of Duncan S. Kemp III

Robert S. Ellis
Courtesy of Martina E. Buck

Jurors in the first trial
Courtesy of Natalie C. Salter

Give [this] to Mrs. Calmas

=I=

=2=

New Orleans La
May 21/24

Mrs Blood thirsty =

This letter to advice you to save
the sy Condemed mens live's if
you want to save your life, you
Say that you not Bloodthirst But
we all say you are, to pay you want
to send this sy to this gallows
Now Mrs Calmas if you was God
enough to be present Wednesday before
the pardon board, You can to prevent
mor mor before Governor Parker and
ask for Clemency for those sy Condemd
men, if you don't do what we say
in this letter before May the ninth we
will kill you next, it is say mor
say mor plenty mor time for you
to change your mind
Mrs. Calmas these men have been

suffering for three years in prison,
don't you think they have enough
punishments they are half dead now
without being hung. Now Mrs. Calmas
its left to you what you entent to
do, be sure and don't delay as we
will get you any when you go.
We want sou to be gold friends to you
as we teen, if you ever thade men
enes. So remember these wed and we mean
every thing we say don't take it
husa take take this serres we mean
it. think that sy men cannt to
hang for one, do it for the sake I
your husand and let his soul rest
if you want to.

We sign

S. E. J. F. M. M C G. B. Q.

From unknown Ten.

Joseph Bocchio (*left trap*) and Andrea Lamantia (*right trap*)
Reprinted from Clement C. Hearsey, *The Six Who Were Hanged*

Roy Leona (*left*) and Natale Deamore (*right*)
Reprinted from Clement C. Hearsey, *The Six Who Were Hanged*

After one week of jury selection and another week of state testimony, which included forty witnesses, the defense offered only twelve witnesses during its day and a half of testimony. Making no serious attack upon the state's circumstantial evidence, George Gulotta and his colleagues presented a defense that consisted of a mystery man, seen only by the defendants, and a christening as the reason for their being in Tangipahoa. After considering all of the evidence, the jury was probably justified in reaching a guilty verdict. Although the jury had the choice of returning a noncapital verdict, that was a most unlikely response—given that courtroom spectators applauded the evidence against the defendants and that some of the state's judicial officers were probably members of the Klan. The full verdict of *Rini et al.*, guilty of first-degree murder, was, therefore, a harsh one.

9

Summary Justice Averted

At the end of the trial, Governor Parker notified Secretary of State Hughes about the verdict. On the same day, June 29, Parker also congratulated Ellis, Reid, and Bowden, for "the splendid way" in which they handled "the case against the Italians."

The next morning, Purser feverishly began to prepare the application for a new trial without the aid of one of his associates because Lewis Morgan announced his immediate withdrawal from the appeal process. No reason was given, but perhaps the issues of bribery and the results of the trial affected his decision.[1]

In an unusual evening session on Saturday, July 2, at five o'clock, Judge Ellis heard the defense's motion to set aside the June 29 verdict. Purser also requested that the defense be granted more time to file additional bills of exception, and Ellis agreed. The motion for a new trial alleged numerous errors during jury selection. In addition, the defense maintained, the alleged bribery charges were prejudicial to the defendants. In regard to testimony, the defense argued that Ellis erred in allowing Charles Pulliam, Robert Thompson, and Thomas Craven to testify about Deamore's conversations with them, because the statements were made under duress. Finally, the defense said, public demonstrations during the trial, extensive newspaper coverage, and the enormous crowds affected the due process of the trial.

On July 7 and 14, Ellis allowed additional time for the stenographer to finish transcribing the testimony. When the hearing finally convened on Saturday, July 16, Judges Robert Ellis and Columbus Reid were again sitting as a panel. The defense, which now

1. Parker to Hughes, June 30, 1921, in Deamore, N., *et al.*, File So. 311.6521, Department of State, NA; Parker to Hughes, Parker to Robert R. Reid, and Parker to Lem H. Bowden, June 30, 1921, all in Parker Papers; New Orleans *Item* and New Orleans *Times-Picayune*, June 30, 1921.

included the former district attorney of Orleans Parish, Chandler Luzenburg, submitted without argument a new trial motion that Ellis promptly denied. Although Ellis permitted the defense to file another motion in arrest of judgment on the grounds that the verdict, "guilty as charged," was vague and indefinite, he denied it also. Sentencing was postponed until July 30. The court stenographer still had not completed the transcript, and the defense wanted more time to review testimony upon which an appeal would be taken to the Louisiana Supreme Court.

On Saturday morning, July 30, the well-dressed defendants appeared before Ellis and Reid for sentencing. Displaying no emotion, they paid little attention to the two hundred spectators. Not one of the defendants' relatives was in the crowd. When Ellis asked whether they had any reasons why the sentence should not be imposed on them, Bocchio replied, "They have got the wrong men. We are innocent."

Ellis stated that they had received a fair trial, and he would not discuss the jury's findings with them before pronouncing sentence: "That you, Joseph Rini, and you, Andrea Lamantia, and you, Roy Leona, and you, Joseph Giglio, and you, Joseph Bocchio, and you, Natale Deamore, be each hanged by the neck until you are dead, and may God have mercy on your souls."

"Thank you," Bocchio replied in a serious tone, probably much to everyone's amazement.

Bowden quickly removed the defendants under heavy guard to await the one o'clock train to New Orleans. At the Amite station was a large gathering—people apparently wanted only to see the prisoners. With great relief, Bowden placed them on the train. At two of the main stops, Independence and Hammond, there were sizable crowds. Curiosity seekers tried merely to get a glimpse of the prisoners.[2]

With Rini and the others safely back in New Orleans, George Gulotta filed the appeal with the Louisiana Supreme Court. One of the bills of exception in the appeal brief cited the existence of extreme prejudice toward the Italians in Tangipahoa. Although

2. New Orleans *Item*, July 8, 16, 30, 1921; New Orleans *States*, July 23–24, 30–31, 1921; Ponchatoula *Enterprise*, July 8, 22, 1921; *State* v. *Rini*, TOA, No. 24,914, pp. 40–48, 99, 238–44.

not specifically cited in the brief, that sentiment surfaced again before the sentencing. Two Italians were arrested in Ponchatoula because they had crossed the infamous "deadline" to peddle bananas without a license. "Just why these Italians summoned up enough nerve to come to Ponchatoula," stated the *Enterprise*, "when they know they are not wanted here is not known, but they lost no time getting out of town as soon as they were released. . . . Ponchatoula does not want Italians and it is only a fool who goes where he is not wanted." Several weeks later, the *Enterprise*, in one of its usual anti-Italian diatribes, stated that "the farmers of the north central part of the parish are selling their holdings and heading for our little town, getting away from the Italian element and coming in among the cleanest American settlement in the state, a place where the Ku Klux isn't necessary, because we are all red-blooded American citizens."[3]

Apparently, the heavy security and all the publicity during the trial had discouraged any threats against the Italian communities. But in early October, parish officials received reports that the Italian merchants in Kentwood were ordered to take their children out of school and to leave town within fifteen days. The Italian consulate sent in an investigative team, and Governor Parker ordered several state officials to gather information. Although most townspeople thought the incident was a prank by some irresponsible person, local officials were concerned.[4]

Anti-immigration articles in local newspapers followed the Klan-like disturbance in Kentwood. The *Louisiana Sun* (Hammond) argued that "more rigid immigration laws would have to be obtained" because "Italy has dumped a most undesirable element into the United States. . . . It is painful to note that of the large Italian element in Louisiana, and in Tangipahoa Parish, mighty few of them seem interested now in the outcome of the noted case. They appear evasive when approached in regard to assisting the prosecution. They do not care to donate to any fund that might possibly be paid the lawyers assisting the state. Why is this?

"We'll venture the assertion," added the paper, "that one-half of

3. Ponchatoula *Enterprise*, July 15, September 23, 1921.
4. *Florida Parishes Times* (Amite City), October 8, 1921.

the population of Italians are not citizens of the United States. Out of the lot, we'll venture further and say that a number would be found who would commit the same crime that caused Dallas Calmes to be sent to his eternity."

The *Sun* concluded by commenting on the unusual sentence meted out by Judge Ellis. "'Six Italians should not die for the killing of one American' is pretty well circulated these days. But we believe that six Italians will die for the murder of one American and we believe further that if necessary one hundred would suffer the same fate if circumstances warranted. This is certainly not a time to express any sympathy for these murderers. They deserve the death that the legal processes demand, no matter if all were subjects of Italy."

The *Sun* article enraged the Italians in Tangipahoa. Submitting a letter to the editor, several leading Italians reminded citizens of the parish that Joe Graziano served as the official trial interpreter and received no compensation. They also noted that Dr. Anthony J. Strange, an Italian, and Mayor Charles Anzalone assisted the state on numerous occasions before and during the trial. Further, Anzalone, a close family friend, led a parishwide fund drive to help pay off the Calmeses' mortgage. Finally, almost as a warning, they reminded everyone that "a large amount of the wealth of this parish, particularly that coming from the culture of strawberries, is the result of the labor of the Italian farmers." Economic strength, sometimes a source of prejudice against the immigrants and their children, was a weapon that Italian leaders were not afraid to use against Tangipahoa's powerful political factions.[5]

The fund referred to by the *Sun* had support throughout the parish. The money raised was to defray the expenses for the two special prosecutors, Reid and Ponder. Responding to the fund drive, three major banks contributed $100 each.[6]

As Tangipahoa residents awaited the state supreme court decision, which would decide the fate of the six Italians, Sheriff Bowden made the arrangements for the execution. According to one newspaper account, he planned to build one large platform

---

5. *Louisiana Sun* (Hammond) clippings, in Dallas Calmes Scrapbook; New Orleans *Item*, May 13, 28, 1921.

6. *State* v. *Rini*, TOA, No. 25,583, pp. 97, 149.

with six traps so that the six could be hanged at once. Sure that the execution would occur shortly after the supreme court's decision, Bowden sold the Hudson at auction. Norman P. Vernon, the parish tax assessor, purchased it as a family car. He did not inspect the car closely—what was in the lining of the car roof remained hidden. For three years, the Vernon family, not knowing that their lives were in danger, used the Hudson extensively.[7]

While preparations for the execution went on in Tangipahoa, an unannounced visitor at the Orleans Parish Prison asked to see the warden. Archie Rennyson happened to have a reporter in his office. So, for perhaps the first time in history, New Orleanians read the comments of the city's official executioner. Known only to Rennyson and one deputy, and summoned by a secret message, the executioner was a building contractor with a wife and children. Having served the previous prison administration, the hangman had performed seven executions.

"I am not blood thirsty," he said to the reporter, who requested an interview. "But I do love the thrill of adventure, and I need the money. I work as hard as any man, but I am always behind.

"I am excited for a few days before each hanging," he continued. "I am nervous almost to prostration when I am ready to spring the trap, and I am depressed and upset for a few days afterward. Then it all seems like a dream, and I am a normal human being."[8]

The Louisiana Supreme Court was studying the legal briefs filed by the defense and by the state. Finally, on Monday, January 2, 1922, it issued its decision. Speaking for the court, Justice Winston Overton announced a unanimous reversal of *State of Louisiana* v. *Joseph Rini et al.* Having to examine thirty-six bills of exception, the court quickly dismissed many of the defense's technical objections, such as the attempt to quash the grand jury indictment on the grounds that a jury commissioner held another public office. But the court was especially interested in Deamore's

7. *Florida Parishes Times* (Amite City), December 3, 10, 1921; newspaper clipping, in Dallas Calmes Scrapbook; New Orleans *Times-Picayune*, April 13, 1923.
8. Newspaper clippings, in Dallas Calmes Scrapbook.

statements in Albany and in New Orleans. The court noted that the pistol-whipping had occurred an hour and a half before Deamore spoke to Pulliam and "was not done with the end in view of bringing about the making of a statement." The court also found that Bowden's slapping Deamore "was attributable only to the indirect manner in which Deamore answered questions, and was . . . not intended to elicit any particular answer." Justice Overton concluded that "while Deamore was mistreated by the officers prior to the time he made the statement, yet the mistreatment did not cause him to make it, either by putting him in a state of fear or otherwise." According to Overton, "the motive for making the statement appears from the statement itself, wherein he condemns those who got him into the trouble, and offers to assist the officers in finding them. Therefore, finding that the statement was freely and voluntarily made, it was admissible as evidence."

The court discussed the admissibility of Deamore's statements to Craven in New Orleans. "As to whether the statement was voluntarily made," stated Overton, "depends upon whose evidence should be accepted. . . . A careful review of the evidence leads us to the conclusion that it was voluntarily made, and, having been thus made, there can be no question that the objection urged against its admissibility was properly overruled."

The justices then grappled with the issue of Ellis' jury charge, which was partially oral and partially written. After citing sections of the Revised Statutes of Louisiana, the court ruled that "a charge orally delivered and stenographically taken is not within the requirements of the statute." Although the defense waited until the judge finished and then excepted, the court held that the defendants did not thereby waive their right to a charge entirely written. It was sufficient that the bill was reserved before the jury retired. "The nature of the right conferred," wrote Overton, "is such that for a defendant to seek to enforce it then and there would probably result in his delaying the trial to his injury." Therefore, the Louisiana Supreme Court ruled that "the refusal of the judge to comply with it by not giving a written charge when requested, is fatal."

The truly fatal error in this case occurred when the state supreme court refused to examine the bills of exception relating to the "incidents surrounding the trial." Maintaining that passing on them would serve no useful purpose, the court refused to examine the charges of prejudice toward the Italians in the parish and toward the defendants—as revealed by "the applauding of spectators" when the prosecution scored a point and the need to have three national guard units available in the event of a not-guilty verdict.[9] The state supreme court, in effect, remanded the case to the Tangipahoa court, where the Klan was influential in the judicial system and where many residents and newspapers expressed open hostility toward Italians. Although the defendants were granted a new trial, there was serious doubt about the possibility of an impartial judicial proceeding.

An *Item* reporter brought the news of the reversal to Rini and the others. There was, at first, complete silence, but then they cheered, shook hands, and did a "snake dance" on the exercise floor. Throwing their caps into the air, they wrestled vigorously, pulled each other's hair, and threw playful blows at each other. Then all six men ran to the gate and called for Captain Rennyson to send them "lots of spaghetti" for a celebration.[10]

The immediate response of the defense attorneys was that if the trial were conducted again in Amite, they would ask that Parker provide troops. Chandler C. Luzenburg, the son of the prosecutor in the Hennessey case, announced that the Italian ambassador in Washington suggested the use of federal troops, should the trial be held in Amite.

After the supreme court decision, Governor Parker advised Secretary of State Hughes of the reversal and warned that feelings ran "very high in Tangipahoa Parish where violence before was narrowly averted." Parker also informed Hughes that "an earnest effort is being made for a change of venue on this trial."[11]

---

9. *State* v. *Rini et al.*, 91 So. 665 (1922); New Orleans *States* and New Orleans *Item*, January 2, 1922; *Florida Parishes Times* (Amite City), January 7, 1922.

10. New Orleans *Item*, January 2, 5, 1922; New Orleans *Times-Picayune*, January 3, 1922; newspaper clipping, in Dallas Calmes Scrapbook.

11. New Orleans *Times-Picayune*, January 3, 1922, September 15, 1950; Parker to Hughes, January 7, 1922, Henry P. Fletcher to John M. Parker, January 18, 1922, both in Deamore, N., *et al.*, File So. 311.6521.

District Attorney Allen announced that he would study the decision, to determine whether to request a rehearing. Should a rehearing be refused, Allen stated that he would oppose any attempt to change the venue. Bowden's reaction to the decision was that he hoped that the new trial would not lead to mob rule in Amite.

There were no outright demonstrations in Tangipahoa at the news of the supreme court's decision. Although many people in the parish were surprised by the ruling, some local attorneys believed that several of the bills of exception had merit. Some businessmen interviewed in Amite felt that the trial had been fair, but one Amite merchant came closer to the truth, perhaps, than anyone else when he told the press, "The six men were lucky to have been given a court trial of any kind."[12]

After the Louisiana Supreme Court ruling, the talk of a change of venue began in earnest. According to Hammond newspaper editor George Campbell, who kept Parker abreast of the latest events, Robert Reid stated confidentially that the parish would "return to pioneer days of outlawry," should a second trial be held in Amite. The editor, urging a change of venue, also told the governor that Sheriff Bowden feared that there would be violence. Parker concluded that a change of venue was absolutely necessary, and he so notified State Attorney General Adolph V. Coco. Parker admitted that the neighboring parishes of St. Tammany and Washington were not suitable because "it would be equally dangerous." He suggested moving the trial to East Baton Rouge Parish, the location of the state capital, and housing the defendants at the state penitentiary. The governor also requested from Adjutant General Toombs the number of national guard troops available in Bogalusa and Franklin and their readiness for active duty.[13]

Amid the growing controversy over a possible change of venue, George Campbell sent to Governor Parker reports that certain officials were attempting to delay the second trial for political rea-

---

12. New Orleans *Times-Picayune*, January 3, 1922; New Orleans *States*, January 2, 1922; *Florida Parishes Times* (Amite City), January 7, 1922.

13. New Orleans *States*, January 2, 1922; Campbell to Parker, January 2, 1922, Parker to Campbell, January 3, 1922, Parker to A. V. Coco, January 2, 1922, all in Parker Papers; Parker to Toombs, February 24, 1922, in John M. Parker Correspondence, Department of Archives, Troy H. Middleton Library, Louisiana State University, Baton Rouge.

sons. Although Reid believed that the state could not be ready by spring, it was, according to Campbell, Judge Ellis who wanted to delay the trial until after the September primaries. Ellis planned to be a candidate to succeed his uncle on the court of appeals. Campbell also noted that the delay disturbed the police jury[14] because the cost to the parish would be great. Moreover, the editor castigated Ellis for his judicial error, which would probably cost the citizens of Tangipahoa another twenty thousand dollars.[15]

Although this report disturbed Parker, he was also embroiled in a major campaign to destroy the Ku Klux Klan in Louisiana. During this crusade and just prior to the second trial, many supporters warned Parker that the greatest threat posed by the Klan was its control of jury systems. One of the governor's admirers suggested disqualifying from public office and jury service any person who refused to sign an affidavit disavowing the Klan or its sympathizers. Three days later, Parker announced his plan to bring that up at the May session of the legislature.

Parker's stand against the Klan brought hostile comments from prominent residents of Tangipahoa. Campbell thought that someone was attempting "to hoodwink" the governor in reference to the Klan's true nature. The Tangipahoa Klan, he said, contained "the very best element of citizenship—the same element instrumental in your election; the same element instrumental in a fair trial for the six Italians." The Hammond editor warned Parker about "the power wielded in this parish by the Klan at Kentwood, Amite, and Ponchatoula." Referring specifically to the upcoming trial, Campbell noted that "the slowness of justice, the technicalities always ferreted out in many important trials, has caused the Klan in this section to determine that justice move more firmly, the guilty punished as the law prescribes and the immunities granted under a subterfuge be completely eliminated."[16]

Although Parker also received confidential reports from his own operatives that the Klan controlled the parish's law-enforcement and judicial system, he never attempted to expose the hooded order

14. The police jury in Louisiana is comparable to the county commission.
15. Campbell to Parker, March 5, 1922, in Parker Papers.
16. William Hill to John M. Parker, March 24, 1922, John M. Parker to Walter Burke, March 27, 1922, Campbell to Parker, March 26, 1922, all in John M. Parker Papers, Southern Historical Collection, Walter Royal Davis Library, University of North Carolina, Chapel Hill.

in Tangipahoa. The governor criticized the Klan's lawless acts, but he always defended his part in the 1891 killing of the eleven Italians. Even though he opposed the Klan, Parker's basic philosophy was similar to the Klan's in the areas of crime and immigration. In the *Rini et al.* case, the Tangipahoa Klan had nothing to fear as long as there was no violence. Their staunch ally firmly believed that society should rid itself of Italian criminals, especially those associated with the Mafia.[17]

As the second trial approached, the Klan sent Parker warnings with obvious references to *Rini et al.* "Bear in mind," wrote one Klansman, "you are not dealing with niggers and foreigners. The country and particularly this state is being owned and controlled by Catholics and foreigners—Italians, Greeks and Jews and others. Come what may, we are determined to Americanize this state."[18]

Probably aware that their case had attracted the attention of Louisiana's Klan members, Rini and his cohorts awoke early Monday morning, March 13, 1922, to hear that they were going to Amite for arraignment. On the train, they laughed and joked among themselves and spoke to two of their attorneys, George Gulotta and A. D. Henriques, who had recently joined the defense. Henriques had vast courtroom experience in defending Italians. A former assistant prosecutor for Luzenburg, he was the son of one of the defense attorneys in the Hennessey case. Keen observers undoubtedly noted that the sons of the attorneys involved in that famous case were engaged in *Rini et al.*

News of the prisoners' unannounced arrival spread quickly through Amite, but there were no demonstrations or large crowds in the courthouse. After they pled not guilty to the charges, Judge Ellis set the trial for Monday, May 1. Although there were reports that Allen would not oppose a change of venue, the defense counsel, to everyone's surprise, did not file such a motion.[19]

On Monday, April 3, the defendants were again in Amite. Every-

17. New Orleans *Item*, April 7, 1922.
18. I.H.M.K.K.K. to John M. Parker, n.d., in Parker Papers, University of North Carolina.
19. New Orleans *Item*, March 13, 1922; New Orleans *States*, March 13, 1922, May 9, 1924; New Orleans *Times-Picayune*, March 14, 1922, August 5, 1935; newspaper clipping, in Dallas Calmes Scrapbook; *State v. Rini*, TOA, No. 25,583, p. 17.

one expected a change-of-venue hearing, but Gulotta, Purser, and Henriques shocked everyone when they filed a motion to recuse Ellis. The judge, who was stunned, announced that he would rule the following morning, and the prosecution wanted at least a day to study the motion.

Accusing Ellis of being hostile toward the defendants, the attorneys charged that the judge had expressed his prejudice by stating that the defendants were guilty and should hang. Without specifically referring to Ellis' Klan membership, Gulotta maintained that many jurors would unwittingly yield to the judge's known prejudice. Furthermore, the defense claimed, Ellis had discussed the case with Dallas Calmes's relatives and state witnesses, and he had privately advised the state attorneys.

The following day, Ellis denied none of the charges against him. The motions were, he said, "vague and uncertain and specify no remarks or language used in the discussion." He found no reason to recuse himself or to refer the issue to another judge for a hearing.[20]

Tangipahoa papers condemned the recusal motion and commented on the approaching change-of-venue hearing. One paper stated that "the idea of sending any man . . . away from this parish in order to give him a fair and unbiased trial does not smack so good with the populace." Another paper editorialized that "the outside would grasp the impression that a man, or men, convicted of murder in this parish cannot get a fair, impartial trial." Despite press assurances of a fair trial, Governor Parker, wishing to take no chances, ordered national guard troops in Washington Parish to be on standby.

On Thursday, April 13, Purser, Gulotta, and Henriques filed a written statement by the defendants, waiving their rights to be present for the hearing. According to the motion filed by the defense, one of the grounds for granting a change of venue was that the size and prominence of the Calmes family made a fair trial impossible. The serious talk of lynching the defendants was further proof that the second trial should be held in another parish.

20. New Orleans *Times-Picayune*, April 4, 1922; *State* v. *Rini*, TOA, No. 25,583, pp. 20–21, 78, 83–87, 145; newspaper clippings, in Dallas Calmes Scrapbook.

The defense argued that a recent case in which an Italian was to hang for murder in Tangipahoa, was highly prejudicial to the defendants.

Just before the noon hour, Adjutant General Toombs, a reputed Klansman, testified that in his judgment, the defendants could not get a fair trial in Tangipahoa. Other state witnesses, however, said that most parish residents believed that the right men had been captured, that they were guilty, and that they should hang. Trying to show that Dallas Calmes's family and in-laws were not that numerous, the state hoped to dispel the defense's argument that their influence would affect the outcome of the trial.

The prosecution then called two prominent Italians to testify. Joe Graziano, the first trial's interpreter, testified that there was no prejudice toward Italians in Ponchatoula or in southern Tangipahoa in general. Although he had reservations about hanging all six, he thought that the defendants could get a fair trial. Mayor Anzalone stated that there was some prejudice toward Italians in Independence, but he attributed his reelection to non-Italians, who he claimed were the voting majority.

Despite reports in local and New Orleans newspapers about "the applauding of spectators," Meigs Frost of the *Item* stated unabashedly that he thought the audience showed restraint during the proceedings. The owner of the Hammond *Vindicator* and correspondent for the *Times-Picayune*, George Campbell, denied knowing about an anti-Italian flare-up in Kentwood, an incident widely reported by that New Orleans paper.

After Thursday's testimony, court adjourned; there would be no sessions on Good Friday. On Saturday, April 15, the state and the defense concluded the change-of-venue hearing. Most witnesses said it was possible for the defendants to get a fair and impartial trial. The issue was submitted without further argument, whereupon Ellis denied the motion.[21]

As the trial approached, the New Orleans newspapers reported

21. New Orleans *States* and New Orleans *Item*, April 17, 1922; *Florida Parishes Times* (Amite City), April 15, 1922; New Orleans *Times-Picayune*, April 14, 1922; newspaper clippings, in Dallas Calmes Scrapbook; Campbell to Parker, March 5, 1922, in Parker Papers; *State* v. *Rini*, TOA, No. 25,583, pp. 23–27, 88–95, 153–60, 179, 187–89, 193, 211, 225–26, 251–337.

that one of the major witnesses, Thomas Craven, had received a Mafia letter. The note had a poorly drawn hand in black ink, as well as sketches of a bleeding heart, a dirk, and a skull and crossbones. It developed, however, that the threat against Craven was for his having released an "underworld" bootlegger charged with killing a rival gang member.

On Monday, May 1, 1922, the second trial opened, and the New Orleans press pondered the relationships between the killing of an Italian in Chicago and the recent fatal shooting of bootleggers in New Orleans. Rather than specifically mention the Mafia, the *Times-Picayune* asked: "Has the long arm of the New Orleans vendetta reached to Chicago and cut down one of its victims?" On that same day, the press carried the news of a murder involving two Italians who were on their way to attend the trial. The newspapers did not imply that it was a Mafia killing, even though elements of a long-standing feud were reported.[22]

The New Orleans press also reported on the jury selection, but the articles were relegated to the back pages. The process again proved to be difficult because of the defense's seventy-two peremptory challenges. Before a small group of spectators, the defense continued to question the veniremen as to whether they were prejudiced toward Italians, and few, if any, answered affirmatively.

During the jury selection, the *Times-Picayune* found it most unusual that nearly all of the jurors chosen were farmers who lived in the Second Ward, which was near Mississippi. The defense attorneys did not comment on this issue, and the impaneling of the jury continued until May 8.[23]

As in the first trial, controversy plagued *Rini et al.* At the outset there was an incident that brought about suspicions and charges of criminal interference. The home of Dr. Strange, who was to testify again on behalf of the state, was completely destroyed by fire in the early morning of May 9. Although the cause

22. New Orleans *States* and New Orleans *Times-Picayune*, May 1, 1922; New Orleans *Item*, April 26, 1922; newspaper clipping, in Dallas Calmes Scrapbook.
23. New Orleans *States*, May 1, 4–8, 1922; New Orleans *Times-Picayune*, May 1–7, 1922; New Orleans *Item*, May 1, 3–4, 8, 1922; Baton Rouge *State-Times*, March 25, 1923; Ponchatoula *Enterprise*, May 5, 1922; newspaper clippings, in Dallas Calmes Scrapbook; *State* v. *Rini*, TOA, No. 25, 583, pp. 29, 31, 33, 35, 37, 39, 41, 123, 338–526; *State* v. *Rini et al.*, 95 So. 406 (1923).

was classified as unknown, the fire was inevitably rumored to be connected with the trial. Then District Attorney Allen, after conferring with Ellis and Bowden, ordered the arrest of a Livingston Parish resident for trying to persuade a neighbor to change his testimony about the Hudson's tire tracks. The bribe was said to be an attempt to cloud the issue of how many tracks the escape car left.

These controversies notwithstanding, the state used the same witnesses as in the first trial. Mrs. Calmes, still clad in mourning, again told the jurors she saw only one man shoot her husband; and the defense attorneys still refused to cross-examine her.

Since the second trial was virtually identical to the first, the New Orleans press did not cover each day's proceedings. The reason for that close resemblance probably was that the prosecution provided for its witnesses a copy of the first trial's transcript. In an anteroom near the courtroom, witnesses searched through the four volumes for their previous testimony. Although the defense objected, Judge Ellis saw nothing unusual in the procedure.[24]

By the second week of the trial, the Italian consul in New Orleans requested that Governor Parker provide protection for the defendants, because "strange men are seen about the place who come and go from the Courtroom in groups." Then the Italian ambassador in Washington raised with Secretary of State Hughes the question of preventing mob violence at the Amite trial. When Hughes advised Parker about the ambassador's concerns, the governor stated that Sheriff Bowden had taken the necessary precautions. Nevertheless, the ambassador warned Hughes that he had received reports of "secret understandings" between the Ku Klux Klan and trial officials after each day's session. Furthermore, he said, Klan leaders were permitted to visit the court one day to intimidate the jury. A verdict without capital punishment would result in violence toward the defendants that the sheriff could not stop. Finally, the ambassador requested federal protection for the defendants and for the Sicilian strawberry farmers in Tangipahoa.

Secretary of State Hughes again expressed to Parker his con-

24. Ponchatoula *Enterprise*, May 12, 1922; New Orleans *States*, New Orleans *Item*, and New Orleans *Times-Picayune*, May 9–11, 1922; newspaper clippings, in Dallas Calmes Scrapbook; for testimony, see *State* v. *Rini*, TOA, No. 25,583, Vols. 1–4.

cern over these reports. The governor's response was to assure Hughes that violence was not likely in Tangipahoa, because there were no crowds at the courthouse and little excitement over the second trial. But Parker urged the United States marshal in New Orleans "to prevent any trouble in the trial of [the] Italians."[25]

Toward the end of the first week of testimony, the number of spectators increased because the berry season was ending. But those attending the trial found the testimony boring and confusing. The defense fought over the admissibility of evidence, and there were numerous bills of exception and requests for written instructions to the jury. So complicated were the legal maneuvers that the court stenographer could not keep them straight. The defense hired its own stenographer because Gulotta and his colleagues requested a daily transcript, which the regular court stenographer failed to provide. Finally, after a week of complaints by the defense, Judge Ellis replaced the official court stenographer, who admitted that he no longer understood the proceedings.

After the first week of testimony, another killing in Chicago sparked the interest of the New Orleans press because of its possible connection with the Amite trial. The *Times-Picayune* carried the headline—"Blackhand Seen in Orleanian's Death in Chicago." Vito Di Giorgio and James Cascio were murdered in a barbershop only two blocks from Chicago's "Death Corner," where a score of reputed Mafia killings had occurred in previous years. The police theorized that Di Giorgio, who had been wanted for questioning in the murder of Gaeto and DiGiovanni, died because of a New Orleans vendetta that dated back to World War I—the New Orleans Mafia sent the assassins to Chicago to kill Di Giorgio exactly six years after he was shot in New Orleans.

The murder of Di Giorgio prompted the New Orleans *States* to rehash nearly every so-called Mafia killing since the shooting of Hennessey. On the other hand, the New Orleans *Item* interviewed Deamore, who denied that he had been arrested with James Cascio. Natale then lied and insisted that he had been in

25. Royal Italian Consul to John M. Parker, May 12, 1922, Hughes to Parker, May 19, 1922, Parker to Hughes, May 19, 1922, John M. Parker to Victor Loisel, May 17, 1922, all in Parker Papers; Royal Italian Embassy memorandum to U.S. State Department, May 13, 16, 1922, Hughes to Parker, May 15, 18, 1922, Parker to Hughes, May 16, 1922, all in Deamore, N., *et al.*, File So. 311.6521.

the United States for only five years and could not have been in New Orleans in 1916.

Three days after the shooting of Di Giorgio, the state announced that it had concluded its testimony. To everyone's surprise, the defense rested its case, without offering one witness. On the morning of Tuesday, May 16, Ellis ordered closing arguments to begin, and word spread through the parish that the trial would be ending shortly. According to the *Times-Picayune*, hundreds of spectators poured into the Amite courthouse "as if by magic."

Just after ten o'clock, Ellis stated that he would allow three hours to both sides for closing arguments. The prosecution and the defense alternated in presenting their summations. Asserting that the accused had murdered Calmes during an attempted bank robbery, the state demanded the death penalty. Also, District Attorney Allen argued that one or more of the defendants shot Calmes, which made them all equally responsible.

After Reid spoke—his presentation was described as strong—more spectators arrived. Ellis allowed them to enter only if there was room. Many had to stand along the walls of the courtroom, outside near the windows, and in the courthouse corridor.

During the defense's closing arguments, Gulotta and his colleagues stressed that the state had failed to present evidence showing who killed Calmes. Therefore, argued Purser, the defendants were innocent. The defense also pointed out that the jury could return different verdicts for each of the six defendants.

At 4:35 P.M., Judge Ellis ordered a recess until 8:30 the following morning because he wanted the jurors to have a good night's rest before they began their deliberations. Since the trial was rapidly drawing to a close, Attorney General Daugherty instructed U.S. Marshal Loisel to have his deputies in Amite. The State Department had expressed concern over possible violence at the end of the trial. The Italian embassy had informed Secretary of State Hughes that its chargé d'affaires in New Orleans reported that the "feeling of the jury and . . . the hostile attitude of the community" caused the defense to decide against placing its twenty-two witnesses on the stand.[26]

26. New Orleans *Item* and New Orleans *States*, May 13–16, 1922; New Orleans *Times-Picayune*, May 12–17, 1922; *Florida Parishes Times* (Amite City), May 13, 1922; Ponchatoula *Enterprise*, May 19, June 2, 1922; Kendall, "Blood on

On Wednesday morning, May 17, Campbell sent Parker an urgent telegram warning that he was "greatly alarmed" over the reports that hundreds of men had gathered that morning in Amite. "We have been tipped off," wired Campbell, "that unless verdict is satisfactory trouble likely to ensue." Campbell also said that many of Parker's followers "were prevailed upon to join certain parties with intentions not calculated to uphold the majesty of the law."

Secretary of State Hughes told Parker that the Italian ambassador was still concerned over the safety of the defendants and wanted adequate protection. Conditions in the parish prompted Marshal Loisel to wire Attorney General Daugherty for further instructions.[27]

Early Wednesday morning, Bowden established heavy security around the Amite courthouse. Taking no chances, the deputies searched each spectator. Also on hand were Loisel's deputy marshals, who kept a watchful eye on the carloads of spectators arriving at the courthouse. There were no demonstrations, and the crowds were silent. Law-enforcement officials were nevertheless concerned.

Ellis was preparing his charge to the jury when Rene Calmes notified him that some citizens were opposed to the defendants' being moved out of the parish after the trial. Ellis told Calmes that they were to be removed after the posttrial proceedings. Twenty minutes later, Sheriff Bowden spoke to Ellis about keeping the defendants in the Amite jail. At the sheriff's insistence, Ellis inspected the jail, where the bars were clearly in need of repair. Ellis agreed that the defendants should be taken to New Orleans immediately after the trial's conclusion.

When seventy-five to one hundred men gathered near the two officials, Ellis explained that the six prisoners would have to be taken elsewhere because the Amite jail was not secure. Ellis later made the same explanation before a smaller group, and some com-

the Banquette," 853; Royal Italian Embassy memorandum (copy), n.d., in Parker Papers; Italian Embassy memorandum to State Department, July 10, 1922, in Deamore, N., *et al.*, File So. 311.6521; *State* v. *Rini*, TOA, No. 25,583, pp. 46, 49, 127.

27. Campbell to Parker, May 17–18, 1922, Hughes to Parker, May 16, 1922, Victor Loisel to John M. Parker, May 17, 1922, all in Parker Papers.

plained that the defendants would "buy their way out" in New Orleans. Robert Reid also joined the gathering and agreed with Ellis.

The crowds appeared to be placated by the officials' remarks, and Ellis returned to the courtroom to charge the jury. After more than half an hour spent reading the general and specific charges, Ellis sent the jury out to deliberate shortly after 9:00 A.M. Wednesday, May 17. While the jurors pondered, the defendants sat calmly, smoking cigarettes and reading newspapers. At 9:50 the jury reached a verdict, and when they returned, Ellis cautioned the crowd. There were to be no demonstrations.

"We the jury," stated the foreman, "find the accused guilty as charged." There was no clapping, but the *Times-Picayune* noted that the spectators seemed "to silently applaud the verdict, just as they did several months ago on the occasion of the first trial."[28]

After the verdict, Bowden escorted the defendants back to the jail, but Rini insisted on speaking to the reporters. "We were prepared for an adverse verdict in Tangipahoa Parish," he said. "We didn't expect a square deal without a change of venue."

"Oh, well," Giglio added, "we beat them once, and we have plenty of money left."

Giglio's remarks angered the crowd, some members of which muttered that the "dagoes" were "juggling with the law" and that there was "unnecessary delay in meeting [sic] out justice." Bowden surrounded the jail with additional deputies because an "unofficial delegation" remained around the courthouse. Since there were two hours before the train left for New Orleans, Bowden decided that he and Ellis should address the three hundred men who were moving closer to the jail.

"I believe in you people," Ellis began. "I trust you and have every confidence in you. If I did not, I would move out of the Parish.

"This jail is unsafe," he continued. "We do not want to trust to its physical weakness. We do not want any rescues. We do not want any jail delivery.

28. New Orleans *Item* and New Orleans *States*, May 17, 1922; New Orleans *Times-Picayune*, May 18, 1922; Ponchatoula *Enterprise*, May 19, June 2, 1922; *Florida Parishes Times* (Amite City), May 27, 1922; New York *Times*, May 18, 1922; newspaper clipping, in Dallas Calmes Scrapbook; *State v. Rini*, TOA, No. 25,583, pp. 50, 695, 704–707, 729, 745; Parker to Hughes, May 17, 1922, in Deamore, N., *et al.*, File So. 311.6521; Parker to Hughes and Parker to Bowden, May 17, 1922, both in Parker Papers.

"Look at your sheriff," said Ellis, hoping to elicit sympathy for Bowden. "The man has worked so hard for you that he is about to collapse. Sleep is a stranger to him. He has been your loyal and faithful servant. Don't you want him to get some sleep? You know that human flesh and blood can't stand up under such a strain any longer.

"Gentlemen," Ellis concluded, "I appeal to your good judgment. I know you. I know that you have been very patient, and I know that you will let the law take its course."

While Ellis addressed the gathering, members of the Calmes family arrived. "We believe in Judge Ellis," said one. "Let's accept the judge's advice." Other relatives told the crowd that they also had confidence in the judicial system.

"Gentlemen," said Ellis, "I give you my personal parole of honor that no matter what the State Supreme Court does, those men will be brought back to Tangipahoa Parish."

According to the *Louisiana Sun*, only after this personal assurance by Ellis "was summary justice averted." Also sensing the seriousness of the situation, a reporter for the *Florida Parishes Times* noted that "one 'come on' and hell in all its fury would have broken loose."

The crowd dispersed quietly. Bowden, three deputies, and two New Orleans police officers transported the defendants to the train station without incident. At the depot, there was a large gathering, but there were no threats or demonstrations. Some spectators appeared eager to talk to the prisoners and the guards, and at each stop in Tangipahoa, a crowd was on hand to catch a final glimpse of the defendants.[29]

With the defendants safely in the New Orleans Parish Prison, Governor Parker informed Secretary of State Hughes that the trial ended with no excitement and no attempts at mob violence. Despite newspaper reports of the angry crowd outside the jail, he assured Hughes that at no time were the prisoners in any danger. "Incidentally," Parker added, "I have never seen more effort made

29. New Orleans *States*, New Orleans *Times-Picayune*, and New Orleans *Item*, May 17, 1922; Ponchatoula *Enterprise*, May 19, 1922; newspaper clippings, in Dallas Calmes Scrapbook; *Florida Parishes Times* (Amite City), May 20, 1922, and *Louisiana Sun* (Hammond), May 19, 1922, quoted in *State* v. *Rini*, TOA, No. 25,583, pp. 133–35, 682–83, 688, 694, 700–703, 708.

to save criminals as in this case, and it looks as though the money they have to spend is practically unlimited."[30]

At the end of the second trial, Parker undoubtedly knew that additional legal efforts lay ahead. After two trials, an appeal to the state supreme court, and several hearings, Gulotta and his colleagues still had other judicial redresses available, such as a second appeal to the state supreme court and possibly an appeal to the United States Supreme Court. To the dismay of Parker and others, these proceedings alone would also delay the final disposition of the case.

30. Parker to Hughes, May 16, 19, 1922, both in Parker Papers.

10

I Could Not Sleep

Less than two weeks after the close of the second trial, Ellis granted the defense attorneys a hearing on their motion for a new trial. The grounds cited were the failure of Ellis to recuse himself, the denial of a change of venue, the difficulty in obtaining jurors, the alleged prejudice in the parish toward Italians, and the circumstances surrounding Giglio's remarks.

On Monday, May 29, 1922, Judge Ellis presided over the hearing, which was to examine only the conditions in which Giglio's statements were made. The major witness was the managing editor of the *Florida Parishes Times*, Lee Lanier. After more than an hour of grueling examination by the defense attorneys, Lanier repeatedly stated that his article, which described a hostile mob that gathered because of Giglio's remarks, was inaccurate. Lanier testified that the crowd was not angry at Giglio's remarks and had only protested moving the defendants to New Orleans.

Judge Ellis, Sheriff Bowden, and Robert Reid substantiated Lanier's statements. In addition, Ellis stated for the record that when he addressed the crowd, he was unaware of Giglio's comments. Reid stated that at no time did he sense that the defendants were in danger. After the examination of Reid, Ellis announced that he would rule on the motion within the week.[1]

It was an unusual hearing. A veteran newspaperman, having reported a near lynching, admitted that he had misjudged the sentiment of the crowd. Although Lanier may have been incorrect, this does not explain the similar article from the *Louisiana Sun*. And the defense attorneys inexplicably failed to call as a witness the

1. New Orleans *Times-Picayune*, May 30, 1922; newspaper clipping, in Dallas Calmes Scrapbook; *State* v. *Rini*, TOA, No. 25,583, pp. 51–52, 123–31, 679, 681–703, 708–10.

author of the *Sun* article, although it was submitted as part of the motion.

Prior to and after the hearing, the Italian embassy continued to protest the handling of the trial. According to one communiqué, the Italian government's firm opinion was that "in the trial excessive consideration was given to the race prejudice which is per public admission prevailing in Tangipahoa County against the Italians." The embassy was also "very painfully impressed" by Ellis' assuring the crowd that the six defendants would return to Tangipahoa Parish no matter what the Louisiana Supreme Court decided. The embassy interpreted that remark as prejudicial toward the defendants, but Ellis was correct. If the supreme court affirmed the decision of *Rini et al.*, the defendants would return to Amite to be hanged, and should the court reverse the decision, the case would probably be remanded to Tangipahoa Parish for a third trial.[2]

While Louisiana officials tried to assure the State Department and the Italian embassy that the defendants were not in any danger, the defense attorneys heard from Kentwood attorney William A. Houghton. On Saturday, June 3, he wrote to Kemp that he had important information that could be helpful in another motion for a new trial. Later that evening, Kemp relayed the message to Purser, who had just returned from Osyka, Mississippi, with additional evidence that might also be grounds for a new trial. Purser asked Gulotta and Henriques to take the next train back to Osyka to continue his investigation. Kemp and Purser drove to Kentwood to speak to Houghton.

Three days later, Judge Ellis denied the motion for a new trial. Since Kemp and his colleagues could not gather their evidence in Kentwood and Osyka in time, they filed a supplemental motion on Thursday, June 8, on the grounds of newly discovered evidence. One affidavit, signed by William C. O'Brian, a juror in the second trial, charged that he and another juror, Ritchie Hope, were intim-

2. Italian Embassy memorandum to State Department, May 24, 1922, Parker to Hughes, May 29–30, June 5, 1922, Newton A. Sanders to John M. Parker, June 2, 1922, all in Deamore, N., *et al.*, File So. 311.6521; John M. Parker to Italian Vice Consul at New Orleans, May 29, 1922, in Parker Papers.

idated into voting for a verdict with capital punishment. The other affidavit, signed by a convicted murderer from Osyka, alleged that Ritchie Hope accepted a twenty-five-dollar bet with him that the six defendants would be convicted and hanged.

After Purser read the affidavits to Judge Ellis and Judge Columbus Reid, District Attorney Allen objected to their introduction as evidence because they were filed after Ellis' denial of a new trial. Purser explained that the defense was given permission to use the affidavits only the day before, Wednesday, June 7, but Judge Ellis sustained Allen's objection. Purser gave notice that he would seek a writ of mandamus to permit the filing of the supplemental petition. The following day, however, the Louisiana Supreme Court ruled that Purser had chosen the wrong judicial remedy to correct any alleged errors by Judge Ellis. The judge's rulings could be remedied by bills of exception or by a direct appeal, which could not be acted upon until the fall term.[3]

After the state supreme court decision, Purser announced that he would still attempt to delay the sentencing through other legal maneuvers. But on Monday morning, June 12, Allen withdrew his objections to the supplemental motion, and Ellis agreed to conduct a rehearing on Monday, June 19.

On the weekend before the hearing, sensational bribery charges were lodged against the defense attorneys by a Tickfaw resident, Comer Rogers, whom the New Orleans press dubbed the "Bootlegger King of Tangipahoa." Swearing to an affidavit in the *Florida Parishes Times* offices, Rogers charged that during the second trial, one of the defense attorneys offered him $5,000 to bribe some jurors. If Rogers was successful, he was to run his hand through his hair twice. Rogers claimed that he had refused. He had remained quiet because there was a second conviction, but O'Brian's statement prompted him to reveal his information.

Rogers' allegations caused a furor in Tangipahoa. District Attorney Allen said that there would be a full investigation, but the

3. New Orleans *States*, June 9–10, 1922; New Orleans *Item*, June 9, 1922; New Orleans *Times-Picayune*, June 10–11, 18, 1922; Ponchatoula *Enterprise*, June 2, 16, 1922; *Florida Parishes Times* (Amite City), June 10, 1922; newspaper clippings, in Dallas Calmes Scrapbook; *State v. Rini*, TOA, No. 25,583, pp. 54, 136–38, 141–42, 789–806.

issue would not be part of the hearing on Monday. The defense attorneys wanted the public to consider Rogers' record. Gulotta laughed about the affidavit and stated that "the sum of $5,000 which Rogers says he was offered is far greater than the share of the [defense] lawyers."[4]

On Monday, June 19, a crowd filled the Amite courthouse almost to capacity. Even though the defendants were not present, the proceedings had the appearance of a trial, and at the request of the state, all witnesses were sequestered. The first witness to take the stand was William C. O'Brian, who had been arrested by Bowden. O'Brian, who was illiterate, stated that he signed an affidavit claiming that he and Ritchie Hope originally voted for a verdict of guilty as charged without capital punishment. But after further deliberation, he and Hope changed their vote to make the decision unanimous. However, he said, they had not done so because of intimidation by the jurors or fears of violence from the crowds. In addition, O'Brian claimed that the defense attorneys offered him $2,000 to sign the affidavit.

Under cross-examination by Henriques, whom O'Brian continually called Henrickerson, he again repudiated most of the affidavit that he had signed before Kemp and Houghton outdoors at midnight. Although he denied that the affidavit mentioned jury intimidation and fear of mob violence, he later recanted part of this testimony. He would have gone along with "that getting scared business," he said, had the defense attorneys given him the $2,000, thus unwittingly committing perjury.

Mrs. O'Brian was next on the witness stand, and she stated that she had overheard Kemp offering her husband $2,000 to sign the affidavit. Then several former jurors testified that they had not feared the courthouse crowd and had not intimidated Hope or O'Brian. Hope concurred with their statements and denied that he made a $25 bet with anyone.

What was to be a hearing on a motion for a new trial turned

4. New Orleans *Times-Picayune*, June 18, 1922; New Orleans *States*, June 1, 9, 18–19, 1922; New Orleans *Item*, June 1, 12, 18–19, 1922; Ponchatoula *Enterprise*, June 9, 16, 23, 1922; *Florida Parishes Times* (Amite City), June 17, 1922; newspaper clippings, in Dallas Calmes Scrapbook; *State* v. *Rini*, TOA, No. 25,583, pp. 55–58.

into a proceeding in which the defense attorneys had to deny serious charges. Stating that O'Brian understood fully all parts of the affidavit that he had signed, Kemp said he had not offered the former juror $2,000 as a bribe. O'Brian had asked for a gun and for money to hire someone to harvest his crop, requests that Kemp refused. Houghton's testimony substantiated Kemp's, but Ponder's grueling examination questioned Houghton's motives for taking an affidavit at midnight behind a barn. Kemp and Houghton testified that O'Brian at the time feared for his life. He apparently did not want to sign anything in a lawyer's office or in his home, where his neighbors might see. So he took the attorneys behind his barn.

When the defense concluded its testimony, Ellis stated that he reopened the motion, even though the state supreme court had not ordered him to do so. Knowing that the court would probably have to rule on a bill of exception dealing with his original denial of the supplemental motion for a retrial, he announced that he wanted in the record what had just transpired.

The hearing, which began at 9:00 A.M., lasted far into the night. The spectators crowded about Ellis' bench, but they were not unruly. According to the *Item*, "You could have heard the proverbial pin drop to the floor with the sound of broken crockery, so intense was the silence." When the hearing concluded, little testimony had been given in regard to a new trial. Nevertheless, the five anxious attorneys stood behind their respective tables and awaited the judge's decision. "Gentlemen," Ellis said to the defense, "I am going to deny your motion for a new trial."[5]

After the hearing, Governor Parker sent to Secretary of State Hughes local press clippings about the proceedings. Interpreting Ellis' denial of the retrial motion as proof of a bribery attempt by the defense, Parker insisted that Hughes forward the articles to the Italian ambassador so that his government could see how the six defendants tried "to corrupt the channels of justice in Tangipahoa Parish, to the end that they might escape the legitimate penalty of their crime."

5. New Orleans *Times-Picayune*, June 20, 1922; New Orleans *Item*, June 19, 1922; newspaper clippings, in Dallas Calmes Scrapbook; *State* v. *Rini*, TOA, No. 25,583, pp. 713–16, 722–26, 730–33, 744–78, 783–825, 836–37.

In view of the many times Parker corresponded with Hughes about the case, the State Department solicitor advised Hughes to send a "friendly letter" to thank the governor for his communications and detailed statements about the two trials. The solicitor warned, however, that another telegram to Parker "would do no good and might be harmful." He recommended that Hughes write the Italian ambassador and merely mention the bribery charges. This communiqué should explain that the feeling against the six defendants arose from the nature of their crime, not from their nationality.[6]

By the end of the week, a Tangipahoa grand jury indicted O'Brian for perjury and Houghton and Kemp for subversion and attempted bribery. Bowden arrested them immediately. Kemp, having posted his $1,500 bond, stated that the indictment was "based on unsupported testimony of a self-confessed perjurer." Castigating the parish officials involved in prosecuting *Rini et al.*, Kemp observed that "the public mind in this parish is so extremely wrought up over this Italian case that there is a wide-spread disposition on the part of the people to condemn anyone connected with the defense of the case."[7]

After the bribery scandal, Governor Parker, mindful of Tangipahoa's notorious reputation, wanted Hughes to ask the Department of Justice to send federal agents to Amite for the upcoming sentencing. Although the governor never personally met the defendants, he was "constrained to believe that they are criminals of the worst class." Parker wrote that "there is no feeling against the Italians in Tangipahoa Parish but the feeling against the Mafia, Malivita [*sic*], Black Hand and other secret organizations that have terrorized a number of Italians themselves is very great, and the attitude of these prisoners in boasting that they had unlimited money and influence has created an exceedingly bad state of feeling throughout Tangipahoa Parish."

Having received a similar request from the Italian chargé

6. Parker to Hughes, June 19–20, 1922, Solicitor to Hughes, June 24, 1922, both in Deamore, N., *et al.*, File So. 311.6521.

7. New Orleans *Item*, June 23–24, 1922; New Orleans *Times-Picayune*, June 24, 1922; Ponchatoula *Enterprise*, June 30, 1922; Nelson H. Williams to John M. Parker, July 17, 1922, Parker to Coco, July 18, 1922, Coco to Parker, July 31, 1922, all in Parker Papers.

d'affaires in Washington, Hughes contacted Attorney General Daugherty, whose staff told him that the Italian government feared for the lives of the six men. Daugherty ordered the director of the Bureau of Investigation to have the New Orleans office send three agents to Amite.[8]

Sheriff Bowden also exercised unusual caution. He announced casually that he would be on a fishing trip Saturday, July 15, in Bay St. Louis, Mississippi. But he actually took a train to New Orleans, where he was joined by several of his deputies and a parish police juror. Aided by the Orleans Parish Sheriff's Office and the New Orleans Police Department, Bowden took Rini and the others at 12:40 A.M. Sunday to the train station. When they arrived in Amite at 2:30 A.M., the town was in total darkness. Since no one expected them, someone had to awaken the jailer. The prisoners were put in cells, where they waited for the opening of court.

Ellis was on the bench promptly at 8:00 A.M., Monday, July 17. There were only two spectators in the courtroom. Attorneys Henriques and Gulotta, who had accompanied their clients from New Orleans, filed another new-trial motion, which was promptly denied by Ellis before he pronounced the sentence.

Standing before Ellis without handcuffs and shackles, the six men showed no emotion. "Do you know any reason why sentence should not be imposed on you men today?" Ellis asked. They did not answer.

"I now sentence each of you to hang by the neck until dead, and may God have mercy on your souls."

Bowden and his deputies quickly took the prisoners to his office, where they were handcuffed and shackled again. They went right to the depot to catch the nine o'clock train for New Orleans. At the station, a crowd gathered to watch the six men who were shackled wrist-to-wrist and foot-to-foot in pairs. While Giglio smoked and returned the stares of the onlookers, the other pris-

8. Parker to Hughes, June 13, 1922, Hughes to Parker, August 3, 1922, both in Parker Papers; Parker to Hughes, July 13, 1922, Hughes to Parker, July 24, 1922, Italian Embassy memorandum to State Department, June 21, 1922, William Phillips to Harry Daugherty, July 22, 1922, Daugherty to Hughes, August 3, 1922, all in Deamore, N., *et al.*, File So. 311.6521.

oners appeared tense, and perspiration began to pour down their faces.

When the train arrived, the prisoners' relief was visible. Once aboard, they discussed their case with reporters. Each stated that they did not have a fair trial and hoped that their second appeal would be successful.

"Our main trouble was that the newspapermen who reported our trial were too wild with their pencils," Rini said.

"Oh, the reporters were all right," countered Bocchio, who was chained to Rini. "They only believed what other people told them. Let's forget that and put our minds on those seven good men in the Supreme Court. All the judges on the Supreme Court are very good men, and we place our trust in their hands."

"Well, all I hope is that we won't have to go to Amite again," added Lamantia, who was putting his head out the window at each stop. Andrea seemed anxious to get completely out of Tangipahoa.

"I guess you do," Rini said. "If we have to go back there it will mean just one thing—." Rini jerked his head as if he were being hanged.

The train stopped at Kenner, where Superintendent Molony and several policemen got on. They had heard that an attempt would be made to rescue the six prisoners while the train was en route to New Orleans. Molony announced that he had more police ready at Union Station.

In New Orleans, the police surrounded the train and brought up a well-guarded patrol wagon. Rini and the others entered the vehicle. A procession of police cars went to the Orleans Parish Prison, where deputies thoroughly searched the prisoners and placed them in their cells.[9]

Bocchio, the youngest of the six, wrote a letter to his brother in Sicily. Joe had written frequently since his arrest to his mother and to his sister Angela, but he never told them about his plight. Although he knew his attorneys planned an appeal, he finally told his brother that he was sentenced to hang for murder. Bocchio al-

---

9. New Orleans *Times-Picayune*, July 18, 1922; New Orleans *States* and New Orleans *Item*, July 17, 1922; Ponchatoula *Enterprise*, July 21, 1922; newspaper clippings, in Dallas Calmes Scrapbook; *State* v. *Rini*, TOA, No. 25,583, pp. 59, 840.

ways believed that he would be set free, but as he pondered his future he wrote in his diary that "I could not sleep that night." He had finally realized that it was highly possible that he and his five comrades would eventually hang in Amite.[10]

While Bocchio and the others lamented their plight, the Louisiana Supreme Court granted two delays, which prompted criticism by the Tangipahoa press. However, in early November the court announced that it would hear the *Rini et al.* appeal. Had the court delayed any longer, Robert Reid would probably have had to recuse himself—he had been elected to the high court and was scheduled to take his seat January 2, 1923.[11]

Just prior to the hearing, Governor Parker received the first letters asking for clemency for the six defendants. In these pleas, religious references often underscored the point that the state should not execute the prisoners. The plight of the men attracted the attention of death-penalty abolitionist Emma Lambert from West Virginia. She corresponded with Bocchio for several months and wrote letters of clemency to Governor Parker, other state officials, and the Louisiana Supreme Court.[12]

The court, however, was more interested in reading the briefs and transcripts of *Rini et al.* Filing over forty bills of exception, the defense, which no longer included the Amite attorneys, again charged that Judge Ellis erred in refusing the motion to recuse himself as trial judge. Gulotta, Henriques, and Luzenburg also alleged that Ellis was "acting as an attorney in the case . . . by privately conferring and advising . . . the state." They charged that Ellis had a "highly disorganized state of mind." His *per curiam*, which was "teeming with misstatements of facts and half truths," included a note: "A fair and impartial jury *was* secured and cer-

---

10. Bocchio, "Last Days of a Condemned Man," New Orleans *Item*, January 30, 1924.
11. Ponchatoula *Enterprise*, July 14, 1922; newspaper clippings, in Dallas Calmes Scrapbook; Motion for Time to File Transcript, Motion for Time to File Briefs, both in *State* v. *Rini*, TOA, No. 25,583.
12. C. T. Riley to John M. Parker, October 20, 1922, John T. Matney to Parker, November 12, 1922, W. S. Concannon to Parker, November 24, 1922, Emma Lambert to Parker, Lieutenant Governor Hewitt L. Bouanchaud, and A. V. Coco, November 4–5, 1922, all in Parker Papers; newspaper clippings, in Dallas Calmes Scrapbook.

tainly had not been tampered with, bribed or approached by any person interested in the prosecution." Then, in a most unjudicial commentary, Ellis added, "Can the defendants show the same?"

In regard to the bill of exception charging an error in denying a change of venue, the defense maintained that the incident following Giglio's remarks "shows that the condition of the mind of the public in the town of Amite was such that, if these defendants had not been convicted, they, probably, would have suffered bodily harm." The defense also cited the unusual security precautions at the trial as grounds for granting a change of venue. The attorneys noted that "no man in that parish could testify for the defendants on their application for a change of venue without incurring the displeasure of his neighbors." Urging "a reading between the lines of the testimony," Gulotta and his colleagues requested that the court realize that "the very atmosphere surrounding . . . these proceedings was surcharged with hostility towards these defendants."[13]

Unfortunately, the defense attorneys were not privileged to read Governor Parker's official correspondence, which showed that parish and state officials shared their reservations about holding a second trial in Amite. Nor did the defense provide proof of the Klan's influence in the parish and in the trial proceedings. However, the attorneys probably knew they would never be able to prove that in court. Furthermore, Gulotta and his associates, not knowing whether the supreme court justices were themselves Klansmen, probably did not want to risk antagonizing the state's highest court.

As in the first appeal, the defense objected to the introduction of Deamore's conversations as evidence. In addition, the attorneys argued that William O'Brian was now an incompetent and partial juror, as evidenced by the testimony included in the hearing on the supplemental motion. Finally, the defense argued that Ellis erred again in charging the jury.[14]

13. Supplemental Brief on Behalf of Defendants and Appellants, pp. 1–12, 32, and Original Brief on Behalf of Defendants and Appellants, pp. 2–18, both in *State v. Rini*, TOA, No. 25,583, and p. 838.

14. *State v. Rini*, TOA, No. 25,583, pp. 584–91, 603–604, 641–48, 669–75; Assignments of Error, p. 1, and Supplemental Brief on Behalf of Defendants and Appellants, pp. 18–20, both in *State v. Rini*, TOA, No. 25,583.

On Friday, December 29, 1922, the Louisiana Supreme Court issued a twenty-six-page decision, one of the lengthiest in recent times. In regard to the recusal motion, the high court found nothing illegal in Ellis' discussing the case with prosecution witnesses or anyone else while in his official capacity. Noting that the defense failed to cite specific conducts or subjects of discussion that were improper and prejudicial to the accused, the court concluded that the charges failed to prove a cause for recusation.

Discussing the denial of a change of venue, the court was impressed by the frankness of the witnesses during the hearing and the veniremen called for examination. The defense failed "to sustain the idea of a prejudiced attitude in Tangipahoa except for the lower end of the parish around Ponchatoula." The justices considered the election of an Italian mayor in Independence, as well as the testimony of Mayor Anzalone and Joe Graziano: "The great majority of the witnesses, and the evidence . . . indicated that the prevailing sentiment of the parish was that the accused should have the benefit of all the orderly processes of the law." The court remarked upon "the orderly conditions" at the trial and found no reason to grant the change of venue.

The court found nothing unusual in the jury selection, and it dismissed the incident after Giglio's comments as without proof. The justices further concluded that Judge Ellis properly charged the jury and that "the statements of Deamore were voluntary." Consequently, the court found "nothing in any of the motions justifying our disturbance of the verdict." But in a dissenting opinion, Chief Justice Charles O'Neill wrote that the defendants should have been granted a change of venue and that Deamore's statements were not made voluntarily. In addition, he contended, the statements by Pietro Leotta and his son were not admissible because they were probably coerced.[15]

Upon hearing the decision, Gulotta stated that if a rehearing was denied, he planned to appeal to the United States Supreme Court, claiming a violation of the Fourteenth Amendment. "Our men did not receive a fair trial at Amite," a dejected Gulotta said, at his home. "I was actually stunned by the decision of the Su-

15. *State* v. *Rini,* 95 So. 400–413 (1923).

preme Court—so confident was I that a new trial would be ordered and a change of venue granted."

As soon as Captain Rennyson heard about the supreme court's decision, he ordered the six prisoners into an exercise yard while deputies stripped their cells. When they returned, Rini and the others found that the deputies had removed all items that could be used in a suicide attempt. Rennyson announced that they would each be placed in a solitary cell with a guard stationed outside. Nor could they use the outside corridor or have visitors other than relatives and those on official business.

Once they were in their cells, the warden told them about the decision, and Giglio and Leona expressed confidence that the United States Supreme Court would overturn their conviction. Rini and Lamantia agreed, but Deamore only shook his head and muttered in Italian. Showing signs of uneasiness and loss of hope, Bocchio said, "If I am hanged, an innocent man will die."

When local reporters visited them later, they appeared eager to talk. "It is much disappointment," said one of them, "that even the supreme court will not see we get a fair trial. But the law is so funny. The judges of the supreme court must have surely done what they thought right."

"Everyone knows," Giglio charged, "that there was much prejudice against us. We were almost mobbed. They hit me twice in the stomach and they kicked my shins. The law is so funny. The supreme court thinks that is all right."

"And they struck me twice over the head," Leona added, from the next cell.

"We never confess, not one of us!" Rini shouted proudly, from near the end of the tier.

"We're all Catholics," Giglio said. "We don't know what's going to happen beyond this world. We believe what they told us to believe and so we think that even if they do hang us, we'll get a square deal some place."

"But I don't want to die," Leona said. "No one wants to die."

"I was planning to make a model," said Bocchio, who wanted to experiment with an electric motor, "when the supreme court gave us a new trial. But I won't do that now."

"There's no use to be put down by the court's decision," Deamore said optimistically, from the far end of the tier. "We're all innocent. Things will come out right." Deamore then began his rendition of "O Sole Mio."

Later that night, Bocchio wrote in his diary: "My cell became a tomb after the supreme court of the state affirmed our conviction four days after Christmas, 1922. Everything was taken from our cells, including books and what little accommodations we had thus far enjoyed."[16]

On Saturday, January 27, 1923, Bocchio and the others received more distressing news. Rennyson told each prisoner that the Louisiana Supreme Court denied their application for a rehearing. Giglio only smiled at the warden. Bocchio also smiled and wondered whether the case would be appealed further. A short while later, Gulotta arrived. After a lengthy conversation with his clients, he announced that they would appeal to the United States Supreme Court. Upon hearing the news, Rini and Lamantia only shrugged their shoulders as they paced their cells. Finally, they sat down and placed their heads in their hands.

On Saturday afternoon, Rini let it be known that he wished to speak to reporters. Sitting in his cell, he stroked Toots, a small dog he had gotten shortly after his arrest. "I guess the next thing is Washington," he said. "Perhaps some of the boys, or one of them, will confess the actual shooting. I wish they would. Then I'd have a chance." Realizing that the possibility of escaping the hangman's noose was now diminishing, Rini was the first to imply their involvement in the Calmes slaying.

On Sunday, January 28, the New Orleans police announced that there was evidence of a plan to help the prisoners escape. A package of twelve sticks of dynamite, three yards of fuse, and six percussion caps was found at the local American Railway Express station. The police traced the recipient—Giacomo Bucaro, who had been arrested for hiding his cousin Cipolla. Bucaro insisted, however, that he did not know what was in the package. Detectives searched his backyard and found under a woodpile sixteen sticks of dynamite, five yards of fuse, and thirty percussion caps.

16. New Orleans *Times-Picayune*, New Orleans *States*, and New Orleans *Item*, December 30, 1922; Bocchio, "Last Days of a Condemned Man," New Orleans *Item*, February 1, 1924; newspaper clippings, in Dallas Calmes Scrapbook.

Since he had been visiting the prisoners constantly, he was arrested for possession of the explosives, a riot gun, and a sixty-gallon copper still.

Federal authorities joined the New Orleans police in investigating the incident, which officials believed was a plan developed in Chicago. Within a few days, law-enforcement authorities developed a theory surrounding a plot by a "nationwide gang" to free the six prisoners. Although the police did not specifically refer to the Mafia, officials believed that gang members planned to throw dynamite against the Orleans Parish Prison wall at Franklin Street on an evening when the six men exercised in the yard. Simultaneously, other conspirators were to set off dynamite at Saratoga near Gravier Street by the First Precinct Station. The police would rush to the station, and the prisoners would escape.

The police believed that this theory had substance because they found that the six prisoners had had a Louisiana road map for at least the last three months. They had studied it, authorities were convinced, for a possible escape route. As a result, Rennyson doubled the number of deputies guarding Rini and the others.[17]

Although there was talk that the execution would occur in early 1923, the warden was aware that an appeal to the Supreme Court might take several months or more than a year. Rennyson had had little trouble with the six prisoners, but now that their hope for gaining freedom was fading, he could not afford to take any chances.

Known as Little Napoleon, Archie Rennyson was fond of the six prisoners, who were polite to his staff and who violated few rules. The warden normally granted every convenience the men requested, if it was not prohibited by law. For example, he allowed them to prepare special meals; to receive food from friends and relatives; to construct their own writing tables; and to keep books in their cells. One unusual sight was all the clothes—the accumulation took up a surprising amount of space. Rennyson also allowed all six prisoners to use the corridor outside their cells,

17. New Orleans *Times-Picayune*, January 28, 1923; New Orleans *Item*, January 27–28, 1923; newspaper clippings, in Dallas Calmes Scrapbook.

but this privilege was rescinded after the denial of their second appeal.[18]

Lamantia kept a small oil stove so he could prepare his specialty—a savory oyster soup with tomatoes. When not cooking meals for the others, Andrea would lie in his cell and think about the barbershop that he had planned to open, often recalling how he had saved money for it. But he knew that his plans were probably in vain.

Leona had tuberculosis and was ill most of the time. Although Gulotta had tried to get special treatment for him, he showed no signs of recovery. Throughout the three years, he said little to reporters, and he spent most of his time quietly in his cell.

Deamore would often sit and wonder whether anyone still remembered him in the city where he sharpened knives and scissors. He was known to his customers and friends as Uncle Christmas. Natale was melancholy because he had been unable to be with his wife when their baby daughter died. Although his grief seemed to have abated, Natale appeared to be mentally exhausted and dispirited.[19]

Deamore was the saddest of the six, but Rini was generally the most jovial. Recalling his youthful days on Chicago's West Side, Joe would lie on his bunk and comfort Toots, the Chihuahua given to him by the prison chef. Rini also found consolation in his visits with his father, who came often from Chicago.[20]

Giglio received few visitors and spent most of his time writing letters to his mother in Italy. Joe had an ingenious plan whereby his brother would deliver the letters periodically. "My mother, she's 79 years old," he explained, "and she ain't going to live so long any more. So she gonna keep right on getting a letter from me once in a while, through my brother, and maybe she will die without ever finding out what really happened to me."[21]

---

18. New Orleans *States*, December 30, 1922; Bocchio, "Last Days of a Condemned Man," New Orleans *Item*, February 10, 1924; New Orleans *Item*, January 2, March 13, 1922, May 7, 1924; Hearsey, *The Six Who Were Hanged*, 11.

19. Newspaper clipping, in Dallas Calmes Scrapbook; Bocchio, "Last Days of a Condemned Man," New Orleans *Item*, January 30, February 10, 1924.

20. Bocchio, "Last Days of a Condemned Man," New Orleans *Item*, February 8, 1924; New Orleans *Item*, April 29, May 7, 1924.

21. New Orleans *Item*, April 29, 1924.

Bocchio, who had broken his engagement with Patrina, continued to keep the truth about his predicament from his mother, whom he did not want to worry. In most of her letters, she asked when he planned to return home, but he never answered her. "I should be a man," Bocchio wrote in his diary, "and write back that, perhaps, I never shall. But I cannot do so. I have not the courage. I can tell it to my brother, but not to her. Dreams are good and sweet, and dream-breakers should sometimes be killed."

When Bocchio entered the Orleans Parish Prison, he was illiterate in English. With the help of Father Raymond Carra and William Warrington, a settlement house worker, Bocchio taught himself to read and write English. His knowledge of the language was considered so remarkable, Rennyson and others compared him to Arthur Brisbane. One of the first newspaper columnists in the United States to be syndicated, Brisbane wrote for the New York *Sun*, the New York *World*, and the New York *Journal*. He included anecdotes in his articles, and his writing was distinguished by his use of short words, sentences, and paragraphs.

While in prison Bocchio also worked on his secret invention—a new type of electric motor. Realizing that Joe was sincere, Rennyson sought permission for tools and other implements, but local officials denied the request because of possible security risks. Rennyson did provide Bocchio with a private cell as a workroom for two months.

Undaunted, Bocchio relied on his drawings. "I got the idea," he said one day to a visitor, "while I was a student at the academy in Italy. I thought it out for some time, but it was not until I came to America seven years ago that I had an opportunity to make a working model."

Before the second appeal, Bocchio had also been developing an automobile engine. "I am sure it will work," he bragged to one reporter, "and I know that if it works it will work on half as much gasoline as an ordinary six-cylinder engine."

Refusing to discuss his work in detail, Joe said that his plans were in his attorney's safe. "If bad luck overtakes me it goes to my brother," he said. "If I get a new trial I want to build a model. I can't tell anyone about my inventions until they are safe. There are too many crooked people in the world," he added wryly.

While in the Orleans Parish Prison, Bocchio volunteered as a worker in the city's drug rehabilitation program. One day an addict offered him a cigarette. Not knowing that it was marijuana, he returned to his cell to smoke it. After a few puffs, Joe began to gasp for breath and became dizzy. He lay down on his bunk. His mouth was dry and he felt paralyzed. At first he was scared, but then he got angry.

Bocchio thought his cell was "an assembly of nervous tears and dizziness. I walk in it and become unsteady. I lie down and my ribs start to complain." His bunk was so unbearable that he often chose to sleep on the damp floor. One night he was so uncomfortable that he argued about a lumpy mattress with a deputy, who placed him in solitary confinement for one hour. "This was my greatest punishment," Bocchio wrote.

The "extreme solitude" of prison life, Joe found, was "good for some souls, but I do not like it." And he frequently contemplated suicide. "But I have gotten over that stage," he wrote, in early 1924. "Suicide is only a cowardly slap in the face of fate that does no good. Above all, I hope to die in a Christianly manner."

His thoughts of dying were constant. "I hope here, at this moment, I may escape the scaffold," began one entry in his diary. "Why fool myself saying I don't care if I die? People who say that usually are liars. But I do say: Perhaps I shall live again. Yet even with these thoughts, I hate to leave just now. There's plenty of fun in life, plenty of music. I want my record to play a little longer."

Although he received assistance and comfort from prison reformers and religious workers, Bocchio was skeptical: "Reading the Bible has not made a bigot of me as it does of some," he noted. "I abhor fanatics. I learned, however, from my reading that one must pray often, but the real praying is not simply grumbling words."

One particular reformer for whom Bocchio had immense respect was Emma Lambert. They corresponded for nearly two years, and she helped him develop a concern for prison conditions. Joe was especially bothered that many of his fellow inmates could not spell their names. Although he admitted that he was no authority on prison reform, he sincerely believed that compulsory education should be used to rehabilitate inmates.

In addition, Bocchio was evidently a pacifist. Joe recalled talking to numerous prisoners who fought in World War I. "They brought the war of the Argonne to me," he wrote, "and the bombs which painted the night. They gave me pictures of men dropping down to die. And from this, I have formed a conclusion: War is sin."

What astounded prison officials and gained the attention of many citizens was his having learned English so quickly and then undertaking to study the law through a correspondence course. Knowing by heart many passages from the works of Shakespeare, Dante, and Kipling, Bocchio was so enthusiastic about his studies that he was able to encourage a convicted murderer to read poetry.

During the long, dull hours, he often sat at his writing table and composed blank verse rather than study his blueprints. When reporters visited him, he frequently gave them copies of his latest verse, which appeared in local newspapers. One piece was entitled "Condemned." "Take it," he said to a newspaperman, "as a souvenir from Joe Bocchio." The reporter read the first three lines about the gallows: "My lady of death,/ She will be with me on that long road which winds into the shadows,/ But I go unafraid."

Another poem was dedicated to his mother. One, written on the day a fellow prisoner was hanged, was published in early 1924:

> Within a catacomb, a prison cell,
> Wherein dark solitude reigns as king,
> Blithing men with its silent touch,
> I sit, a mannikin of fate, a pawn,
> To wait till destiny shall draw the bolt
> And let the sunlight of tomorrow in.
>
> Tomorrow's shameless jade, how often you,
> With rouged lips and powdered cheeks have sped
> The fair, till, as today, thou must unmask
> And stand revealed a hag from torment sprung,
> Whose soul a duplicate should only find
>   between these walls
> Where men are held, whom men decree must die.[22]

22. Bocchio, "Last Days of a Condemned Man," New Orleans *Item*, January 28–30, February 1–8, 1924; newspaper clippings, in Dallas Calmes Scrapbook; New Orleans *States*, April 25, 1924; Hearsey, *The Six Who Were Hanged*, 29; Charles East, "Six for One," Baton Rouge *Morning Advocate Magazine*, January 18, 1951, pp. 3, 12; Lambert to Parker, May 4, 1924, in Parker Papers.

Although Bocchio's prose and verse were at times sophomoric and contained grammatical errors, he displayed an intellectual capacity which captured the attention and sympathy of officials, reformers, and the public. When first arrested, he could communicate only in Italian, but within three years he was able to quote classical works, study the law, and write and read English proficiently. His working drawings for an advanced electric motor and a gasoline engine demonstrated that Bocchio possessed exceptional mechanical ability. However, what was probably noticed by those who followed *Rini et al.* closely for three years was that Joe Bocchio exhibited qualities that set him apart from the Orleans Parish Prison population and the preconceived ideas about the *mafiosi*.

11

I Am a Klansman

During the second trial, the Tangipahoa Klan remained silent. But two days after the sentencing, a night watchman was found murdered alongside a railroad track in Hammond. The gang of youths charged with the crime was released with low bonds—and one of the leaders was an Italian from Baton Rouge. Furthermore, the Klan was still disturbed about the continuing delays in *Rini et al.*

At midnight on Wednesday, July 19, Klansmen in thirty automobiles drove through Hammond's business district toward Amite, where the Italian gang member was in Sheriff Bowden's custody. Promising to rid the communities of all undesirables, the Klan stopped in Independence, Amite, and Roseland, but there were no reported incidents. For the rest of the summer of 1922, the Klan paraded against bootleggers and other criminals and made frequent donations to Protestant churches. On the night of Thursday, August 24, nearly twenty cars of Klansmen drove from Ponchatoula to Hammond. Carrying an American flag and a large banner emblazoned "Beware Bootleggers, Gamblers, and Loafers," they drove down the main street and out of town without incident.[1]

Throughout 1922, Governor Parker continued his crusade against the Klan with great enthusiasm and solicited the assistance of Attorney General Coco, who supported virtually his every move. Coco, of Italian, French, and English ancestry, had always opposed clandestine groups. In the 1890s he had joined the forces against the White Caps, an organization similar to the Klan. During that same period, both he and Parker were staunch anti-Lotteryites. But in 1896 he became a charter member of the Ring (Choctaw Club), an organization that Parker opposed throughout his politi-

1. New Orleans *Item*, July 19–20, 1922; Baton Rouge *State-Times*, July 28, August 25, 1922; Ponchatoula *Enterprise*, July 21, 28, 1922.

cal career. Nevertheless, Coco and Parker were in 1922 working together to rid Louisiana of the Klan.[2]

In the late summer of 1922, two men were missing and presumed dead in Morehouse Parish. The wife of one of them asked Parker to investigate because she suspected that local Klansmen were involved. The bodies of the two men were found in December, and Parker ordered Coco to conduct a full hearing on the murders and to use national guard troops if necessary.[3]

These actions caused blistering attacks from the Klan in Louisiana and other parts of the South. In addition, Parker's political enemies saw this as an opportunity to attack the governor, and many of his detractors argued that his anti-Klanism was only a part of his overall plan to gain national office. Several Louisiana sheriffs and district attorneys, who extolled the virtues of the Klan, warned Parker that he had lost their political support. Blasting Parker for his supposedly inept handling of the Klan issue, a Shreveport attorney commented on Parker's involvement in the Hennessey affair: "I have never been in favor of mob law in any form, nor would I take part in a mob under any circumstances, which is more than you can say for yourself since you did take part in a mob in New Orleans which took the law in their own hands and shot to death a number of Italians." A pro-Klan minister also referred to the Orleans Parish Prison incident and called Parker and Coco "Lyncher John and Dago Cocacola."[4]

But many southerners praised Parker for his stance against the Klan and the Mafia, especially in regard to the trial of Rini and the others. A letter from Winnfield, Louisiana, warned Parker in a friendly manner that the Klan "might do like the Italians done chief hennesey [*sic*] of New Orleans, La.," because "this Ku Klux is working on about the same principles as that Italian black hand society."[5]

2. Harrell, "The Ku Klux Klan in Louisiana," 157; Charles T. Haas to John M. Parker, September 4, 1922, in Parker Correspondence, Louisiana State University; New Orleans *Times-Picayune*, May 25, 1924.

3. Harrell, "The Ku Klux Klan in Louisiana," 215, 217, 221, 225–27, 236, 244, 258–59; New Orleans *States*, December 28, 1922.

4. Harrell, "The Ku Klux Klan in Louisiana," 160, 252–53; Schott, "John M. Parker," 437, 445; Thomas W. Robertson to John M. Parker, December 26, 1922, in Parker Papers.

5. To John M. Parker: L. D. Fondren, January 12, 1923, Fred Dupree, January 13, 1923, J. F. Hester, December 31, 1922, all in Parker Papers.

As a member of Louisiana's planter society, Parker considered the Klan a threat to the state's class structure. Throughout his life he disliked and distrusted all secret organizations, especially those among the lower class. Specifically, he considered all Klansmen cowards, because they hid under their robes and masks. He nevertheless held to many principles that the Klan espoused. Expressing a belief in white supremacy, Parker told one of Louisiana's United States senators that it would be a "grave mistake" to appoint a black man as the New Orleans surveyor of customs. In regard to immigrants, the Klan and Parker were again in basic agreement: "In this day and period, when unrest and dissatisfaction stalk . . . over the country," Parker wrote, "a very large percentage of it is due to the undesirable class of immigrants who have been vested with the power of the ballot and who never have and never will absorb American ideas and ideals."[6]

Adhering to these nativist beliefs, the governor continued to ignore the Klan's growing power in Tangipahoa and surrounding parishes. In the fall of 1923, George Campbell resigned as the *Times-Picayune*'s correspondent in Hammond because of the newspaper's anti-Klan campaign. In addition, a Tangipahoa resident had warned Parker that Amos Ponder was supposedly organizing small groups in the parish to defend the Klan.[7]

Parker undoubtedly hoped that he would not have to open a second attack on the Klan in Tangipahoa. But in January, 1923, Robert R. Reid died, having served only two weeks on the high court. Both Judge Columbus Reid and Judge Robert Ellis announced for the vacant seat. Judge Reid tried to be somewhat evasive about his Klan membership, but Ellis acknowledged during the campaign that he was a dues-paying member of the Amite chapter.

In 1923, Parker had refused to appoint known Klansmen to the bench or support their candidacy for any office. He and other anti-Klan forces urged Judge Harvey F. Brunot of Baton Rouge to enter the race. Brunot and his supporters charged that in the Catholic sections of the Fifth Judicial District, Ellis was denying his Klan

6. Schott, "John M. Parker," 410–12; John M. Parker to W. P. McGuire, November 18, 1922, John M. Parker to Joseph E. Ransdall, November 24, 1922, Parker to Hughes, June 13, 1922, all in Parker Papers.
7. Schott, "John M. Parker," 454; C. F. Hyde to John M. Parker, February 21, 1923, J. Edmond to John M. Parker, May, 1924, both in Parker Papers.

membership. Ellis retaliated by denouncing Parker for not supporting Klansmen as judges. Fearing no political repercussion, Ellis finally issued a public statement: "I am a member of that organization. . . . There is nothing in the obligation taken by a Klansman in the least inconsistent with or paramount to his oath."[8]

Some of the main participants in *Rini et al.* were involved in this volatile election. Lewis Morgan, a defense attorney in the first trial, announced at a rally in St. Tammany Parish that his allegiance, formerly to Judge Reid, was to Judge Brunot. Amos Ponder supported Ellis, whose campaign manager was Lee Lanier, the Amite editor who had had difficulty distinguishing between an angry mob and a crowd of concerned citizens. Lanier traveled throughout the district and charged that the Brunot forces were distorting Ellis' record. He wrote to the editor of the Baton Rouge *State-Times*, reminding voters that Parker had praised Ellis and Tangipahoa residents for their orderly conduct during the two trials.[9]

On the eve of the election, the first major public Klan demonstration in the campaign occurred in Baton Rouge. The crowd loudly applauded Ellis, who explained how he and the late Judge Reid were the first two Klan organizers in Amite. Ellis, who was being supported by Senator Delos R. Johnson, a reputed Klansman, freely admitted that he had worked closely with the Klan to prevent mob violence during *Rini et al.*

"I had no more idea," said Ellis, "when I entered this campaign that I was entering any other campaign than the usual sort, where the qualifications of the men were considered. I was grieved when the religious issue was entered, and at no time have I denied that I was a klansman. The religious issue was injected in this campaign by Governor Parker, the press, and the bootleggers."[10]

8. Schott, "John M. Parker," 443; Harrell, "The Ku Klux Klan in Louisiana," 167, 324–26; "Judge Ellis Issues Statement," March 17, 1923, in Parker Papers; Charles C. Alexander, *The Ku Klux Klan in the Southwest* (Lexington, Ky., 1965), 119–20; New Orleans *Times-Picayune*, January 3, 15, March 16, 29, 1923; New Orleans *Item*, January 28, 1923; Baton Rouge *State-Times*, March 26, 1923; Ponchatoula *Enterprise*, January 19, March 16, 1923.

9. Ponchatoula *Enterprise*, March 30, 1923; Baton Rouge *State-Times*, March 26, 1923.

10. Baton Rouge *State-Times*, March 26–27, 1923; New Orleans *Times-Picayune*, March 27, 1923; "KKK Lists," in Parker Papers.

According to the New Orleans and Baton Rouge press, the supreme court race in the Fifth District was the first contest in Louisiana history between Klan and anti-Klan forces for a major political office. "Don't be confused on this issue," editorialized the Baton Rouge *State-Times*. "This is strictly a klan and anti-klan fight." The New Orleans *Times-Picayune* stated that the Klan and its sympathizers controlled political affairs in the parishes of Livingston, St. Helena, East Feliciana, and Tangipahoa, where Hammond politicos had predicted that Ellis and Brunot would be in a runoff election. However, the *State-Times* found an especially strong anti-Klan following in Tangipahoa. Despite the predictions, Brunot defeated both Ellis and Reid by 600 votes. But the two Amite jurists refused to concede and charged that there were voting irregularities.[11]

During this political contest, some of the major participants in *Rini et al.* came forth to prove by their statements what had long been suspected—that the Klan strongly influenced the judicial proceedings and that the Louisiana Supreme Court erred in not ordering a change of venue. Although the Klan was defeated in this election, Robert Ellis, Columbus Reid, and other members of the hooded order remained in control of Tangipahoa's judicial process.

11. New Orleans *Times-Picayune*, March 27, 29, April 8, 1923; Baton Rouge *State-Times*, March 17, 26, 31, 1923; Ponchatoula *Enterprise*, March 30, 1923; Hammond *Vindicator*, September 14, 1934.

12

We've Got to Die

In the spring of 1923, Gulotta and his associates filed a voluminous brief with the United States Supreme Court. There was, however, a backlog at the Government Printing Office. So the lengthy document could not be printed right away, and the case was delayed for nearly a year.

The main argument of the brief of *Rini et al.* was that the defendants were denied their rights under the due-process clause of the Fourteenth Amendment. Citing errors during the trial, Gulotta and his colleagues stated that Ellis should have recused himself and that a change of venue should have been granted because of extreme prejudice against the defendants' nationality.[1]

Rini et al. gained further notoriety when Tangipahoa Tax Assessor Norman P. Vernon decided to reupholster the Hudson. Tearing the roof lining off, a workman discovered a stick of dynamite, which had been constantly exposed to the sun's heat. According to experts, the slightest jolt could have caused the dynamite to explode. Officials attempted to determine which of the six men had placed the explosive there, but they all denied knowing anything about it.[2]

For the rest of 1923, *Rini et al.* was not front-page news in New Orleans. In late January, 1924, the United States Supreme Court refused to entertain the appeal of the case, "for lack of a federal question." Reporters learned of the decision and rushed to the Orleans Parish Prison. Bocchio heard a rustling sound near the front of the tier, and he looked down the corridor and saw some movement. Straining to see who was there, he noticed a newspaperman who seemed to be about to leave.

"Good morning!" Joe shouted.

1. Newspaper clippings, in Dallas Calmes Scrapbook.
2. *Ibid.*; New Orleans *Times-Picayune*, April 13, 1923; Crowell, "Stern Justice Took Six Lives for One," 1–E.

The reporter turned around again and walked down the corridor to Bocchio's cell. "I've some news for you, Joe."

"What is it?"

"We've just got some news from Washington. The Supreme Court has decided your case."

Joe was attentive—this was news they all had been waiting for.

"Do you want me to read it?" asked the reporter, who looked at Joe anxiously.

The newspaperman cleared his throat and began to read. Joe turned pale and decided to lie down on the floor of his cell. "Don't get so white," pleaded the reporter. But he continued to read the decision; becoming more nervous, he crumpled the paper in his hands.

"I'm sorry," said the newspaperman.

Sensing the sincerity, Joe smiled and reached out to shake the reporter's hand. "I still have hope," Bocchio said.

"It's foolish to give up hope," said Rini, who was the next to be informed about the decision. He laughed and said, "Well, I'll have to send a telegram to my father . . . in Chicago. I'm glad my mother isn't alive."

"My conscience is clear," Lamantia insisted, in the next cell. "I still have hope that my good friends will intercede.

"I have faith in God, and I do not believe the good people of Louisiana will fail to give justice." Lamantia wept and spoke of his seventy-two-year-old mother, his wife, and his children.

The reporters walked down to Deamore, who protested, "I am innocent of any crime. I've never known anything about the murder.

"I am glad of one thing, though," he said. "My wife, who has been in the hospital for eight months, is getting better. She is now at Harvey with our two children."

"I'm surprised," stated Giglio, in the next cell. "We have been deprived of a fair trial and equal rights. I am sure the people of Louisiana do not want to see six men hang on circumstantial evidence. If we're guilty, we would not ask for mercy."

Leona's only comment was, "I am appealing to the people of Louisiana because we are innocent and convicted on circumstantial evidence."

Rini, who had been smiling, was now bitter. "Nine men were

157

indicted," said Joe. "We six were strangers and were tried and convicted. The other three were local men who never have been called to answer the charges contained in the indictments."

The reporters left, and Andrea sat alone in his cell. From the floor above he heard the black female prisoners moving about, singing, and cursing. Then one of the women shouted down to him, "I'm sorry." He heard other women offering their condolences.

Word of the Supreme Court decision apparently spread through the prison, and Rennyson immediately provided more guards that Monday morning. The warden had received a warning that the jail would be bombed unless the six prisoners were freed.[3]

Numerous letters and telegrams, urging clemency for Rini and his cohorts, arrived at Parker's office. The pleas, coming from small towns in Louisiana, Mississippi, and Alabama, often were based on biblical quotations. Ironically, one of the letters was from Dallas Calmes's niece who lived in New Orleans. "I do not believe," Bertha Calmes stated, "that the execution of six men . . . would prove justice."[4]

When Parker signed the death warrants, more letters poured into his office. The requests for clemency came from individuals and from several Italian societies and organizations in Chicago, Montreal, Detroit, and San Francisco. A former state senator from Louisiana reminded the governor that "the people of New Orleans murdered a bunch of Italians after our courts decided they were not guilty," and the Italian Chamber of Commerce in Detroit said that Tangipahoa was "notoriously hostile toward Italians."[5]

Parker also received a complaint from the Klan, which charged that the governor "sat idly by" and allowed the law to be "twisted, warped and bent into every conceivable shape." The Klan maintained that "when anyone tried to punish one of them, you and

3. Bocchio, "Last Days of a Condemned Man," New Orleans *Item*, February 9–10, 1924; New Orleans *Item*, January 21, 1924; New Orleans *States*, January 21, 1924; newspaper clippings, in Dallas Calmes Scrapbook; *Joseph Rini et al.* v. *State of Louisiana*, 44 Supreme Court Reporter 230 (1924).

4. New Orleans *Item*, January 30, 1924; to John M. Parker: W. C. Robertson, January 23, M. H. Stewart, January 24, William C. Ermon, January 31, Joe Printz, February 1, J. F. Mitchell, February 3, Bertha Calmes, January [?], 1924, all in Parker Papers.

5. New Orleans *Times-Picayune*, May 10, 1924; A. Battista to John M. Parker, March, 1924, and several similar letters, all in Parker Papers.

your Koco, Katholic Kronies promptly steps forward and says, 'Nay, Nay, Pauline.'"

Besides the criticism, there were many letters of support for Parker. One was from an old personal friend who yearned for "a return to the good old days of *Judge Lynch*, whereby the people themselves can purify the moral welfare of their community as San Francisco did in the early 50's." He also suggested that hanging a few criminal lawyers was desirable. Parker's response was, "You don't know how much I appreciate your letter."[6]

While the public reacted to Parker's signing the death warrants, George Gulotta prepared to request a special meeting of the Louisiana State Board of Pardons. Elsewhere, Sheriff Bowden thought a new gallows was needed. The existing structure was in poor condition and had not been used since the hanging of Avery Blount. The sheriff's office and police jury decided that the new gallows would have a double trap to accommodate Rini and the five other prisoners.[7]

During the last several days of March, Parker carefully read the voluminous record of *Rini et al.*, and on the night of April 1, he decided to set the execution for Friday, May 9, 1924, three years and one day after the death of Calmes. When New Orleans reporters heard of Parker's action, they again rushed to inform the six condemned men. Rini and the others generally shrugged their shoulders, saying they still had faith that they would not hang. For the most part, they were philosophical about their plight.

Rini stood up in his cell, and he wrapped his fingers around the bars and gazed out the window. He decided to cover Toots with some clothing to protect the dog from the spring chill.

"Well, I still have hope," Rini said finally. "When does the pardon board meet?"

When a reporter told him that it would be after the execution, he said, "Isn't there a chance the governor will reprieve us? Well, I

6. To John M. Parker: [Klan member], n.d., Citizen, March 14, S. S. Anderson, March 26, Jean M. Gordon, April 4, J. W. McClelland, April 3, Omar C. Ritchie, April 4, 1924, Parker to Ritchie, April 7, 1924, all in Parker Papers; New Orleans *Item*, April 14, 1924; New Orleans *States*, May 3, 1924.

7. Newspaper clippings, in Dallas Calmes Scrapbook; Ponchatoula *Enterprise*, March 21, 1924.

still have hope and I have little fear of death. I faced death many times during the war, when I served on the *Leviathan*."

After Bocchio received the news, he said, "Well, it does seem a bit unjust that six men should die to pay for the death of one. But I have great faith in God, and I don't believe I am going to die. Surely the governor will reprieve us." Joe then talked about his mother in Italy.

"Are you going to write to her now?" the reporter asked.

"At this stage of the game? No, I guess not." Before the reporter left, Bocchio repeated, "I don't believe I'm going to die. I think God will help me."

Giglio, who was described as the Rudolph Valentino of the group, became angry. "People who hate us in Tangipahoa were responsible," he said. He recalled the two trials and the threats by the courthouse mobs. Although he did not refer specifically to the Klan, Giglio blamed an anti-Italian faction in Tangipahoa for the capital verdict. Finally, Joe said he had faith in Parker, but he knew now that the governor would not commute the sentence.

Lamantia was so startled, he asked the reporter to repeat the news. "I could hardly believe my ears," Andrea said. He smiled and shrugged his shoulders as he paced his cell. "Well, for a long time," he said, "I've been expecting that. Still I have hope."

Deamore was playing cards with a cell mate when he heard about the execution date. "Yeah, well, I been expecting it," he said gruffly and returned to the game. But then he paused. "Course I feel bad, how you expect me to feel?"

Sitting alone at his table, Leona had little to say. He took a hairpin and ran it down each tooth of his comb. Roy refused to comment.

The *Times-Picayune* sent a reporter to George Gulotta's home to get a comment. "I have not exhausted all the legal remedies," Gulotta said. Although he refused to make further statements until he consulted with his associates, Gulotta admitted that they had a possible course of action. In the Leo Frank case (1913–1915), the attorneys' last resort was applying to a United States district court for a writ of habeas corpus, which, if refused, would place the case before the United States Supreme Court for review. According to Gulotta, this legal procedure might delay the execution for another year. Nevertheless, his most immediate action was an appeal to the Board of Pardons.[8]

The regular quarterly meeting of the Board of Pardons had occurred in March. According to rumors, the defense attorneys wanted to delay the execution until a new board met in June. The board as presently constituted, they said, would not be merciful. Gulotta and his associates were probably correct. Members of the board included the trial judge, Robert Ellis; the state attorney general, Adolph Coco; and the lieutenant governor. Hewitt Bouanchaud had resigned recently to become a member of the Louisiana Tax Commission, so the new lieutenant governor and third board member was the former president *pro tem* of the state senate, Delos Johnson. A reputed Klansman, Johnson had supported Ellis in his bid for the state supreme court seat in the spring of 1923.[9]

And all sorts of rumors circulated. A confession from one or more of the prisoners would implicate residents of Independence. Or one of the six would take dramatic action shortly. Or the prisoners had drawn lots to see who would confess. When contacted by reporters, however, the defendants referred to the many stories as "bunk."[10]

Friends of the six prisoners had commutation petitions with fifteen thousand signatures. One of the leaders of this movement was William Warrington, who had befriended the six men over the last three years. Claiming that their plight would receive national attention, Warrington said that he, friends, members of the prisoners' families, and city organizations had circulated another petition to raise funds for the defense appeals to the federal courts and the Board of Pardons.

Many Tangipahoa residents considered these petitions "outside influence, not home influence." Doubting that the hanging would be delayed, Bowden announced that the double gallows was ready. Surrounded by high walls to discourage spectators, the gal-

8. New Orleans *Times-Picayune*, April 2, 1924; New Orleans *Item*, April 2, 1924.

9. New Orleans *Times-Picayune*, April 3, 6, 1924.

10. *Ibid.*, April 5, 1924; New Orleans *Item* and New Orleans *States*, April 6, 1924.

lows was connected to the jail by a covered wooden passageway.

Shortly after Bowden's announcement, the sheriff's office received numerous letters from professionals and from inexperienced men who wanted to hang the six prisoners. Although the executioner had not been chosen, it was rumored that one of Bowden's deputies had also volunteered. Bowden said that he planned to allow the six men to decide the order of hanging.[11]

In early April, it was said in New Orleans that Leona was hemorrhaging. A few days later, a doctor from the Board of Health confirmed that conditions at the parish prison had caused Leona's relapse. He feared that the others had contracted tuberculosis.[12]

Knowing that their clients' poor health would not delay the execution, Gulotta and Henriques requested a meeting with Parker on Tuesday, April 15, at 2:00 P.M. to ask for a reprieve. After listening to the attorneys for more than an hour at the governor's mansion, Parker replied that the six men had had adequate counsel and had received a fair trial. He said there would be no reprieve unless startling new evidence was disclosed.[13]

Upon hearing the news, Deamore and the others became despondent. "I've got nothing to say," Natale said. He was seated at a table made from packing boxes. "Let the lawyers talk. If those are to be the arrangements, what can we do? I am going to continue to pray to God. I don't think God wants an innocent man to be hanged, and God knows I am innocent."

Lamantia, who was next to Deamore, came to the front of his cell. He leaned forward into the sunlight that filtered into the jail. Listening to the message, he appeared to be unmoved by Parker's refusal. He bowed his head, and his fingers gripped the steel grating. Finally, his face revealed that he was visibly shaken.

"There is nothing to say—nothing," Andrea said. "There is nothing to do—nothing but pray. And I am praying to God to save my life. What difference does the hour when we die make, if God wants us to die?"

11. New Orleans *Times-Picayune*, April 2, 5–6, 1924; New Orleans *Item*, April 6, 15, 1924; Crowell, "Stern Justice Took Six Lives for One," 1–E.

12. New Orleans *Item*, April 8, 15, 1924.

13. *Ibid.*, April 14, 1924; New Orleans *Times-Picayune*, April 15–16, 1924; New Orleans *States*, April 15, 1924; newspaper clipping, in Dallas Calmes Scrapbook.

Rini shrugged his shoulders and said, "I am not going to die. I am praying to God and he has heard my prayers. I know it."

When asked about Bowden's plan to allow them to choose the order of their hanging, Rini said, "Let the sheriff decide our turns. I don't want the privilege."

"I want to be the last one to go to the scaffold," Bocchio interjected, "because I have two things which will give me hope. I have faith in God and my clear conscience. Truly, if I had committed a murder or had done anything, I couldn't stand here and talk to you like this. I want to go last because I feel something is going to happen to save me—a reprieve or something like that."

Giglio was not happy about Bowden's offer. "The sheriff isn't doing me a kindness when he tells me I can choose my turn of going to the gallows," he said. "You're not giving any innocent man, whom you are going to hang for a crime he did not commit, a favor when you let him pick his turn. You might as well tell me they're going to give me ice cream and cake on the gallows. First or last, what does it matter?"

When the reporters reached Leona, they found him fatalistic. "If God says we've got to die, we've got to die—that's all," said Roy. "What difference can it make whether I am killed first or last? And that doesn't mean that I have given up hope. I have not. But if it should come—well, I don't care anything about my turn. They can take me first, if they want to."[14]

Within a three-month period, the case of *Rini et al.* suffered three major setbacks—the United States Supreme Court denied the writ of certiorari, the execution date was set, and Parker refused to grant a reprieve. Nevertheless, there were still some reasons for hope. The attorneys planned to file a writ of habeas corpus in federal district court and to apply for a hearing before the Board of Pardons; and numerous petitions requested commutation of the sentences. Despite these efforts, Joe Rini and his companions, who for nearly three years never really believed that the state of Louisiana would execute all of them, now realized that they had only three weeks left.

14. New Orleans *Item*, April 16, 1924.

13

This Decision Is Final

As the execution neared, rumors of a confession were revived. For several days, reports circulated that the prisoners had come to a major decision. Despite the persistence of these rumors, all six prisoners denied that there would be an eleventh-hour confession.

Amid all these denials, Father Raymond Carra called Rennyson and asked for a press conference in the warden's office at 8:00 P.M., Monday, April 21, 1924. At the arranged hour, Rosario "Roy" Leona, Rennyson, Father Carra, Mrs. Fernand May, known as the "Parish Prison Angel," and reporters from the major newspapers met in the warden's small office on the second floor of the main prison. As soon as Leona entered, everyone noticed his pallor.

Leona read the prepared confession in Italian, and only Father Carra understood him. With Father Carra translating, Roy explained that Vito Di Giorgio had told him and Giglio about the opportunity to rob a bank in Independence without harming anyone. When Roy reached the part about going to Independence on Saturday night, he said that only he and Rini left the car. "As I jumped over the fence," Leona explained, "one of the pickets broke and the noise must have awakened Mr. Calmes. Mr. Calmes opened the door and shouted 'Halt!' and fired four shots at me. Being surprised and frightened, I fired two shots in the direction that the fire of Mr. Calmes' revolver was coming from, but unfortunately for him and me, I killed him. I was alone when Mr. Calmes shot at me, and I alone returned the fire which killed Mr. Calmes.

"I make this statement," Leona continued, "because I now feel and I know that I cannot be saved. I make this statement in justice to my own soul and to the other five men who had nothing at all to do with the killing of Mr. Calmes."

"And now, Leona," a reporter asked, "what did Cipolla, Gaeto and DiGiovanni have to do with this thing?"

Leona stared blankly for a few moments. "They didn't have nothing to do with it," he answered finally. "That shooting was something else I don't know anything about. It just happened that night—that's all. The only [man] outside who had anything to do with this was Di Giorgio with his talk about easy money, easy money, easy money."

"I am glad they killed him—glad," Roy added. "They ought to have killed him before."

After speaking to Mrs. May about his family, Leona wept convulsively. He buried his face in his handkerchief. Then he raised his head to speak again.

"I made up my mind last Saturday. I told myself on Saturday, this is the last Easter for me. I think in my heart that if it was them, they would not be so cruel as to let me be that one that's gonna pay for something they did. So I'm gonna see that it's straight, because nobody else was there. So I say to the others, 'I'm going up to confession and take communion and tell the truth. I want you boys—you I want to be in the clear.'"

There were repeated questions from the reporters about details of the shooting. At first, Roy hesitated to answer but then changed his mind.

"I and Rini was the only ones that left the car," Leona insisted, "and the car was two–three blocks away from the bank. I don't know where Rini went, but he didn't come with me. It was dark, and I suppose he stayed behind somewhere because I know I was alone when I broke the picket in jumping over a fence. And nobody else but Mr. Calmes and me were shooting. I couldn't see him—black—but it was raining, too. So I shot at the fire from his [gun] and I hit him both times. But he didn't hit me at all."

"Oh, if it had only been the other way!" Leona said. "If he had only killed me instead of me killing him—all this trouble wouldn't have been."

Leona stopped speaking, and there was another flood of questions. Roy finally put up his hands and protested.

"Don't, don't," he pleaded. "My head will get mixed up, and if I shake my head yes to a question, I should be shaking it no; and I don't want to do that.

"Look," he said, "what shows we didn't want bloodshed. When we try to escape and all those people in an automobile following us, we could have put out our lights and shot them when they came up. We didn't. We got out of our car and hid in the woods till they got past.

"We didn't go there to kill nobody," Roy said.

Leona returned to his cell, and the press requested permission to visit the other five prisoners. Rennyson, who generally allowed newspapermen to interview any inmate, agreed.

When an *Item* reporter told Natale about Leona's confession, he shrugged his shoulders and said nothing. He suspected that the visitor wanted to trick him.

"Oh, Roy," the reporter called. "Deamore won't believe you've made a statement. Holler loud so that he can hear you, and you tell him yourself."

From a cell at the far end Leona's Italian crackled through the tier. After hearing Roy repeat his statement, Deamore had a gleam in his eyes.

"If he says he did it, he did it," Deamore said. "What he says is so. Don't be mad. I can't make no statement. I want to talk to my lawyer. I can't say nothing till I talk to my lawyer."

Lamantia listened to the conversation with Deamore. When the reporter approached him, he stuck two fingers through the grating to shake hands.

"I'm glad, more glad for Roy than for myself," Lamantia said, "because his conscience is easy now. It was good for him to free his conscience, even if it makes no difference in what they do to us. No matter what happens now, people will know we others didn't do no killing."

The reporters continued down the corridor to Rini's cell and disturbed Toots, asleep on Joe's bunk. "I—I've been praying for something like this," Rini exclaimed. "Yes, I've been praying. But I don't know what you want me to say. Am I glad or sorry? I'm not anything at all.

"Boys," Joe continued, "just put yourself in this cell for three years for a killing you didn't do and wouldn't have done. Get a date fixed for your hanging and then let someone say: 'Roy has confessed that he was the only one that did any shooting.' Could you think of anything to say?"

Looking up from his copy of O. Henry's *Heart of the West*, Bocchio greeted his visitors. "I can't be so very happy," he said thoughtfully. "Of course I am glad in one way. It shows I didn't do any killing and it must be good for Roy to free his own conscience. And maybe it means that they will not be so hard on the rest of us.

"But down here," Bocchio went on, "it isn't like it is on the outside. I didn't know Roy before we got into trouble. I just met him that time. But you get to know people who are in the condemned cells with you for three years, and Roy has been with us. And when I think of Roy and what this means for certain for him— don't you see?

"Then I can't be very happy," he said. "I can't be so very glad."

"It doesn't make any difference now if they hang me or not," Giglio said. "We all got to die sometime, and I'm not afraid to go when my turn comes. But I have an old father and mother back in Italy, and if I get hanged and everybody thought I actually really killed somebody, it would have killed them sure. So I been keeping this trouble away from them, and I had it all fixed up to let them know afterwards I just died or something. But now I'm going to write them all about it, because I went there to steal, not because I killed anybody. And my father and mother will know that."[1]

The public reaction to Leona's confession was immediate and mostly negative. The press claimed that his confession was at variance with the trial testimony, but the newspapers also stated that those who believed Leona's confession did so because it did diverge from the witnesses' statements. Their argument was that he could have easily fabricated a story that agreed on all points with the testimony.

Leona's confession disturbed many Tangipahoa residents. Since his tuberculosis was supposedly fatal, District Attorney Allen and Judge Ellis gave little credence to the confession. They also argued that the admission had little bearing on the legal standing of the

1. New Orleans *Item*, April 3, 22, 1924; New Orleans *States*, April 21–22, 1924; New Orleans *Times-Picayune*, April 22–23, 1924; newspaper clipping, in Dallas Calmes Scrapbook; Hearsey, *The Six Who Were Hanged*, 6.

case. But the most vociferous critic was Mrs. Calmes, who described the confession as a "purely trumped up affair."

At her home, she stated, "The confession is a fabrication of a man who is dying of tuberculosis anyway. I am positive there were more persons than one firing at my husband, and I still have the blueprints and charts to show bullets were fired from two different directions." Mrs. Calmes said that she and her family were so indignant over Leona's actions, they planned to request that Governor Parker and the Board of Pardons "let the law take its course."

Mrs. Calmes was so disturbed that a few days later, she wrote a letter to the editor of the *Item*. Claiming that her memory was "fresh and vivid," she insisted that her husband fired in self-defense, his assailant having shot at him first. Clarifying an earlier statement she made to the press, Mrs. Calmes wrote, "I saw only one man in the yard when my husband was murdered, and if the report has been circulated that I saw more than one man in the yard, it is an error on the part of someone, and is no fault of mine." Nevertheless, she believed that there was more than one assailant because of the directions of the bullet holes in the wheelbarrow and other objects. "But," she reiterated, "I saw but one man, one gun, one murderer." Finally, she argued, Leona imagined that it rained the night of the murder. Her recollection was that "never before, nor since, has nature ever blessed the world with a prettier starlit night."

Despite the criticism of his confession, Leona was still content. With his elbows on the table and his face buried in his hands, he appeared to be praying one night and did not notice his visitor. There was a light tapping on his cell door, and Leona straightened up. He had a bandage around his head. He suffered severe headaches, he said, and the bandage provided relief. When the reporter asked whether he had been praying, he replied, "Yes, I have given myself up wholly to God. I have sincerely repented and believe my soul, at least, will be saved. As for my body, I don't care much what they do with it."[2]

Because of Leona's confession, Henriques announced that he

2. New Orleans *States*, April 22–23, 1924; New Orleans *Times-Picayune*, April 23, 26, 1924; New Orleans *Item*, April 22–23, 26, 1924; newspaper clippings, in Dallas Calmes Scrapbook.

was prepared to ask Parker again to grant a reprieve so that a clemency plea could be heard by a new Pardons Board. Should Parker not grant the reprieve, Henriques was prepared to ask for a special session of the current board.[3]

While the attorneys contemplated that special session, Sheriff Bowden arrived in New Orleans on Wednesday, April 23, to read the death warrants. Just before noon, the six men entered Rennyson's office to hear officially that their execution would occur on Friday, May 9, between noon and three o'clock. All of the prisoners appeared tense except Rini.

Before they left the room, Bowden decided to question Leona about some details in his confession. The sheriff maintained that the bullet hole in the wheelbarrow was not in the line of fire between Leona and Calmes. Therefore, Bowden concluded, the physical evidence contradicted what Roy said. Leona did not change any part of his confession and continued to insist that he alone shot Calmes.[4]

After nearly three years, the defense attorneys undoubtedly realized that their failure to challenge Mrs. Calmes's testimony and the physical evidence concerning the directions of the bullets might be a hindrance to future legal proceedings. Challenges to Leona's confession by Bowden and Mrs. Calmes probably influenced Governor Parker, who, after receiving a large number of telegrams urging a reprieve, stated that "no matter if the pardon board should recommend a commutation of sentence for the five men because of Leona's confession . . . , I would refuse to grant a commutation, because in my opinion all six men are equally guilty. . . . This decision is final."[5]

Shortly thereafter, Charles Papini, acting Italian consul in New Orleans, carried a personal message to Parker from Ambassador Celasio Gaetini. Writing unofficially, the ambassador explained that Italy had no death penalty and did not put the responsibility for murder on those not actually present at the scene. His country

3. Newspaper clippings, in Dallas Calmes Scrapbook.
4. *Ibid.*; New Orleans *States*, April 23, 1924; New Orleans *Times-Picayune*, April 24, 1924; New Orleans *Item*, April 23–24, 1924.
5. Newspaper clippings, in Dallas Calmes Scrapbook; New Orleans *States*, April 23, 1924; New Orleans *Times-Picayune*, April 24, 1924; New Orleans *Item*, April 23–24, 1924.

interpreted the impending execution as an act "inspired by race hatred." Gaetani wrote that "this will be substantiated by the fact that . . . such hatred has at times manifested itself in some parts of Louisiana." The ambassador warned that the hanging, as well as new immigration laws that discriminated against Italians and others, would severely harm the relationship between Italy and the United States. Gaetani asked Parker to commute the sentence to life in prison.

The Italian ambassador's plea to Parker received national attention and was quoted in the New York *Times*. The State Department again closely monitored the developments in *Rini et al.* Parker informed Gaetani that he had no power to pardon or to commute a sentence unless the Board of Pardons so recommended. But the governor failed to say that he had no intention of granting such a reprieve—even if it were recommended.

Parker was actually enraged by the ambassador's letter, and he notified Hughes that he considered it "practically a threat." The State Department solicitor advised Hughes merely to acknowledge receipt of Parker's letter. The solicitor, concerned about the tone of the governor's letters for nearly three years, thought Parker's latest communication was "most unusual, to say the least." He also advised Hughes that Parker's statement that the United States Supreme Court confirmed the case of *Rini et al.* was "somewhat misleading." The Court did not pass on the merits of the case but dismissed it for lack of a federal question.[6]

When Giglio heard about Parker's second refusal to grant a reprieve, he said, "Ah, Mrs. Calmes, her I don't blame. She lost her husband, and nobody could blame her for anything. But the governor, him I do blame. I think he must have a prejudice against Italians—he was mixed up in that lynching of a lot of Italians here in New Orleans.

"How can he say that we had a fair trial," Joe said, "when he himself went from one end of that parish to the other preaching

6. Celasio Gaetani to John M. Parker, April 19, 1924, Parker to Gaetani, April 25, 1924, Parker to Hughes, April 25, 1924, Solicitor to Mr. Secretary, April 30, 1924, in Deamore, N., *et al.*, File So. 311.6521; Hearsey, *The Six Who Were Hanged*, 3; New York *Times*, May 10, 1924; New Orleans *States*, April 25, May 7, 1924; New Orleans *Times-Picayune*, April 26, 1924; newspaper clipping, in Dallas Calmes Scrapbook.

them not to lynch us[?] Is that a sign we are going to get a fair trial where even the governor is afraid they are going to lynch us[?] And now he says he won't even listen to what the pardon board has to say after Roy's confession. He's prejudiced, that's all."

Rini found humor in the news. "Mrs. Calmes says she saw a short thickset man back there," he said. "Sure, I am short and thick now, but I have been getting awful fat for three years in jail without no exercise.

"And now you just take a picture of us when we first got in this trouble," Rini continued, "the picture they take up at Amite. Why I was skinnier than Roy Leona then. I wasn't thickset at all. There wasn't a thickset short man in the crowd those days.

"But, then, they got their minds made up, I guess," Joe said. "A tough break, isn't it?"

"Too bad, too bad," said Lamantia softly as he squatted near the small oil stove in the next cell. He was cooking a pot of soup. Andrea got up and went to the cell door. He shook his head mournfully. "Looks pretty bad, don't it?" he asked with a nervous smile. He turned away and said nothing else.

"What they trying to do, these people?" asked Deamore angrily. "What they want? They ain't just killing me. The minute they kill me in that same minute they kill my wife. She drop dead sure right when I die. Two times she been operated on since I been in here.

"Yah, how can they say like they say," Natale said. "You know what I be willing to do. I be willing to show these facts to a jury of jackasses. They don't have to be smart men. Jackasses would know even that all of us didn't do no murder."[7]

Three days after Leona's confession, Bocchio requested an interview with Rennyson on the afternoon of Thursday, April 24. In his cell, Joe told the warden that he wanted to confess. Later that night, Rennyson called a press conference in his office. When Bocchio arrived to prepare his confession, his face was without color, and his neck and arms showed signs of weight loss.

Speaking in measured tones, Joe read his letter to Governor Parker. On several occasions he stopped to make grammatical

7. New Orleans *Item*, April 24, 1924.

changes, in his clear handwriting. Those in the room were surprised at his accuracy. Bocchio stated that Deamore enticed him to go to Independence to make "easy money." Admitting that he drove the car to town that Saturday night, Bocchio said that only Rini and Leona left the car to go to the bank. After the shooting, they drove to Giamalva's farm to decide their next move. Then Bocchio said that Pietro Leotta hid their guns in a strawberry patch for them until they decided to leave for New Orleans.[8]

Bocchio wanted Rennyson to deliver his letter to the governor, who he believed would save him. "I repeat again before you," Bocchio wrote, "before my God and before the grave of my father, that never in my life would I be able to murder or hurt anyone." Unfortunately, Bocchio was probably unaware that Parker described himself as an "earnest advocate of capital punishment." The governor firmly believed that "the death penalty should be inflicted wherever warranted." It was, he said, "not only a deterrent to committing crime" but it removed "very dangerous criminals from further activity."[9]

Parker saw *Rini et al.* as another chapter in his never-ending crusade against what he believed were elements of the Mafia. And in the delays, the reputedly large defense fund, and the "high-class" attorneys, the governor saw similarities to the Hennessey case. In a letter to Secretary of State Hughes, he again denied that he was prejudiced against Italians. However, he admitted that "my attitude today is exactly what it was thirty-two years ago— that we want law-abiding citizens in American and do not propose to tolerate the Black Hand, Mala Vita or similar organizations superseding the law and our duly constituted authorities." Moreover, Parker brought up the eleven Italians who were killed in 1891. "We only acted in open daylight," Parker wrote, "after the courts had failed to function and justice made a mockery."

Parker told Hughes that Hennessey was killed by the "Black

8. *Ibid.*, April 25, 1924; New Orleans *Times-Picayune*, April 25, 1924; New Orleans *States*, April 24–25, 1924; newspaper clipping, in Dallas Calmes Scrapbook; Bocchio to Parker, April 24, 1924, in Parker Papers.

9. J. Bocchio to A. M. Rennyson, April 25, 1924, Bocchio to Parker, April 25, 1924, in Parker Papers; John M. Parker to Victor V. Young, March 5, 1923, in Parker Correspondence, Louisiana State University.

Hand." The governor still believed that the New Orleans Italians, before Hennessey's death, were responsible for ninety-four murders for which there were no convictions. "The result of that gathering," Parker concluded, "was that it has been thirty-two years since we have had any trouble of any kind with these people."[10]

Despite Parker's position, Gulotta filed a formal application on Friday, April 25, for a special meeting of the Board of Pardons. When State Attorney General Coco received the document, he conferred with Lieutenant Governor Johnson and Judge Ellis to set the meeting for the following Wednesday. Coco announced that the six men could personally appear before the board. Sheriff Bowden said that he had an extra squad of deputies ready to provide security at the civil courts building, where Coco's office was located.[11]

The news of the special meeting did not cheer the six condemned men. Giglio and Rini remained composed, but Deamore, the oldest, showed "unmistakable signs of going to pieces under the strain." When he attempted to talk, he often burst into tears, fell on his bunk, and buried his head in his arms. Once when visitors arrived, he shrieked uncontrollably, jumped around in his cell, and for nearly ten minutes, beat his head with his fist.

Leona had given up all hope of being saved from the gallows. He embraced religion as his solace and appeared to be more relaxed. It seemed, though, that he counted each minute of the day. When Giglio spent more than his allotted hour to exercise in the steel-encased corridor in front of their cells, Roy looked at his watch and said, "Joe took ten minutes of my time. He was walking an hour and ten minutes by the watch."[12]

Although Giglio exhibited no fear of his impending execution, he was often angry over what he considered extreme bias against him and the others. "Prejudice, that and nothing else has convicted us and consigned us to our death!" he shouted to a reporter.

10. Parker to Hughes, April 25, 1924, in Deamore, N., *et al.*, File So. 311.6521.
11. New Orleans *Times-Picayune*, April 26, 1924.
12. *Ibid.*, April 27, 1924; New Orleans *States*, April 25–26, 1924; New Orleans *Item*, April 3, 27, 1924.

His voice carried through the tier. "Leona confessed that he alone fired the shots that killed Mr. Calmes. Why then make us, too, pay the extreme penalty[?]

"I know now that I am going to die," he shouted, in another burst of rage. "Some statements have been made in this case, but before I die I am going to make a few statements myself. I am going to say something that will open somebody's eyes."

"Are you prepared at this time to make a statement of any kind?" asked the reporter.

"No, I am not prepared yet," Joe said softly as he regained his composure.

When the reporter questioned Giglio and the others about rumors that an effort to rescue them was afoot, they responded angrily. "That is calculated to bring more prejudice against us," Giglio insisted. "For three years we have been the best behaved prisoners here. Ask Rennyson, and he will tell you the same.

"You can rest assured there will be no attempt on our part to gain our freedom," Giglio said. "If Governor Parker does not change his mind, then we must and will die.

"We are not the desperadoes that we have been pictured," he said. "We have no gunmen or hardened criminals on the outside as friends who would resort to so desperate a thing as trying to set us at liberty."[13]

Rennyson had decided to live in the Orleans Parish Prison until the hanging, and he had five deputies constantly patrolling the tier where the inmates awaiting execution were. Superintendent Molony also ordered several policemen to patrol a four-block area around the prison. Although the New Orleans police did not officially believe that a conspiracy existed to free the six prisoners, the superintendent and the warden were probably reacting to the arrest of three "suspicious" Italians seen driving around the prison for about a half hour on Friday afternoon, April 25.[14]

Meanwhile, Tangipahoa authorities were preparing to carry out the execution. At Bowden's request, Rennyson purchased one hundred feet of Manila rope, which was put through a block and

13. New Orleans *States*, April 27, 1924.
14. *Ibid.*, April 26, 1924; New Orleans *Item* and New Orleans *Times-Picayune*, April 26, 1924; newspaper clipping, in Dallas Calmes Scrapbook.

tackle to stretch it at least eighteen inches. The sheriff continued to test the gallows, and the warden negotiated to hire an experienced hangman in New Orleans.

Italians in Tangipahoa were especially interested in the execution. Giglio's relatives, living between Hammond and Amite, followed events closely. A boy translated the newspaper accounts for them. Although officials planned the execution for the busiest part of the strawberry season, they predicted that few Sicilian berry farmers would work on May 9, the day of the hanging. Several Italians tried to explain why they would not pick their crop that day, but they only said, "Well, just because—."[15]

Despite two confessions and a plea from the Italian ambassador, the death warrants had been read, and local and state officials worked on final plans for Rini and the others. Although the attorneys petitioned the Board of Pardons for a special session, Governor Parker had announced for the second time that he would not grant a reprieve. With the execution scheduled for the following week, Deamore and the others began to show signs of depression that would only worsen.

15. New Orleans *Times-Picayune*, April 27, 1924; New Orleans *Item*, April 28, 1924; New Orleans *States*, April 24, 27, 1924.

14

It Ain't Right

For the first time in its history, the Board of Pardons decided to meet at the Orleans Parish Prison to consider the appeals of five of the prisoners. At Rennyson's request, Bowden had told the board that extraordinary security would be necessary to transport the men from the prison to the civil courts building. So Coco agreed that the board would meet first in offices adjacent to his to review the records of the case and then recess to the prison to hear the verbal pleas.[1]

As soon as the meeting date was set, Rini and the others announced that they would appear personally before the Board of Pardons to appeal for commutation. Although the appeal was for everyone except Leona, Roy said that he wished to appear also. Giglio had a speech he hoped to deliver that Wednesday morning, and Rini asked for Rennyson's assistance in drafting a letter. Lamantia, who had no education, did not prepare for the hearing. His nervous smile seemed constant, and he showed signs of fear and despondency. To most observers, Andrea was at the "breaking point." When questioned by reporters, he admitted that he feared he would not be successful before the board.

In another cell, Bocchio wrote a statement that he wanted to read to the board. Joe's friends had tried to have a new trial granted for him only. If that occurred, they argued, he could clear himself of the murder charge, but their efforts were in vain. Other sympathizers wrote letters pleading that Bocchio's sentence be commuted to life in prison, and one woman reminded the board that "Mrs. Calmes only saw *one* man in the yard."[2]

1. New Orleans *Times-Picayune*, April 27, 1924; New Orleans *Item* and New Orleans *States*, April 27–28, 1924.
2. New Orleans *Times-Picayune*, April 27, 30, 1924; New Orleans *Item*, April 27, 29, 1924; newspaper clipping, in Dallas Calmes Scrapbook; Virginia Montgomery to Board of Pardons, April 30, 1924, in Parker Papers.

While Rini and the others prepared for the hearing, Ambassador Gaetani announced that he planned to appeal to Secretary of State Hughes and President Calvin Coolidge to obtain a stay of execution, but neither had jurisdiction over the case at this point. The ambassador explained that in his letter to Parker, he had not questioned the fairness of Louisiana laws or the integrity of its judicial system. Since Leona's confession, however, he decided to ask for mercy for the other five men. Italian law distinguished between "material murder" and complicity in a murder by persons not actually or materially participating. Gaetani asked Parker to consider this difference when he made his decision concerning a reprieve or a commutation.[3]

At the prison, Deamore began to fly into hysterical rages. On Sunday afternoon, April 27, 1924, he yelled over and over that he wanted to confess, but he later changed his mind. On Monday night, guards noticed smoke coming from Deamore's cell. Rushing down the tier, deputies found him standing in the center of a pile of flaming newspapers.

"The whole world is burning up!" Natale shouted. "Everything is on fire!"

The deputies extinguished the fire and removed Deamore from his cell. He had slight burns on his legs and hands, and there was a deep scratch on his neck. Doctors attended to him, and he did not have to be hospitalized.

Rennyson had Deamore's cell thoroughly searched, and deputies found a sharpened wire and a small block of wood that served as a handle. The homemade weapon had no blood on it, so Deamore's neck wound was caused by something else. Deputies also found a broken mirror splotched with blood.

Later Monday, Natale appeared to have settled down, but around midnight he fell from his bunk, jumped to his feet, and screamed, "Fire! Fire! The whole world is burning up!"

Deamore's outburst disturbed nearly the whole prison, and crowds gathered outside. The next morning, he refused to eat. He only sipped some coffee. The deputies feared that Deamore was insane. Rennyson, who believed that Natale was faking to delay the execution, nevertheless put him alone with a mattress in a

3. New Orleans *Item* and New Orleans *States*, April 27, 1924.

cell on the death-row tier. Natale pulled off all his clothes except his undershirt. He threw himself on the mattress and shouted, "Everything is on fire. Take the fire away, quick."

Doctors, guards, and newspapermen quietly observed Natale until Mrs. Deamore arrived. When she saw her husband, who was now totally naked, she pleaded with him to recognize her. He shouted, "Take away the big fire" and threw his hands out in a gesture of appeal and began to beat his chest.

Visibly distraught, Mrs. Deamore was led from the prison by her sister. But she heard her husband shout again, and she returned. She insisted on an explanation. Officials told her that the superintendent of Charity Hospital had examined her husband. Deamore's physical condition was good, but there was a slight danger of an immediate mental collapse. The parish coroner would examine her husband to determine whether he was insane.

Although Rennyson believed that Deamore was feigning insanity, he redoubled the guards. No one could enter the third-floor tier unless Chief Deputy James Glynn or himself was present. Rennyson's order applied to all relatives, the press, and other prison employees not assigned to the tier.

Others doubted that Natale was insane. Although he spoke English to the reporters and the prison staff, it was well known that he normally spoke Italian. But during his supposedly insane rages, he only spoke English.[4]

While officials concerned themselves with the sanity of Deamore and perhaps Bocchio and Lamantia, William Warrington announced that he had 35,000 signatures from all parts of the United States and Canada on a clemency petition, which he planned to present to the Board of Pardons. In addition, as the hearing date approached, letters poured into Parker's office. Knights of Columbus and Sons of Italy in Texas and Pennsylvania pleaded with the governor to commute the sentences. Considering it "ghastly to hang these men," a New Orleanian asked Parker specifically to spare Bocchio, who she believed was "quite incapable of murder and can even accomplish much good by being permitted to live."

4. New Orleans *Item*, April 29–30, 1924; New Orleans *Times-Picayune*, April 29, 1924.

Another resident stated: "How Amite City will be able to hang six men in one day is difficult to understand."[5]

Besides the pleas for clemency, death threats arrived in the governor's mail on the day of the hearing. One letter, which reminded Parker about his part in the Hennessey episode, threatened the governor with death if he allowed the execution to take place. Trying to make Parker believe that the messages were from the Mafia or Black Hand, the authors, in an amateurish manner, signed the letters with the imprint of a full-size hand in black ink.

Other citizens praised Parker's handling of the case. The vast majority of the letters came from Louisiana and generally commended him for not granting clemency. Some of the governor's staunchest supporters were Baptist and Methodist ministers. Parker had support from other quarters as well. For example, a bank president in Tangipahoa informed Parker "that the representative American citizens of this Parish heartilly [sic] commend your action."[6]

Parker was not the only public official receiving mail on behalf of Rini and the others. On the morning of the Board of Pardons meeting, Rennyson received a letter that offered him $50,000 and Superintendent Molony $25,000 to release all the prisoners except Leona. The message also threatened to wreck the train if all six men were brought to Amite to hang. The letter was typed on a Western Union telegraph blank and dated April 29, Independence, Louisiana, but the postmark was Grenada, North Carolina. Although the note was signed "Italiana," New Orleans officials thought that it was a hoax. Nevertheless, Rennyson ordered all prison guards to remain vigilant.[7]

Federal postal authorities started an investigation of the letter sent to Rennyson. Then Mrs. Calmes and her three children also

5. New Orleans *States*, April 29, 1924; to John M. Parker: Walter R. Stauffer, April 29, Reverend A. Centanni, April 28, Frank Graziano, April 24, 1924, and several similar letters, all in Parker Papers.

6. To John M. Parker: [?], April 25, [?], April 29, J. F. Dezauche, April 29, George F. Hull, April 27, John K. Dyer *et al.*, April 27, H. P. Mitchell, April 28, 1924, all in Parker Papers; New Orleans *Item*, April 29, 1924.

7. New Orleans *States*, April 30, May 1, 1924; New Orleans *Item*, April 30, 1924; New Orleans *Times-Picayune*, May 1, 1924; Washington *Post*, May 3, 1924; newspaper clipping, in Dallas Calmes Scrapbook; Hearsey, *The Six Who Were Hanged*, 6; Crowell, "Stern Justice Took Six Lives for One," 1-E.

received life-threatening messages. These contained crude draw-ings of a gallows and six hanged men with their tongues exposed. The letters deeply disturbed the Calmes family. Although many believed that the Mafia sent the threats, Sheriff Bowden thought otherwise, and he was probably correct. According to Humbert Nelli, it was not uncommon for some non-Italians and even some Italians to use such techniques during well-publicized cases in-volving the Mafia or Black Hand.[8]

On Wednesday morning, April 30, a huge crowd surrounded the Orleans Parish Prison, and Molony ordered extra police pro-tection. However, the defense attorneys announced that their cli-ents would not personally appear after all. So the Board of Pardons meeting was in Coco's office. In one corner of the attorney gen-eral's conference room were four women from the Prison Aid League, who had notified the board that their organization op-posed all forms of capital punishment and favored commuting the prisoners' sentences.

Probably undaunted by the Prison Aid League, Lieutenant Governor Johnson, the reputed Klansman and the chairman of the Board of Pardons, opened the hearing. Gulotta was allowed to withdraw the original petition that asked for commutation of all six men's sentences. He then filed a petition requesting that the sentences for all except Leona be commuted. Gulotta argued that Leona's actions were not part of a conspiracy. The law, Gulotta maintained, distinguished between burglarizing a house and rob-bing a bank at night because the former act could result in mur-der. Since the bank had no guard and was unoccupied, the six men could not have conspired to kill anyone.

Gulotta also offered Bocchio's statement, which, he argued, cor-roborated Leona's and the testimony in the two trials. Henriques submitted Mrs. Calmes's testimony in which she stated that she saw one man in the yard, and Gulotta argued that her statement agreed essentially with Leona's. For the first time in three years, the defense attorneys maintained that Calmes's shots probably went astray, thus creating the appearance of another gunman.

8. New Orleans *States*, April 30, 1924; Shreveport *Journal*, May 7, 1924; Hearsey, *The Six Who Were Hanged*, 21; Crowell, "Stern Justice Took Six Lives for One," 1–E; Nelli, *The Business of Crime*, 79.

In regard to Rini, the two attorneys asked the board to examine his case separately. "It is an absolute fact," Gulotta stated, "that four of the petitioners did not commit murder. They were a block and a half away. They are not deserving of the death penalty."

Expanding on Gulotta's anticonspiracy arguments, Henriques said that their clients were never charged with conspiracy to commit murder. According to Henriques, District Attorney Allen agreed on this point. Gulotta resumed the plea for commutation. At most, he said, they were guilty of attempted armed robbery or conspiracy to commit armed robbery—not murder.

Responding to the defense's arguments, Ellis stated that the physical evidence introduced at the trials showed that the shots were fired from more than one direction. However, he added erroneously that witnesses testified that at least four men were seen running back to the car after the shooting.

Gulotta argued correctly that the evidence was not conclusive on these two points. The board decided to research the transcript on the issues. Then the board asked whether anyone else wished to speak on behalf of the prisoners.

Sitting at the right side of the defense attorneys was Girault Farrar, the son of Edgar H. Farrar, one of the members of the Committee of Fifty in the Hennessey episode. The gray-haired gentleman stated that he was an attorney and wished to speak. Claiming to be a humanitarian, he warned the board that "it is dangerous to hang six men for this one murder—and it is brutal!" Farrar believed "in capital punishment in proper cases," but he argued that the sentence of Rini and the others was "legal murder, or butchery under the law." Taking up the arguments of Gulotta and Henriques, he maintained that there was no conspiracy to commit murder.

Allen began the state's presentation by submitting the criminal records of Giglio and Bocchio. He then argued that Leona's confession was false because it did not agree with the trial testimony. But Allen shocked everyone when he claimed that he had additional evidence to support Ellis' unsubstantiated statement. He presented an affidavit from Victor Simon, who claimed that he saw four men fleeing the murder scene that night. Simon swore that he and another black man were in a shack at the rear of the cookhouse that adjoined the Calmeses' restaurant. He claimed that they heard at least five shots that night, and after the shooting stopped, he looked over the fence and saw four men run from the alley and across a vacant lot to a parked car.

Simon's affidavit contradicted all testimony in the two trials. The defense attorneys were stunned by the convenient introduction of a sworn statement by a witness who had never testified in any of the legal proceedings. Since they could not cross-examine Simon during the hearing, the new evidence was left unchallenged, and Allen resumed his arguments.

After an impassioned plea for clemency by Mrs. Fernand May, Sheriff Bowden was the last witness to testify. He branded Leona's confession false because it was not, in his opinion, supported by the physical evidence. Bowden now claimed that the direction of the bullet holes proved that at least three or four men shot at Dallas Calmes. The sheriff also argued that Leona's statements about climbing the fence were false because it was made of heavy planks, not pickets (as Roy maintained).

After Bowden's testimony, the board went into executive session. At about 1:00 P.M., dispatches arrived from Governor Parker, who perhaps wished to influence the board's deliberations. Announcing that he had received death threats through the mail, the governor stated that he would refuse to commute the sentences of any of the men even if the board so recommended. Parker claimed that the Black Hand sent the threats. He also said that the authors were not well versed in English and that the letters were postmarked New Orleans.

At 2:40 P.M., Chairman Johnson announced the board's unanimous decision that Leona and Rini should hang. However, on a second ballot, by a vote of 2 to 1, the board decided that the other four should also hang. Attorney General Coco's was the dissenting vote.[9]

When the Board of Pardons hearing ended, Rennyson decided to tell the six men immediately. "Boys, I've got bad news for you,"

9. New Orleans *Times-Picayune*, May 1, 1924; New Orleans *States*, April 30, May 1, 1924; New Orleans *Item*, April 30, 1924; Ponchatoula *Enterprise*, May 2, 1924; Atlanta *Constitution* and St. Louis *Dispatch*, May 1, 1924; newspaper clippings, in Dallas Calmes Scrapbook; Victor Simon statement, April 28, 1924, in Parker Papers.

began the warden. "The pardon board has decided that you have got to hang."

Lamantia slumped against the cell bars. His fingers clutched the steel grating. He did not speak; his eyes were blank. Deamore, who was in the middle of a hunger strike, said nothing.

Rini became pale, in striking contrast to his naturally swarthy complexion. "It ain't right, it ain't right, it ain't justice," he muttered. "Oh God! I sure thought we would get a different deal from the pardon board."

Overhearing Rennyson's message, Bocchio collapsed on a chair. He buried his head in his arms and wept uncontrollably. He finally lifted his head and clasped his hands. "Oh God," he looked upward and sobbed, "be good to my mother and help her to stand this."

Hearing Rini and Bocchio, Leona rose from his chair and leaned against the bars at the front of the cell. He hugged himself, seemingly in prayer. But Roy was weeping.

"It's wrong, it's wrong, it's wrong," Leona shouted. "It's all right for me. I know I was dead a long time ago, but it is all wrong for them.

"Those boys didn't do nothing," he insisted. "I'm sorry I didn't go up by myself to rob that bank. They had no more to do with the killing of Calmes than if they hadn't been in Independence at all."

Giglio was silent. Hearing Leona speak, he finally commented, "Prejudice, nothing but prejudice, that is all it is. It is because we are Italians. Italians can't get justice in that parish. Italians can't get justice in this state. Italians can't get justice in this country.

"If we had been six Americans who did that, do you think we'd all hang?" Giglio asked. "No, of course not! Because we are Italians. If it had been 20 of us who went up there, those people would insist upon hanging all 20 of us."

After Rennyson spoke to the prisoners, all personnel, Tangipahoa officials, and newspapermen departed. The intense emotional reaction they had witnessed left them despondent. They considered their task a horrifying one and did not wish to repeat it. But Rennyson returned—he had to ask the condemned men to prepare written instructions for the disposition of their bodies and their possessions.

Later that afternoon, the warden permitted reporters, friends, and relatives to visit the six men, who were still visibly shaken by the decision. "Yes I know they turned us down," Rini said to one visitor. "I don't see how the board could have been unanimous in wishing to hang me along with Leona. I did admit leaving the automobile with Leona, but I was not present when the shooting occurred. I was in another part of the premises."

"That's right," Giglio said. "Joe Rini had got back into the car before the shooting started. But what's the use of bringing it all out."

"May the God above me cause me to strangle for two hours while they hang me if I had one little thing to do with that shooting!" Rini exclaimed passionately. Joe was usually pleasant, but since the decision his anger was obvious.[10]

The decision of the Board of Pardons early Wednesday afternoon spread "like wildfire throughout the city." Many people who had followed the case closely were surprised—they thought the lives of the six men would be spared. The first reaction of the defense attorneys was that they planned to do nothing further. However, Henriques stated that if the coroner declared Deamore insane, he would try to save Natale from the gallows.[11]

Many citizens sent Parker letters concerning the board's decision. Reverend W. A. "Billy" Sunday was thrilled by the governor's stand "in face of Black Hand letters and threats of every sort." One Louisianian said that next to Parker's contributions to Louisiana State University, "this will have been your greatest achievement." A letter from Washington, D.C., commended the governor and stated, "If the Dagos get to [sic] smart we will frame a law on them as we did with Japan." A businessman warned Parker about the Klan influence in the Board of Pardons' decision. "Senator [Lieutenant Governor] Johnson and Judge Ellis," wrote the New Orleanian, "as you know, are both Kluckers, and don't you think that the Klan has had considerable to do with the refusal of the Board

10. New Orleans *Item*, April 30, May 3, 1924; New Orleans *Times-Picayune*, May 1, 1924; New Orleans *States*, April 30, May 1, 1924.

11. New Orleans *Item*, April 30, 1924; New Orleans *States*, May 1, 1924; newspaper clipping, in Dallas Calmes Scrapbook.

to entertain any plea for clemency for the four men who it is generally believed had no hand in the actual killing?"

Since at least the spring of 1923 and the campaign for the seat on the state supreme court, Parker was aware that Ellis and Johnson were two of the state's leading Klansmen. And both were on the Board of Pardons. Although the governor castigated the Klan in all parts of Louisiana, he was unusually silent about its influence over the proceedings of *Rini et al.* He never explained his reticence. A letter from a Crowley, Louisiana, merchant to the governor suggests that perhaps Parker had an agreement of noninterference with Klan leaders: "I am sure glad you are keeping the agreement made with the late Robert E. Reed [*sic*] of Amite. He and I had a talk some time before his death and he told me you would abide by the law."[12]

Parker's constant refusal to commute the sentences virtually ended all possible appeals of *Rini et al.* through the state judicial system. Henriques and Gulotta were aware that the petitions for mercy and pleas for commutation would not halt the execution. Although Henriques stated that there would be "no trifling with the courts for delay," he did not categorically refuse to seek an appeal if justified.[13] The two experienced defense attorneys knew that a writ of habeas corpus before a federal court was their only hope, albeit a very slim one.

12. To John M. Parker: W. A. "Billy" Sunday, May 2, R. M. Gentry, May 4, [?], May 4, Jim Murray, May 1, T. J. McDonald, May 1, F. M. Milliken, May 5, 1924, all in Parker Papers.

13. New Orleans *Item*, April 30, 1924.

15

All Hope Is Gone

During visiting hours, curious men and women tried every means to catch a glimpse of the "six Italians." But Rennyson established the "deathwatch" on Friday, May 2, 1924, and only family members were officially allowed near the cells. The warden also armed each deputy on the tier, and in spots easily accessible to his officers, he placed several high-powered rifles.[1]

As the "deathwatch" began, letters of protest and pleadings for mercy continued to arrive at Parker's office. A Methodist minister from Evansville, Indiana, urged Parker to "remember . . . that Italians are human beings just like Americans." A New Orleans resident stated that the reason for the execution was that the six men were "Dagoes." Parker's response was usually the same: "It is not in the power of the Governor to pardon or commute, and even if it were, that power would not be exercised in this case, due to my strong convictions."

Among the pleas for mercy were special requests for clemency for Joe Bocchio. *Le Fiamme D' Italia*, an Italian-language newspaper in Montreal, Canada, and the Italian Legion in San Francisco and Chicago asked Parker to spare Bocchio's life. Joe sent Parker another letter to request commutation and to explain that he did not understand the laws of the United States. No one told him that he could be a state witness. Furthermore, Leona convinced him that if he kept quiet, the legal fees would be taken care of. Parker's secretary replied in a perfunctory manner that the governor had no authority to commute the sentence unless the Board of Pardons recommended it.

An amateurish letter with the imprint of a hand in black ink arrived at the governor's office. The senders threatened Parker,

---

1. New Orleans *Item*, May 1, 1924; newspaper clippings, in Dallas Calmes Scrapbook.

Johnson, Ellis, and Mrs. Calmes with death if they did not intervene to save the lives of the six men before Friday, May 9. "You say you don't take it serious," they wrote, "but you must take this letter seriously as we mean what we say. It's no dame [*sic*] train going to take those six Italian men to Amite. We watching every train day and night." Finally, they warned, "We don't care if you all get an arrangement of soilders [*sic*] to take those men to Amite. We are going to do what ever we intenting [*sic*] to do. So it's best to change your mind if you want your life to be safe."[2]

Meanwhile, Deamore at last ended his hunger strike—he ate several large servings of macaroni. After the Board of Pardons' decision, Deamore remained quietly in his cell. But on Thursday morning, he caused a disturbance. He screamed "Big-a fire." In a strong baritone that echoed through the prison corridors, he sang the "Sextet" from *Lucia di Lammermoor*, the prison selections from *Il Trovatore*, and the famous quartet "Bella figlia dell' amore" from *Rigoletto*. His dramatic renditions were interspersed with Italian street songs. Contorting his face and grinning fiendishly, Natale often frightened the deputies on the tier and his wife, who could not get him to talk to her.

Later that morning, there was a commotion in Bocchio's cell. He was screaming hoarsely in Italian and throwing his frail body about the cell. Rennyson arrived to comfort him, and after several minutes, there was quiet. Bocchio insisted that he still had hopes that Parker would grant clemency. Finally, he fell into a restless sleep for a few hours.

Shortly before noon, a high-pitched laugh came from the opposite end of the tier. Guards rushed to Leona's cell. Nodding, whispering, and giggling to himself and holding conversations with imaginary figures, Roy was a perfect picture of an imbecile. He insisted that there was no need to hold him in prison any longer because he was already dead. Sometimes he laughed at something that he described as just "over there," and Roy shrank from imaginary objects in his cell.

2. [?] to John M. Parker, May 2, 1924, Clarence D. Royse to John M. Parker, May 2, 1924, F. G. Scott to John M. Parker, May 6, 1924, Parker to Stauffer, May 1, 1924, [?] to John M. Parker, May 5, 1924, Nanni Leone Castelli to John M. Parker, May 6, 1924, Bocchio to Parker, May 1, 1924, David M. Evans to J. Bocchio, n.d., "Americans" to John M. Parker, May 1, 1924, and several similar letters, all in Parker Papers.

"Where's the doctor?" Roy asked. "Call the doctor. I want to show him this bullet."

Roy carefully unwrapped his handkerchief and some newspaper to reveal a bullet which he claimed had passed through his body. Holding a wooden spool whittled into the shape of a bullet, Leona said, "It's not right to shoot me that way. You see this bullet?

"They just shot me right here," he said, indicating his left breast. "And it came out here," he said and pointed to just below his left shoulder blade. "I'm dead already. They should not shoot me that way."

Rennyson was sure that Roy used a knife to whittle the wooden object, and he immediately ordered Leona removed from his cell. The deputies searched all cell areas thoroughly, and the warden personally examined Leona and his clothing. Nothing was found. Some of the deputies believed that Leona might have found the whittled spool on the prison grounds, but Rennyson finally concluded that Roy might have used his teeth to shape the spool.

The warden reminded the guards that no visitors were allowed on the tier. Doubling the number of deputies, Rennyson sent Leona back to his cell, where the knife was still hidden behind a drain pipe. Roy planned to use the weapon again when the right opportunity presented itself.

Leona paced his cell. He continued to shrink fearfully from illusionary figures, and occasionally he shouted, "I am dead now, already I am dead. They cannot hang me, because a dead man would not look well dropping through a gallows trap." Later that afternoon, Leona caused another disturbance during a visit with his brother; and deputies, who thought that perhaps he, too, was losing his sanity, returned Roy to his cell.

Shortly thereafter, Deamore shouted, "Fire! Fire! Nobody believes I'm on fire—I make them believe." He tore the porcelain lavatory from the wall and threw it to the floor. Only when he appeared calm did the guards dare enter the cell. But they promptly exited, taking only the sharp fragments that Natale might be able to use as a weapon.

Deamore began to address an imaginary jury. He instructed them to reach a verdict "right away." After a few moments, he screamed, "Guilty! Guilty! Guilty!" He staggered to the front of his cell and burst into song, but his voice was now hoarse. Finally, Deamore lapsed into incoherent mutterings. "God will save me! Yes, God will save me!" he chanted deliriously.

Rennyson continued to doubt that Deamore was insane, because Natale always raged in English. But Gulotta planned to seek a reprieve from Parker so that there would be enough time to conduct a lunacy hearing in Tangipahoa Parish. Henriques, however, wanted to rely on the medical opinion of the Orleans Parish coroner rather than a lunacy commission. If Deamore were declared insane by the coroner, Henriques said, they could petition Judge Ellis to commit Natale to an asylum.

Since the "deathwatch" had begun, Rennyson was especially patient and understanding. Virtually sleeping in his clothes, he did not leave the prison. When the tempers of the six men flared, he often took them to his office to talk to them privately. He got little sleep and ate at irregular times, but Rennyson managed to remain genial and courteous. Never showing signs of anger, he amazed his staff and the reporters.

Rennyson personally searched and accompanied all visitors to the tier holding the six men. He also placed three deputies armed with riot guns and pistols outside the prison walls on a twenty-four-hour basis. Each officer carried a police whistle to summon aid from the First Precinct Station. At the prison entrance was a squad car loaded with tear-gas bombs, hand grenades, bulletproof vests, and Winchester rifles to be used by the deputies. Although officials did not take the recent threat letters seriously, they felt that they had to be prepared.[3]

On Thursday night, May 1, an unidentified person with what sounded like an Italian accent called Rennyson to ask whether he had received from Independence a letter offering him $50,000 to allow the six Italians to escape. Although the warden tried to keep the caller on the line, the police could not trace the call.

On Friday morning, Rennyson received a threatening letter. It warned that "if they hang, you won't live long after. We will get

3. New Orleans *Item*, May 1–2, 7, 1924; New Orleans *Times-Picayune*, May 1–3, 1924; New Orleans *States*, April 30, May 1–2, 1924; Shreveport *Journal*, May 1, 1924; newspaper clipping, in Dallas Calmes Scrapbook; Hearsey, *The Six Who Were Hanged*, 6–7.

you sure." The letter was signed "THE UNKNOWN SEVEN." The note appeared to be connected with the phone call, but Rennyson refused to take it seriously. Superintendent Molony ordered more patrols around the prison, and he also placed patrolmen with riot guns at strategic points around police headquarters.[4]

Later that afternoon, both Leona and Deamore finally conversed intelligently with prison officials. Roy then spent most of the day sleeping, but Natale resumed his operatic renditions, which disturbed several inmates.

When someone asked Giglio whether he slept the night before, he replied, "No, how could I sleep with a wild man on both sides of me, one yelling that the world was on fire and the other shouting that he was a dead man!

"Now, if I've got to die," he added quickly, "I want to die in my right senses. I don't want to be crazy."

The men's plight continued to attract international attention. Nanni Leone Castelli, editor of *Le Fiamme D' Italia*, wrote to Secretary of State Hughes. Charging that the six men were victims of racial hatred in Louisiana, he asked that the State Department intervene in the case. Undersecretary of State Joseph C. Grew replied that the department had no jurisdiction—only Louisiana officials could grant clemency.[5]

On Saturday, May 3, *Rini et al.* gained further notoriety when George Gulotta informed the *Times-Picayune* that a reliable source had quoted Governor Parker saying that "if they didn't lynch them, I will see that they hang." Parker read the article in the morning edition and dispatched a reply. The governor castigated Gulotta and branded the statement "a deliberate falsehood." Parker's official correspondence, however, revealed that his personal sentiment was such that he could have made the remark. A Louisiana farmer, insisting that he was not a member of the Klan, offered "to string them up" if the execution did not take place in Amite. Parker's response was "I appreciate your offer of

4. New Orleans *Item*, May 2, 1924; New Orleans *Times-Picayune*, May 3, 1924.
    5. Nanni Leone Castelli to Charles Evans Hughes, April 24, 1924, Joseph C. Grew to Nanni Leone Castelli, May 2, 1924, both in Deamore, N., *et al.*, File So. 311.6521.

services and wish to say that it is a pleasure to receive a communication like yours."

In an editorial, the New Orleans *States* said that many citizens believed that Parker wanted the six men to hang because "he hates Italians." Noting that one press dispatch claimed that "the prejudice against Italians here goes as far back as the Hennessy assassination and lynching," the *States* denied that the men's nationality influenced the conviction or the sentence. Displaying a lapse of memory or ignorance of Louisiana's and New Orleans' often violent history, the editor concluded that "the inexorable mandate of the law is being carried out against them only because they were participants in one of the most deliberate conspiracies and murders ever so far to disgrace the fair name of this state."[6]

In the midst of the controversy over Parker's alleged statement, Gulotta and Farrar appeared at the parish prison on Friday, shortly before midnight, with a writ of habeas corpus. Their appearance lifted the spirits of the six men scheduled to hang within a week, and Deamore and Bocchio walked eagerly out of their cells to sign the papers. Natale made his customary mark, apparently fully aware of what was transpiring. Rennyson asked whether Natale understood what he was signing. One of the attorneys said, "Yes," and the warden noted that his "charges seem to have suddenly regained their mental equilibrium." He probably realized, as did Gulotta, that signing the petition made it difficult, if not impossible, for the prisoners to claim insanity.

Gulotta declined to reveal the grounds for the writ. According to reliable sources, however, the attorneys cited the crowds' intimidating the jury and Parker's recent alleged remark. Other issues in the fourteen-page petition were the Bowden-Purser confrontation and the allegations by Ritchie Hope and William C. O'Brian. That their clients had to remain in the Orleans Parish Prison was proof, the attorneys charged, of prejudice toward the defendants.

On Saturday morning, May 3, Judge Rufus Foster refused to

6. New Orleans *Times-Picayune*, May 4, 1924; New Orleans *States*, May 2–5, 1924; New Orleans *Item*, May 3–4, 1924; Shreveport *Journal*, May 3, 1924; Robert A. Conrad to John M. Parker, April 26, 1924, Parker to Conrad, April 28, 1924, John M. Parker to Editor [*Times-Picayune*], May 3, 1924, all in Parker Papers.

grant the writ based on the petition only, but he ordered Bowden and Orleans Parish Sheriff George Williams to appear in court on Monday morning at eleven o'clock to show cause why the writ of habeas corpus should not be granted. If the writ were granted, the execution could not take place until all proceedings in federal court were concluded. That action would certainly have angered many citizens.

Several leading New Orleans attorneys said that there were no grounds for a writ because the United States Supreme Court ruled that *Rini et al.* lacked a federal question. One prominent attorney called the writ "ridiculous" and predicted that Judge Foster would deny the petition. However, if the application for the writ were denied, Foster could issue a writ of appeal without suspending the execution. Gulotta and Farrar could then appeal immediately to the Supreme Court. Similar tactics had been utilized in the celebrated Leo Frank case, but the *Item* recalled that after the appeals and a commutation, a mob lynched the defendant.

On Saturday, reports circulated around New Orleans that the State Department was now considering some type of action if *Rini et al.* was halted by the federal courts. Secretary of State Hughes did not confirm or deny the rumors. He only stated that he had no official communication with Governor Parker or with the Italian ambassador.[7]

Despite the filing of the writ of habeas corpus in federal court, New Orleans and Tangipahoa officials continued to prepare for the hanging. Unobtrusively, the hangman visited the six prisoners that weekend to estimate their weight and size so that he could prepare the nooses. Back in Tangipahoa, Sheriff Bowden abandoned his plans for bringing the six prisoners secretly to Amite. His new transportation schedule included the exact time and day. However, he warned that forty to sixty heavily armed deputies would protect the prisoners. The reasons for his change in plans were Judge Foster's order and especially the recent threatening letters, which angered Bowden. During the weekend, the sheriff also announced that he had tested the gallows successfully. Using

7. New Orleans *Times-Picayune*, New Orleans *States*, and New Orleans *Item*, May 3–5, 1924.

sacks of sand weighing as much as a man, his deputies frequently dropped the double traps.[8]

Late Saturday afternoon, Mrs. Calmes held an interview with a New Orleans *Item* reporter. They sat on the wide front gallery of her hotel. Her chair was a worn wicker rocker. She wore black clothing, and her dark hair was piled carefully on her head.

"On Sunday," she said, "I'm going to the cemetery to Dallas' grave, and on Friday—I'll go over to Amite. Yes, I'll be there Friday. I'll be there, in Amite, some place."

Recalling the night of the murder nearly three years ago, Mrs. Calmes said, "Only one more night, one night later, and there would have been no murder. It was on our last night at the restaurant, in the little rest room of mine in the rear, that my husband was killed. He said to me earlier that evening: 'Bess, I don't like it here, it's not near as comfortable as at home.'

"I agreed with him that we wouldn't spend another night there," she continued. "We went to sleep then, and before morning light he was dead."

Questioned about the "six Italians," Mrs. Calmes said slowly, "The men condemned to be executed claim we're prejudiced against them because they are Italians. That is foolishness. Many of my best friends are Italians. They are our intimate friends before the tragedy—and they are still. We have no prejudices against the six men because they are Italians.

"I read how the men are crazy, or feigning insanity," she said. "Well, now it's their turn. I remember how near my mind came to breaking, my sleepless nights and days, my own grief and sorrow. I'll never forget that night, that starlit night, when my husband was killed. I'll never forget the roaring of the revolvers and how he sagged to his knees, and then to the ground, while his gun blazed forth again and again. It was a night of terror and of death.

"So, when Mrs. Fernand May—that woman from the Prison Aid League who asked for clemency for the men at the pardon board meeting last week—when she came to me and said, 'Why don't you ask the board to commute their sentence to life im-

8. New Orleans *Item*, May 4–5, 11, 1924; New Orleans *States*, May 7, 1924; newspaper clipping, in Dallas Calmes Scrapbook.

prisonment?' When she said that, it seemed I could remember in a flash Dallas' last night, and I just shook my head and I told her to let the law take its course.

"I don't think if I had pleaded for clemency for the men," she concluded, "it would have done any good. They've had their chance in the courts, times enough certainly to prove their innocence if they are innocent."[9]

The interview was over, and Mrs. Calmes continued to rock quietly. Having suffered the loss of her husband for nearly three years, she knew that she had to endure six more days until the hanging.

On Monday morning, May 5, death-threat letters arrived at the homes of Judge Ellis and Mrs. Calmes. The letter sent to Ellis was postmarked New Orleans, and law-enforcement authorities said that the writer's scrawl was an attempt at appearing uneducated. The letter threatened "to make four pair of shoes" out of Ellis, Mrs. Calmes, Governor Parker, and Lieutenant Governor Johnson, and promised to blow up the town of Amite on the day of the execution. On the second sheet was the imprint of a hand, and the black ink had soaked through to the first page.

Although Ellis laughed and said that he was not worried, Mrs. Calmes was very concerned. The flood of "letters are driving me insane," she wrote. Mrs. Calmes had received several that were obscene. On the back of each letter was the black-ink imprint of a hand. She was so disturbed over what the press called the "Black Hand" letters that she urged Parker to state publicly that no action of hers would save the six men.[10]

When the governor heard about the letters to Ellis and Mrs. Calmes, he told Secretary of State Hughes that his office was "deluged" with similar correspondence. Parker had received fewer than five letters, and they were from people who probably wanted him to believe that the Mafia or Black Hand was involved in *Rini*

9. New Orleans *Item*, May 4, 1924.

10. New Orleans *States* and New Orleans *Item*, May 5, 7, 1924; Shreveport *Journal*, May 5, 1924; New Orleans *Times-Picayune*, May 6–7, 1924; Mrs. Dallas Calmes to John M. Parker, May 13, 1924, in Parker Papers; W. S. Watkins to Mrs. Dallas Calmes, May 15, 1924, in Dallas Calmes Scrapbook.

et al. The governor said he intended to stop the sale and delivery of arms and ammunition to Italians in New Orleans and in Tangipahoa. He also suggested that the State Department obtain the United States Post Office's record of money orders from Italians who supposedly donated to the defense fund. Furthermore, Parker urged that the Department of Justice and the Post Office investigate the recent threats because they clearly showed "a determined effort on the part of a large number of Italians to defy the laws of both State and Nation."[11]

The death threats to Mrs. Calmes and Judge Ellis caused considerable concern among the Italians in Independence. Mayor Charles Anzalone, who was a personal friend of the Calmeses', and several other prominent Italians signed a public letter declaring themselves "in favor of law and order and the proper execution of the law." They did not condone such letters and promised to protect the lives of any threatened individuals. Anzalone gathered a group of armed Italian youths to guard Mrs. Calmes at her hotel.[12]

The non-Italian residents of Tangipahoa were also disturbed over the threatening letters. "If a hair on Governor Parker's head is harmed," warned a well-known Hammond citizen who was a longtime friend of the governor's, "as a result of his devotion to law and order and his strict adherence to enforcement of all laws, there is going to be precipitated a serious situation in this parish." He announced that several Hammond residents were on their way to Parker's office that morning to assure him of their loyalty and cooperation. Bowden's response to the letters was that if the writ of habeas corpus was granted, he would parade the five men through the streets of New Orleans and defy anyone to rescue them.[13]

On the morning of the hearing, the largest crowd ever to witness a proceeding in a federal courthouse in New Orleans gathered in the small courtroom. The spectators included men, women, and even children, and nearly every attorney in the city was present. Several relatives of the six prisoners and many residents of Tangipahoa were also in attendance. According to the press, the main

11. Parker to Hughes, May 6, 1924, in Parker Papers.
12. New Orleans *States*, New Orleans *Item*, and New Orleans *Times-Picayune*, May 7, 1924.
13. New Orleans *States*, May 4–5, 1924; New Orleans *Item*, May 3, 1924.

topic of conversation was the rumor that the defense attorneys had assured the condemned men that they would not hang on Friday or any other day.[14]

When the hearing began, Gulotta, citing *Frank* v. *Mangum* (the Leo Frank case) and *Moore* v. *Dempsey*, argued that the conviction and the sentence violated the Fourteenth Amendment. He asserted that the case was a "trial in form" and that the verdict and the sentence occurred under hostile conditions. Mass meetings were held, he said, and citizens urged Ellis to hold a special court session. Further, it was nearly impossible to select a fair and impartial jury because of pretrial publicity.

Although Gulotta did not mention Ellis' Klan membership, he declared that the judge was antagonistic toward the "six Italians." Citing charges from earlier appeals, he maintained that Ellis consulted frequently with the prosecutors in closed session and discussed the case with the Calmes family. Also prejudicial to his clients was Rene Calmes's presence both inside the railing area of the courtroom and on the judge's platform while the verdict was read. The rest of the twenty-five allegations in the petition dealt with the Bowden-Purser confrontation, the recusal and the change-of-venue hearings, Giglio's remarks after the second trial, the use of heavily armed guards during the trials, and Parker's alleged statement.

Gulotta questioned Bowden and tried to show that extraordinary precautions were taken because the sheriff feared that the prisoners might be lynched. Amos Ponder then requested that the writ be denied on the grounds of *res adjudicata*, or lack of a federal question. Judge Rufus Foster denied that request and ordered the state to file an answer. Assistant Attorney General T. Semmes Walmsley said that the state's reply was in longhand and asked for time to have the document typed. After a recess, the state submitted the transcripts of the trials, a copy of the Supreme Court decision, and three typewritten pages which detailed in chronological order all of the legal proceedings in *Rini et al.* for the last

14. New Orleans *States*, New Orleans *Item*, and Shreveport *Journal*, May 5, 1924; New Orleans *Times-Picayune*, May 6, 1924; newspaper clipping, in Dallas Calmes Scrapbook.

three years. Walmsley argued that Parker's alleged remark had been added to the petition because that was the only charge not previously ruled on by the United States Supreme Court. He said that he intended to call Governor Parker, who was sitting in a nearby anteroom. But Girault Farrar quickly announced that they withdrew the governor's comment because the defense's source had "welched."

Then Judge Foster asked for final arguments. Henriques and Farrar argued the law; Gulotta asked Foster to consider that Ellis refused without a hearing to recuse himself and that a majority of the forty-three change-of-venue witnesses testified that it was not possible to get a fair trial and an impartial jury in Tangipahoa.

The state, which was aided by Orleans Parish District Attorney Robert H. Marr, Jr., denied all charges in the petition and argued that Sheriff Bowden was justified in assaulting Purser because of the attorney's courtroom statements. District Attorney Allen said in his argument that the fact that no lynching had occurred was evidence of a lack of anti-Italian sentiment in Tangipahoa. Furthermore, only six out of the nine indicted Italians had been convicted.

The arguments concluded and Foster announced that he would render a decision at 2:00 P.M. on Tuesday, May 6. He then retired to his chambers and researched the case unil 1:00 A.M. Later that morning, he received two anonymous letters. One was written by someone who attempted to appear illiterate, and it was similar to the note Ellis had gotten on Monday. The author threatened Foster with death if he denied the writ. The other letter, written in excellent English, warned that Foster would be killed if he granted the writ.

Undaunted, Foster entered a packed courtroom on Tuesday afternoon. Spectators standing along the wall blocked the windows, and the room was stifling and hot. Ordering the U.S. marshal to arrest anyone who disturbed the proceedings, Foster insisted that he wanted no demonstrations or interruptions. As Foster read his decision no one dared speak. He stated that it was not the prerogative of the federal court to interfere with the administration of justice in the state of Louisiana. "I do not believe there is probable cause," said Foster. "I cannot let my heart control my head."

Then in a quiet voice he said, "I've had a very fine point to decide. However, I have decided that the writ be refused and it is so ordered."

After the hearing, Rennyson returned to the parish prison to inform Deamore and the others. Natale, who had not shaved in several days, paced his cell. When the warden told him the news, Deamore shouted, "Fire! Fire! Fire!" He did not break stride.

Lamantia left his bunk and went up to listen to Rennyson. Shrugging his shoulders, he returned to his bunk and lit a cigarette. He said nothing.

Rini asked whether the decision was the last chance to escape the gallows. He stopped sweeping his cell, and Rennyson replied that it probably was. Rini picked up his broom again and returned to his task.

Bocchio, shirtless, lay on his bunk. Fingering the rosary he wore around his neck, Joe turned and looked at Rennyson. "Somebody give me a match," he muttered. "What time is it?" Joe appeared uninterested in the decision, and he paid little attention to his visitors.

Giglio wanted to know what the next legal steps were and whether they could avoid the gallows. But Leona did not look up. He said nothing and remained lying on his bunk.[15]

After filing the appeal papers with the federal district clerk of court's office at 5 : 00 P.M., Gulotta, Farrar, and Henriques decided to speak to Judge Foster personally once more for a stay of execution. Having prepared the necessary papers, the attorneys also brought with them a local Italian restaurateur, who was prepared to sign any bond necessary for the release of the six men. When they arrived at Judge Foster's home at 8 : 00 P.M., he was hosting a dinner party. The judge escorted his visitors into his library. After listening to the attorneys' pleas, Foster refused to grant a stay order or a "writ of probable cause" to appeal to the U.S. Supreme Court.

15. New Orleans *Times-Picayune*, May 4, 6–7, 1924; New Orleans *States*, May 5–6, 1924; New Orleans *Item*, May 3–6, 1924; newspaper clippings, in Dallas Calmes Scrapbook; Washington *Post*, May 7, 1924; Shreveport *Journal*, May 6, 1924; Hearsey, *The Six Who Were Hanged*, 9.

When the meeting concluded, the three attorneys decided to follow Foster's suggestion. Gulotta and Farrar would seek an appeal and a stay order before Justice Oliver Wendell Holmes. Farrar rushed to catch a train to Washington at 9:10 P.M. However, just outside New Orleans, he realized that Gulotta, with the necessary papers, was not aboard. Farrar, disappointed, got off at Bay St. Louis, Mississippi, to await a return train.

On Wednesday, May 7, Gulotta, who was in conference with three unidentified men in his office, refused to see reporters and to answer questions about any future legal maneuvers for *Rini et al.* According to the *Item*, sources close to the defense attorneys stated that the fund could not cover Gulotta's trip to Washington by train and that money for airfare was not likely to be forthcoming. Friends and relatives of the six men also stated that had the attorneys been able to obtain more money, they would have gone by train to Washington early Wednesday morning.[16]

State and local officials continued to prepare for the execution. Adjutant General Toombs, at the governor's instruction, ordered the 108th Cavalry of the Louisiana National Guard to report for field duty at Jackson Barracks in New Orleans. Toombs proudly announced that he had seventeen hundred soldiers who could be in Tangipahoa with war equipment within three to six hours. Officials there banned firearm sales to everyone from May 6 to May 10.

Tangipahoa authorities were disturbed about the cost of *Rini et al.* Just a couple of days before the execution, a local paper carried an editorial highly critical of the parish's share of the cost of the two trials and the appeals, especially since the six men were not residents of Tangipahoa. Sheriff Bowden, believing the cost was about $30,000, stated that police jury estimates of $50,000 to $75,000 were too high.[17]

Meanwhile, Leona stared blankly at the sky through a grated window. Giglio read a novel or wrote letters and postcards. Laman-

16. New Orleans *Item*, New Orleans *Times-Picayune*, and New Orleans *States*, May 7, 1924; Hearsey, *The Six Who Were Hanged*, 9.

17. New Orleans *Item*, May 6, 1924; New Orleans *States*, May 6–7, 1924; newspaper clipping, in Dallas Calmes Scrapbook.

tia, who had been talkative in the last several days, was now silent. After hearing about Foster's decision, he spent most of his time lying on his bunk.

"Any good news for us, boys?" Lamantia asked, his face close to the grating. "You think we have a chance?"

The evasive answers from Rennyson and the reporters brought a deep sigh from Andrea. "Oh we did no killing. How can they hang so many men who are innocent?"

At the end of the tier, Deamore was silent—no shouts of "Fire!" and no more operas and Italian songs.

On Tuesday evening, Rini wanted to speak to Rennyson and the reporters. He lay on his bunk with his fingers wrapped around the bars, and Toots stood on her hind legs with her forepaws affectionately on his side. Rini stared with large inquisitive eyes at his visitors.

"Toots she love me very much," he said with a sad smile. "And me when I go next Friday, I think of Toots and wonder for her, where she go and who will be good to her."

Toots, a Chihuahua with beautiful white and brown spots, had been Rini's constant companion for over two years. According to reporters and prison personnel, Toots cried and whimpered all day Tuesday as if she knew that it was Rini's last evening in New Orleans.

"You see the dog," Joe said. "She knows something going to happen, and already her cryin'. Toots, when I am gone, maybe my father take her and love her, because I loved her . . . and she loved me."

When Rennyson and the reporters gathered around Bocchio's cell, he spoke about his part in the crime. "As God is my judge," Bocchio insisted, "all I had to do with that crime was to drive the car. I've got nobody to blame but myself for getting in this predicament. I did not leave that car once, and I never fired a shot. I'll say that to my last breath." [18]

Later Tuesday night, Sheriff Bowden, District Attorney Allen, Dr. Jesse McClendon, the Tangipahoa coroner, and several deputies went to Rennyson's office to review the detailed plans for

18. New Orleans *States*, May 7, 1924; Hearsey, *The Six Who Were Hanged*, 7.

moving the six prisoners the next morning. Bowden was assured of national guard troops, and he was glad to hear that Superintendent Molony had offered a score or more of traffic officers to clear the streets from the prison to the train station.

Bowden said that he had tested the double gallows that day. There was a sharp hatchet to sever the ropes that released the traps. And his deputies had kept the trap hinges greased. The police jury carpenters built partitions on the gallows so that the two waiting men could not see the actual execution. Deputies roped off the jail to keep the crowds away from the wooden scaffold.

Bowden asked the warden how the six men were. "They are in a rather bad state tonight," Rennyson said. "And naturally so, but I don't think that they are going to give us any trouble."

"I think you will have no trouble with your prisoners, sheriff," a reporter said. "And from my experience, I dare hazard the opinion that they will go boldly. . . . There's one at least I'm sure of and that's Rini."

"What was that, Rini?" Rennyson asked.

"Yes, Rini," the reporter said again.

"They'll have to carry him," the warden said. His reason for that comment was unclear—Rini was one of the strongest of the six.

Another newspaperman then related the gloomy, hideous details of the thirty-six hangings he had witnessed.

"In all the men you have seen hanged," Bowden asked, "was there ever an instance where it was necessary to carry the culprit to the scaffold?"

"No," answered the reporter. "I have seen some weak and faltering victims of the noose, but never a man in the actual state of collapse.

"In my experience as a newspaperman," he continued, "I have seen many criminals strangle horribly, and such a mode of capital punishment has no place in a civilization such as is ours."

"What do you think of the electric chair?" Bowden asked.

"I know nothing of electricity and have never seen the chair in operation," replied the reporter. "But I am told that there are some constitutions which resist the current until their very flesh fries and burns."

"How about the guillotine?" asked a younger reporter.

"It may be quick and certain if the machine is good, but disgustingly bloody and unsightly," answered the veteran newspaperman.

"What mode of capital punishment would you suggest?" Bowden asked.

"The lethal chamber," the reporter stated quickly. "There is a clean, a certain, and a painless way for society to rid itself of its objectionable units. There would be no failure in this. Have a nicely fitted up condemned chamber, with the gas openings concealed from view. Set no certain time for the execution, but have a period of death during the term of a week at the sheriff's discretion. Drug the prisoner's food some night during the period, and when he has fallen asleep turn on the gas. There'd be no struggling torture, no horror attending this, and the lethal chamber would express the humane in legal executions."

Almost everyone in the room agreed with the reporter's suggestion that the gas chamber was the best method of execution. But someone reminded the officials that if the terror was removed, the execution would not be a deterrent.

"Fire! The world is on fire!" Deamore shouted.

When officials and reporters reached Natale, he was pacing his cell and gesticulating wildly. William Warrington tried to speak to him, but Deamore appeared not to recognize him. After Natale settled down in his bunk, Warrington visited Lamantia, Rini, and Giglio, who all greeted him with handshakes.

"Is there no more hope?" Rini asked.

"All hope is gone, it seems," Warrington replied. "But whatever you do, go as brave men."

Warrington tried to visit Leona, but Roy lay on his bunk and mumbled to himself. He refused to respond to his visitor.

At midnight, Rennyson began to make his rounds. Lamantia slept soundly but Deamore was restless. He opened his eyes, mumbled something, and only stared at the warden and his party.

When Rennyson reached Rini's cell, Toots barked loudly because the warden had his Saint Bernard. Joe stirred, but did not awaken.

Bocchio sat on his bunk and appeared much calmer. He smiled when he saw Rennyson and asked about his attorney's trip to Washington, D.C.

"You might say how much we appreciate," Bocchio said to the gathering outside his cell, "what those who have tried to be kind to us have done in our behalf. And we hold no hard feelings, no grudge, for those who have been our enemies. We will pray for all—enemies and friends alike—until we are taken away for good."

"That's right," Giglio added. "Just say that we appreciate and thank those who have tried to show us their sympathy. Five of us are dying innocently, and to those who have believed in us we want to give the thanks of dying men."

During the 2:00 A.M. rounds, Rennyson found everyone asleep except Bocchio, who sat on his bunk. "What time is it?" he asked in a husky monotone. "What time is it?" Bocchio appeared delirious and fearful again.

At 4:00 A.M., the warden saw that all six prisoners were sleeping, and he and his party returned to his office. There was a clap of thunder, and it began to rain lightly as they continued to talk about the impending execution. Had they known what lay ahead, they would have tried to get as much sleep as possible.[19]

19. New Orleans *Times-Picayune*, May 7–8, 1924; New Orleans *Item* and New Orleans *States*, May 7, 1924; newspaper clipping, in Dallas Calmes Scrapbook; Hearsey, *The Six Who Were Hanged*, 9–16.

16

You've Got to Get Ready

"Get up, boys," Rennyson shouted as he rattled the heavy padlocks to awaken the prisoners at 4:15 A.M., Wednesday, May 7, 1924. After leading five of the men into the dayroom, the warden and a deputy returned to the tier to check on Leona, who was still lying on his bunk. "Come on, Roy," said Rennyson. "Let's go. You've got to get ready to go out of here." Leona finally rose and leaned against the bars, his back to Rennyson. He looked upward and beat his chest savagely with a closed fist. When Roy raised his hand above his head, Rennyson finally saw the small knife and rushed toward Leona. Before the warden reached him, Roy stabbed himself again in the right breast and neck.

After subduing Roy, the deputies searched his cell. They found what was commonly known as a Texas Jack—a pocketknife with a three-inch springblade. They did not know where Roy had hidden the weapon, which he had probably used to whittle the wooden bullet.

Charity Hospital doctors arrived almost immediately and examined Roy. Finding that one of the wounds had penetrated the left lung, they insisted that he be hospitalized. Rennyson, however, had to consult Tangipahoa authorities.

In obvious pain, Leona writhed and moaned in a chair. Two deputies had difficulty restraining him. "I die," said Roy. "I die. Let me die." His eyes were closed tightly, and his face was pale.

From across the dayroom, Deamore began to rave, "Fire! Fire!" But he made no attempt to move.

"God knows we are going to our death innocently, and God is the judge of judges," Rini insisted as he rose from the bench. Toots, whimpering loudly, pressed against Rini's shackled ankles.

Shortly thereafter, Dr. McClendon arrived and examined Leona carefully. Finding that the wounds were not fatal, he refused to allow Roy to be hospitalized. While Leona was being treated, officials and newspapermen asked about his hiding place for the knife. Although they persisted, Roy only said, "I had it."

While deputies questioned Roy, Rini explained that he also thought about suicide, but he decided against it. Kissing Toots, Rini talked about the injustices of their case. He gave a forced laugh and withdrew a cigar awkwardly from an upper coat pocket. One of the deputies lit it, and he jammed the cigar in his mouth and said, "But why worry. I'm going to die anyhow. No need of killing myself. Might as well make the best of it."

Rini puffed furiously on the cigar, and his knees shook. "To hell with them," he added. "We only die once. Don't tell them a thing. We never did anything."

"It's all because we are Italians," Giglio insisted. He was dressed immaculately and was composed. "The newspapers have been unfair. If we had been Americans they wouldn't have commented so much until we were sentenced.

"How can anyone say we got a fair trial," Giglio went on. "If we had got a change of venue there would have been a different story. Our attorneys did the best they could for us. It's just because we are Italians that we are being hanged. I've been a better American than many who are not sharing my fate."

Rini then asked to see the prison chef. Joe told him to leave Toots with his brother, William Rini. After giving instructions on the dog's care, Joe looked at his pet and said sadly, "Well, Toots, I guess I'll never see you again!"

Other officials and reporters in the room questioned Bocchio, but he said little. Then he blurted out, "Why should I die? I have done nothing. I have been three years in cells. One disappointment after the other. I have made a man of myself during those three years. I did not know the world when I came to jail. I have studied it since. I have read. I have not read lately. I have only prayed for a way to save us."

In response to a question, Bocchio said, "What would I do if I were freed now? Well, I studied to be a priest. I would be a reformer. I would teach young boys of my experience. I would go to all penitentiaries. I would tell them to be good. I have made a mistake, but should I hang for such a mistake?"

As officials prepared for the departure, the prisoners gave some of their possessions to the deputies as gifts. One of them and Leona gave a deputy letters to mail. Roy's letter was to his wife, who still did not know that he was to be hanged on Friday. He wrote, "I knew I had not very much longer to live as my lungs couldn't last much longer at best. So I told the police that I alone was to blame—that I done the killing. But it did no good. They will hang the others too. I am innocent."

Seeing that it was time to leave, Rini held the dog closely in his lap. As the deputies neared him he raised the yelping animal with difficulty, because of the shackles, and kissed her forehead several times. In tears, Joe handed the dog to a deputy.

The order to leave came, and officials escorted the prisoners into the yard. It was a foggy, chilly morning, and the only sound was the jangle of the shackles. Deamore, Giglio, and Rini entered a patrol wagon, which was protected by a police cordon, at the rear of the prison. The other three prisoners exited through the main gate, which was sealed off by sheriff's deputies. Also surrounding the prison were forty heavily armed national guard soldiers.

At 6:00 A.M., Rennyson telephoned Captain George Royan, special agent for the Illinois Central Railroad, that they were ready to leave the prison. Bowden and Rennyson then joined Molony, who would be in the lead car in the procession, behind the officers on motorcycles. With several riot guns and tear-gas bombs in his car, the superintendent was prepared for an attack. The two patrol wagons, with uniformed officers on the back and front, followed closely. A high-powered police car, loaded with heavy weaponry, was next; and an officer carrying a knapsack full of grenades rode on the running board. There were also a dozen or more cars with deputies, policemen, reporters, and photographers.

It had rained earlier, and the streets were still slippery. Molony ordered everyone to drive carefully. As they approached the train station, the police sirens wailed. Railroad whistles shrieked. Seeing a crowd of nearly one thousand, Molony ordered the entourage to the rear entrance, which was guarded by another forty soldiers. But before the prisoners left the patrol wagons, the crowd rushed into the area. Molony immediately established a line of officers around the railroad cars, and the troopers positioned their automatic weapons. The spectators, however, were orderly and only wanted to see the "six Italians" for the last time. In order to maintain security, Molony decided that anyone allowed near the train would have to have a special pass.

Illinois Central workmen attached three cars to the train for the soldiers' weaponry and equipment, the press, the police, and the prisoners. Each car had soldiers with rapid-fire weapons. In addition, Royan arranged for four armed railroad detectives to precede the train, examining the railbed for explosives and watching for suspicious characters. Royan said that all this rivaled the security measures for President Woodrow Wilson's trip through the South.[1]

The train departed from Union Station on schedule, and three hundred yards ahead was the railroad motor car with Royan and the railroad detectives. As the train moved out of the New Orleans area some of the prisoners spoke in a friendly manner with reporters and the soldiers assigned to guard them. Lamantia, however, sat silently, refusing to speak to anyone. Sitting behind Andrea, Bocchio, who was pale but calm, told the soldier next to him his story of the last three years.

"As God is my judge," Joe said, raising his right hand, "all I had to do with the crime was to drive the car. I've got nobody to blame but myself for getting in this predicament. I did not leave that car once, and I never fired a shot. I'll say that to my last breath."

For the first time in nearly two weeks, Deamore spoke in a rational manner. "I am in this trouble because I've got no brains," he said bitterly. "Another man planned this robbery, and I just followed along. I didn't know what would happen. I didn't fire no shots. My poor baby, the baby what I never spanked. I'll never see that baby any more. Oh, my God!

"Fifteen years I live in New Orleans," he continued. "I don't believe in stealing. I don't believe in killing. I work hard all of the

1. New Orleans *Item*, May 7, 9, 1924; New Orleans *Times-Picayune*, May 7–8, 10, 1924; New Orleans *States*, May 6–7, 9, 1924; Ponchatoula *Enterprise*, May 9, 1924; Shreveport *Journal*, May 7, 10, 1924; Louisville *Courier-Journal* and Atlanta *Constitution*, May 8, 1924; New York *Herald Tribune*, New York *Times*, and Washington *Post*, May 10, 1924; St. Louis *Dispatch*, May 4, 7, 1924; newspaper clippings, in Dallas Calmes Scrapbook; Hearsey, *The Six Who Were Hanged*, 8, 16–17; Crowell, "Stern Justice Took Six Lives for One," 1–E.

time and look!" Deamore raised his manacled hands for all to see.

After repeated proddings from a *States* reporter, Lamantia finally talked. "I wrote my wife last night that I was gone," he said. "I didn't tell her when, not the exact date, but I told her I was gone. I'll never see her or my three baby girls in New York again. There's no justice, I tell you. I'll say up to the last minute they spring the trap on the scaffold that I never fired a shot. I hope my three babies learn their father's troubles and obey the law all their lives."

Giglio sat quietly, looking at his manacles and shackles. Then he said to a *States* reporter, "Of course I'll go to the gallows swearing I never fired a shot. I was sore because there ain't no justice. I'm still sore. We been railroaded. But up to the minute they hang me, I'll be telling the world I ain't guilty of no murder. Before I die I want the world to know that I forgive those who helped convict me, and I want to thank all those who assisted me."

Rini had little to say during the sixty-eight-mile trip to Amite, but a *States* reporter finally encouraged him to comment. "Gee," said Joe, "I feel lost without that dog Toots. Well, I've made myself right with God anyway. I hope I'll get a square deal in the Hereafter. I ain't had one here. I'll die swearing I never fired a shot."

The train slowed for the bridge over Pass Manchac, which connects Lake Maurepas and Lake Pontchartrain. Two railroad agents signaled Royan and the detectives that it was safe to cross the trestle, which had been guarded since Tuesday night.

Then the train entered Tangipahoa Parish. In Ponchatoula a hard rain kept most curiosity seekers away, though at least 150 spectators were at the station to catch a final glimpse of the condemned men. In Hammond a solid mass of onlookers gathered around the depot—the Hammond *Vindicator* had announced when the train would arrive. The townspeople were tense because of rumors about suspicious-looking Italians and the disappearance of a newly arrived Sicilian grocer. Hammond's chief of police and several sheriff's deputies were on duty, but the crowd was orderly.

The train stopped in Independence, directly in front of the Farmers and Merchants Bank. The prisoners had a clear view, but they generally ignored the 100 spectators gathered around their coach. Several passengers got out to look at the bank. In front of the Calmeses' restaurant, a man sat reading a newspaper. Mrs. Calmes saw the train and became so upset that she went to bed.[2]

The train arrived in Amite at 9:00 A.M. The town was relatively quiet, and the sky had started to clear after the early morning rain. A crowd of between 200 and 300 stood on the platform. Among them was Roy Calmes. Although the gathering was orderly, he recalled that three years ago, a "spirit of vengeance" had prevailed in Tangipahoa. As soon as Bowden reached the platform, he called Calmes aside to tell him that Bocchio wanted to speak to Mrs. Calmes, Judge Ellis, and District Attorney Allen. Roy said he would relay the message to his aunt.

The prisoners entered the waiting vehicles. Thirty to forty national guardsmen with fixed bayonets assembled in single file on each side. Bowden started his car and led the procession slowly to the jail. The troops intently watched the crowd, which was described as sympathetic toward the "six Italians." Residents of Amite stepped out onto their porches or pulled back their curtains to see the condemned men.

When they reached the prison, the troops broke their single lines and cordoned off the wide pavement that led from the prison door across the courthouse square to the street. As the prisoners passed the steps that led to the gallows, they appeared to shudder. By 9:25 A.M., the transfer was over. The crowd dispersed, and the sun grew brighter.[3]

Guardsmen, dubbed the "Amite Expeditionary Forces," pitched a half dozen tents at the southwest corner of the jail and set up a kitchen in the courthouse basement. Having been sent for a three-day field assignment, they were fully equipped. Several soldiers patrolled the prison area, and others established a checkpoint at the courthouse entrance. The townspeople walked up to the rope barriers and stared silently at the prison walls.

Although Amite was quiet, the telephone lines were congested

2. New Orleans *States*, May 7, 9, 1924; New Orleans *Item*, May 7, 1924; New Orleans *Times-Picayune*, May 7–8, 1924; newspaper clipping, in Dallas Calmes Scrapbook; Hearsey, *The Six Who Were Hanged*, 17.

3. New Orleans *Item* and New Orleans *States*, May 7, 9, 1924; New Orleans *Times-Picayune*, May 8, 1924; Chicago *Daily News*, May 7–8, 1924; Hearsey, *The Six Who Were Hanged*, 17; Crowell, "Stern Justice Took Six Lives for One," 1–E.

with long-distance calls. Hotels and boardinghouses were filled with crowds from surrounding parishes and from New Orleans. But women and children, fearing possible violence, continued to leave Amite for the countryside. There were reports of "mysterious strangers" in powerful cars, and people were buying an unusual quantity of shotgun shells in Hammond—which prompted lawmen to stop all unknown persons and cars.[4]

After being placed in different sections of the jail, several of the prisoners requested liquor. Dr. McClendon brought a flask of whiskey for all six, but Deamore refused to drink anything. "I never touched a drink of whiskey," he said, "and I ain't startin' now."

Bocchio again told Bowden that he wished to speak to Judge Ellis, District Attorney Allen, Mrs. Calmes, and Rene Calmes. Bowden said that he had already delivered the message, and the other prisoners expressed a desire to speak to Mrs. Calmes. But Leona refused to see her, and he alone did not put on a clean shirt and collar in anticipation of the visit.

"Well, I guess it is all over," Giglio said to reporters. "We can trust in God! You know God is good, even though it is hard to see that at times. We must trust in His goodness."

Leona, who was wrapped in bandages, said to a group of reporters that he was "feeling pretty bum." Bocchio and Lamantia refused to speak to the newspapermen, and Deamore did not respond to their questions.

A short while later, Bowden's messenger returned to the jail to report that Mrs. Calmes was distraught. Unable to leave her home, she said that her brother-in-law, George Harpole, would meet the prisoners. Later that afternoon, Ellis, Allen, Bowden, and Harpole visited only Bocchio, who wanted no reporters present. For one hour in a dimly lit cell, Bocchio repeated his earlier confession and proclaimed his innocence of conspiracy to commit murder. Stressing that he only drove the car, Bocchio insisted that he never left the automobile on the night of the murder. He begged them all to ask Parker to grant him a reprieve and recommend commut-

4. New Orleans *Times-Picayune*, May 7–8, 1924; New Orleans *Item*, May 7, 9–10, 1924; New Orleans *States*, May 6–7, 1924; newspaper clipping, in Dallas Calmes Scrapbook; Harrell, "The Ku Klux Klan in Louisiana," 122; Schott, "John M. Parker," 437.

ing his sentence. Allen and Harpole said that they would consider it, but Bowden and Ellis made no promises.

After that meeting, Harpole, a highly respected strawberry broker in Hammond, said that he would appeal to Parker to grant a reprieve. "Bocchio looks life straight in the eye and never falters," he said. "He told us that he wanted to tell his story several times, but Leona wouldn't let him. He was the only one of the six without money or friends, he said, and Leona warned him to 'stick,' saying they would all go free if they stuck together."

Later that Wednesday, Harpole and other Tangipahoa residents began a parishwide movement to save Bocchio's life. Harpole also asked Dallas Calmes, Jr., to see Parker in Baton Rouge and to determine what effect a strong clemency petition for Bocchio would have on the governor. Saying that Mrs. Calmes supported the effort, Harpole urged Dallas to assist him.[5]

On Wednesday afternoon, Farrar announced that he and his colleagues planned to go to Washington, D.C., by airplane. Although Gulotta and Henriques refused to comment on any further action on behalf of the prisoners, Farrar said that he wanted to file an appeal with Justice Edward T. Sanford, who was assigned to the circuit containing Louisiana. Should the United States Supreme Court deny the appeal, Farrar said, he would ask Secretary of State Hughes and possibly President Calvin Coolidge to intervene. Although Gulotta and Henriques denied any further legal pleas, the *Item* reported that the attorneys were negotiating with Gates Flying Circus to fly one of them to Washington, D.C., with an appeal to stay the execution.[6]

Two nuns arrived from the Sacred Heart Mission in New Orleans to comfort the six men on Wednesday afternoon. Later that evening, Mrs. Calmes was feeling better, and she notified Harpole that she wanted to meet with Bocchio the following morning. Believing that Joe knew more about the murder than he admitted, she wanted to clarify certain details. And she would speak to any prisoner who wished to see her. However, she strongly doubted

5. New Orleans *States*, May 7–8, 1924; New Orleans *Item*, May 7, 1924; New Orleans *Times-Picayune*, May 8, 1924; Hearsey, *The Six Who Were Hanged*, 18.
6. New Orleans *Item* and New Orleans *States*, May 7, 1924; New Orleans *Times-Picayune*, May 8, 1924; newspaper clipping, in Dallas Calmes Scrapbook.

that any clemency movement for Bocchio would influence Parker or members of the Board of Pardons.

The prisoners were pleased to hear that Mrs. Calmes would visit them Thursday morning. They retired for the night with the hope that she would intervene on their behalf and save them from the gallows.[7]

7. New Orleans *Times-Picayune*, May 8, 1924; New Orleans *Item*, May 7, 8, 1924.

17

We Are Going to Hang

After breakfast on Thursday morning, May 8, the rhythmic sounds of picks and shovels were heard. Adjutant General Toombs had ordered guardsmen to dig a trench around the courthouse. Soldiers would man the fire hoses to fill the moat. There would be only one bridge constructed.

Fifty soldiers were on duty at all times, and Toombs ordered that sentries be relieved each hour. Fred Beckler and Paul Surcouf, New Orleans police officers, walked the grounds casually with their knapsacks over their shoulders. They appeared to be innocent observers, but the veteran policemen carried tear-gas bombs and hand grenades. Six soldiers from Battery A of the 141st Field Artillery (Washington Artillery) set up three machine-gun emplacements at strategic points on the courthouse grounds.

On Thursday morning, all the prisoners were talkative as they awaited Mrs. Calmes's arrival. Leona described his attempted suicide, but he became angered over the persistent questions about the knife.

"What good would it do to tell," Roy said. "I had it, that's all."

"Holding the knife in my left hand," Leona said, "I tried to bury the blade in my brain. I stabbed at my left temple twice, but could not force the blade through my skull. Then I tried to stab my throat. The blade struck my collar bone. Then I changed the dirk to my right hand, and tried to strike it in my heart. I didn't have enough strength left to force it in deep enough.

"I'm all right now, only when I move," he said. "When I move or when I cough I can feel my lung go *ph-phtt, phtt* like a sponge when you squeeze it. But it's all over now—only I was hoping I'd be dead already."

Later Thursday morning, Mrs. Calmes spoke to an *Item* reporter about Bocchio's part in her husband's murder. "The question that is still puzzling me," she said, "is whether any other persons than those mentioned had anything to do with the planned robbery. Someone put the lights out in the bank on the night of May 7. That was three years ago last night. Dallas saw them out before he went to bed.

"I'm going to ask Bocchio who else was in the plot," she continued. "I'm going to find out, if I can, the truth about this crime. I'm not sure we know all of it. Bocchio, of the six, seemed to be the only man who had any sympathy for me in my grief. During the trial the others stared at me, brazenly, sneeringly, but when Bocchio's eyes met mine, he dropped them. He seemed to grieve at my sorrow, my loss.

"The others called Bocchio the weakling, and the traitor," Mrs. Calmes insisted, "because he wanted to tell the authorities the truth. They told him to keep quiet and 'we'll pay a lawyer for you,' at least, that is what I'm told. So Bocchio, without funds, kept quiet until now. A day away from the gallows and death, he pleads for mercy.

"Mr. Harpole favors clemency for Bocchio," she resumed. "He wants the man saved. I'm trying to hold steady. I don't want to break down. If this man deserves mercy and clemency, I want him to get it."[1]

The eleventh-hour clemency movement for Bocchio included, besides Mrs. Calmes and George Harpole, Judge Columbus Reid, former district judge W. S. Rownd, and a large delegation of prominent women from Hammond and Amite. Although District Attorney Allen was not part of the movement, he stated that Bocchio was the least culpable of the six. Even Dallas Calmes's brother, Rene, agreed.

Early Thursday morning, a committee of citizens—Harpole and Judge Reid among them—visited Judge Ellis at the courthouse to solicit his support. After listening to their pleas, Ellis refused to join the movement. "I have had three years to think this over and I have made up my mind," he said.

Judge Ellis later talked to the press. "If I had to pick out any one

1. New Orleans *Item*, May 8, 1924; New Orleans *Times-Picayune*, May 9, 1924.

of the six to let live," he said, "I'd say poor Deamore. He seems to be the worst scared. . . . He is so scared now, he would be straight and honest all the rest of his life.

"But it is 'hands off' for me. I'll stick with Governor Parker in that," Ellis said.

"We must remember that this was organized crime," he said. Ellis was probably one of the first public officials to use *organized crime* in reference to Italian criminals. "Now organized crime is far more dangerous to the country, and it is a far more serious offense than individual crime. These men joined together and plotted a robbery and its consequences. Under the law we can't separate the band and declare some less guilty than others. The law must take its course and particular[ly] in such cases as this of organized crime."[2]

After Ellis' refusal, the committee decided to go to Baton Rouge to see the governor. Parker's office was now deluged with letters and telegrams asking for clemency, especially for Bocchio. "In the name of God and humanity save Bocchio's life and America's good name," wrote Emma Lambert. Two of Dallas Calmes's relatives from Ponchatoula and Kenner pleaded with the governor to spare Bocchio's life. Frank M. Edwards, an Amite resident, requested that Parker commute the sentence of the youngest prisoner. But George Campbell informed Parker that he believed that the parish residents were equally divided on Bocchio's fate.

Parker's response on numerous occasions was that he favored capital punishment because "a life sentence in Louisiana . . . is reduced by good conduct to ten years and six months." Furthermore, the governor still believed that the Mafia was involved in *Rini et al.*, and he insisted on hanging the six defendants because he was determined that "the Camorra, Malavita [*sic*] or Black Hand shall never control this country."[3]

2. New Orleans *Item*, May 8, 1924; New Orleans *Times-Picayune* and Atlanta *Constitution*, May 9, 1924.

3. New Orleans *States*, May 5, 8, 1924; New Orleans *Item*, April 7, 1922, May 3, 1924; to John M. Parker: Emma Lambert, May 7, Joseph Kopfler, May 8, William P. Kopfler, May 8, Frank M. Edwards and Dr. F. H. Murphy, May 8, Campbell, May 8, Phillip Manno *et al.*, May 8, Peter F. Morettini, May 8, J. Emil Nelson, May 9, 1924, John M. Parker to Dr. C. J. Owen, April 29, 1924, and several similar letters, all in Parker Papers.

Earlier that Thursday morning, Dallas Calmes, Jr., who now lived in Baton Rouge, phoned Parker to relay his family's request that the governor stay the execution of Bocchio. But Parker refused to intervene. Calmes told his uncle, but Harpole and the delegation traveled to Baton Rouge anyway and urged the governor to commute Bocchio's sentence. Parker again insisted that justice would be best served by hanging all six men.

Harpole returned to Tangipahoa Parish and went to tell Bocchio that the clemency movement on his behalf had failed. But the news preceded him. Harpole and Rene Calmes came to visit Bocchio. "Joe, I'm sorry to tell you there is no hope," Harpole said. "And now that the last chance is gone, I wish you would tell me all that you know, the whole truth, every bit of it. Now don't keep back anything."

"You are about to die," Calmes added. "So why don't you tell us the whole story of the attempted robbery."

"As God is my judge," Joe replied, "what I've told you is the truth."

Harpole said that he believed him. "And right then I knew that Joe Bocchio was telling the truth," Harpole said later. "I broke down and cried. I just couldn't help it."[4]

Shortly after Parker's denial of a reprieve for Bocchio, the defense attorneys announced that Justice Sanford had denied their petition to stay the execution. Refusing to reveal how they reached Washington, D.C., Henriques said that they had exhausted every legal remedy on behalf of their clients. Farrar, however, was still determined to stop the execution. On Thursday morning, he sent a telegram to the governor-elect, Henry L. Fuqua, to urge him to intervene or cancel the inaugural festivities planned for May 19. Farrar insisted that ending one gubernatorial term with a mass hanging and then beginning another with a fancy inaugural ball did not appear proper.[5]

After hearing of Parker's refusals, Mrs. Calmes's relatives urged

4. New Orleans *Item*, New Orleans *States*, and Shreveport *Journal*, May 8, 1924; New Orleans *Times-Picayune*, May 9, 1924; San Francisco *Chronicle*, May 9, 1924; newspaper clippings, in Dallas Calmes Scrapbook; Hearsey, *The Six Who Were Hanged*, 18.

5. New Orleans *States*, May 8, 1924; newspaper clipping, in Dallas Calmes Scrapbook; Hearsey, *The Six Who Were Hanged*, 21.

her to cancel her visit to the prison. It would be a harrowing experience, they said, and she was neither physically nor emotionally strong enough. Although she desperately wanted Bocchio to clarify the details of her husband's murder, she agreed not to go.[6]

When the prisoners heard that Mrs. Calmes had canceled her visit, they spent the rest of the day praying or watching the crowds around the courthouse. Cars from surrounding parishes and counties in Mississippi drove slowly around the square. People parked where they could and walked to the jail. They watched as special telegraph wires for the news services were strung to the cupola. The New Orleans *Item* also hired Gates Flying Circus to take a photographer to Amite on Friday. Within an hour of the hanging, the plane would be in New Orleans with pictures for the afternoon edition.

Elsewhere in Amite, the residents tried to ignore the activities around the courthouse. There were no street-corner gatherings, and no one would discuss the hanging. The residents were aware of the threats to blow up the town, and the reports of women and children leaving for the countryside continued. In addition, the Tangipahoa Parish School Board ordered all schools closed on Friday.

According to the *Times-Picayune*, the Italian communities were quiet on the eve of the execution. Traveling around the parish, a *Times-Picayune* reporter found only a few Italians willing to discuss the execution with him. "They are bad men," said one. "They violated the law, and the law must be observed. They came to steal our money out of the bank in which we deposited it for safekeeping, and when they were prevented from getting it, they killed a good man. We feel sorry for any men who have to die, but they brought it upon themselves."

"Do you think these men are to be hung just because they are Italians?" asked the reporter.

"No." The farmer was emphatic. "I did not understand how it could be right for six men to die for the killing of one, but now I understand that everybody in a conspiracy is equally guilty."

6. New Orleans *States*, May 8, 1924; newspaper clipping, in Dallas Calmes Scrapbook; Hearsey, *The Six Who Were Hanged*, 21; New Orleans *Item*, May 8, 1924.

Another parish resident was willing to speak. "If we talk much and it is published, then the bad fellows kill us," said one Sicilian.

"What bad fellows? The Black Hand?"

The man was startled. He glanced back sharply and gave a quick nod of his head.

"Are they in Tangipahoa Parish?" asked the reporter.

"No, no, way off."

"Have they ever bothered you?"

"No," he said, smiling in such a way that the reporter knew he would say no more.[7]

While reporters combed the towns and countryside for interviews, Mrs. Calmes went to Amite on Thursday afternoon to talk to Sheriff Bowden about the execution. As she stood in the courthouse corridor, Mrs. Deamore and her two children arrived to obtain permission to visit Natale. Although Mrs. Calmes's back was toward the door, Mrs. Deamore still recognized her.

When the children saw Mrs. Calmes start to leave the courthouse, they ran toward her, crying and begging her to help save their father from the gallows. Mrs. Calmes, visibly shaken, said that she could do nothing.

Mrs. Deamore approached rapidly. "For God's sake have mercy on me and my children," she said, "and if you can, save my husband. Forgive him."

"I do forgive your husband," replied Mrs. Calmes, "but remember I am going out to my husband's grave at once. You know what I went through and now you must face the same. I forgive your husband, but you must suffer as I have.

"I am powerless," she said. "I am not the judge. I cannot interfere with the operation of the law." Mrs. Calmes turned away, obviously upset, and called for her daughter. The two women left to go to the cemetery, which was two blocks away.[8]

Later that afternoon, Rini's father and brother visited the jail. Joe had often said that he would go to the gallows bravely. But when Sal clutched him through the bars and kissed him, Joe wept.

7. New Orleans *Times-Picayune* and New Orleans *States*, May 9, 1924; New Orleans *Item*, May 8, 1924; newspaper clipping, in Dallas Calmes Scrapbook.

8. New Orleans *Times-Picayune*, May 8–9, 1924; New Orleans *States* and Shreveport *Journal*, May 9, 1924.

After speaking to his father in Italian for a short while, Joe regained his composure. But when the visit ended, Sal was so distraught that William had to lead him away. Joe had thought he would talk to the reporters, but the visit so overwhelmed him that he could no longer speak.

For the first time in three years, Joe Giglio's relatives visited him. During their short stay, he controlled his emotions and gave his nephew a message for his wife and children in Brooklyn. Elated by the visit, Joe later said that he was not bitter. "I do not feel that I will die tomorrow," Giglio said. "I am not guilty of murder, and I feel something will save me."

Lamantia, who had no visitors that afternoon, said that he was ready to die at noon on Friday because he prayed for God's forgiveness. "I am sorry for my wife and children," he said. "For myself I am ready."

It was near the close of the day and the men heard the soldiers outside. As the bugler sounded taps, Giglio said, "I remember that in the army. They play that music over dead people, and it's just as well for them to play it for me, because I was in the army."

Smelling the aroma of the troops' supper, Rini and Giglio gripped the bars of their cell and continued to talk to the reporters and the deputies. Both men insisted that they would not die on the gallows the next day. They felt confident that someone would save them.

A visit by the Deamore family after supper interrupted the peaceful spring night. When Natale saw them, he shouted warm greetings in Italian. Through the bars of his cell, he held his children and his wife desperately. The Deamores' farewell lasted for fifteen minutes. Profound weeping and the children's pitiful screams so disturbed the guards that they left the cell area. Walking slowly down the stairs, several soldiers and deputies had tears in their eyes.[9]

After the Deamore family left at 7:00 P.M., the deputies locked

9. New Orleans *Times-Picayune*, May 8–9, 1924; New Orleans *States* and Shreveport *Journal*, May 9, 1924; Hearsey, *The Six Who Were Hanged*, 1–2, 18–19; New Orleans *Item*, May 9–10, 1924; Crowell, "Stern Justice Took Six Lives for One," 1–E. It should be noted that Rini and Giglio were in the same cell, and Hearsey credits Rini with this statement. However, Rini had served in the navy and Giglio was an army veteran.

the outer doors for the night. Bowden ordered his officers and the New Orleans policemen to search the cells thoroughly for contraband. When the cells were cleared, a deputy walked down the narrow corridor. "Boys," he said, "Mrs. Calmes asked me to come over here to say that she doesn't want you to die believing there is any bitterness in her heart against you. She wants me to say that for what you did three years ago, she has forgiven you and hopes you will find the forgiveness of God."

Leona remained silent and only nodded in acknowledgment of the message. He still appeared to be in intense pain from his wounds.

Although Deamore heard the message, he showed no signs of understanding it. With tears on his sunken, unshaven cheeks, he clung to the window bars, trying frantically to get a final glimpse of his family.

"See my baby, see my baby, my beautiful little baby," he sobbed. "Oh my pretty, pretty baby. Never I whip my baby. All the time I do what I can for my baby. Never whip and never scold. And now my baby never going to see her papa no more. And her papa never going to see his beautiful baby no more. Oh God! Oh God! Be good to my beautiful baby."

Natale finally dropped his arms and turned to face several men standing at the cell door.

"Oh, boys, boys," Deamore said, his arms wide in appeal. "See what's become of me because of another man. Tell my little Santo, my little boy, he shouldn't never listen to nobody but his mother, only his mother. And if he do that he never get in trouble like his poor papa. Never, never."

Several reporters and deputies went down the corridor to Giglio's cell. "Thank the poor lady for us," he said slowly. "Never in all these years, when I felt as I was bound to feel, that we were not being dealt with fairly, have I ever felt the least bitterness against her.

"I had not the heart to blame her for anything she might have done," Giglio said, deeply affected by the message, "for she lost her man and his love. That is terrible. I know how my wife and children are going to feel. Thank Mrs. Calmes for the message and tell her it will be easier for me to die now. Those words and Roy Leona's confession have made it easier for me. . . . Even though my children will have to say, 'Our papa was hanged,' still they will know I shot nobody. And I feel peaceful now."

"Yes, that's true," Rini added. "I feel better after wiping the bitterness out of my heart. Mrs. Calmes could not have been blamed for being bitter, and it will be a comfort to take with me the thought that she forgave us.

"She lost her man—her husband," he said. "But, oh, it is awful to think that we are dying for a crime we did not commit—the crime of murder. Boys, boys, I hope that this will be the last hanging ever, ever held in this country. I hope never another gallows will be built in the United States.

"It is—it is—it is," Rini said, "a thing that ought not to be."

Lamantia nodded gently that he understood the message, and Bocchio muttered a few words of gratitude.

Having spent nearly night and day with the six prisoners for the last month, the New Orleans reporters found themselves in an awkward position. After the final interviews, no one knew how to say good-bye. Finally, one newspaperman said, "God bless you, boys," and they all rushed out.

As the reporters departed Rini shouted, "For God sake you gentlemen there from the newspapers tell the world for us how terrible is capital punishment. I hope that God will grant this prayer, that we six will be the last men to die on the gallows. Often I have heard of innocent men dying by the rope. But I said no; it cannot be. Now I know it can be, because I, an innocent man, must die on the gallows tomorrow."[10]

Later that Thursday evening, Rennyson took the executioner to an Amite hotel. Known only as Joe the Hangman, he had stiff sandy hair, a short gray moustache stained with tobacco juice, and bushy eyebrows. His payment, according to the newspapers, was three hundred dollars. Although the hangman had executed at least a dozen men, a veteran police reporter stated that some of them had strangled to death. The executioner also had a reputation for consuming large amounts of whiskey before each hanging.[11]

After a Catholic priest administered Communion that eve-

10. New Orleans *Item*, May 9, 1924; Hearsey, *The Six Who Were Hanged*, 18–20.

11. Hearsey, *The Six Who Were Hanged*, 18–20; New Orleans *Item* and New Orleans *States*, May 9, 1924.

ning, the men asked that no one else be allowed near their cells. They planned to spend the rest of the night in prayer and sleep. But Deamore, who rarely initiated a conversation with newspapermen, later called for a reporter from the *States.*

"Did you see my wife and two children?" he asked. "Did you see my baby?

"She say papa come with me," he said. "Please come with me. And I can't go." Natale, overwhelmed with grief, sagged against the cell door. Seeing that Deamore was distraught, a national guardsman ordered the reporter to leave.

Around 11:30, Bocchio asked to speak to the newspapermen. Still hoping for a last-minute reprieve, he wept bitterly about the order of the hanging. The arrangement was alphabetical, and he would be first.

"If my life had been spared I know I would have become a useful man," Bocchio said after a pause. "I believe I have improved myself to the extent of taking a course that would have eventually made me a big man. But I have dispelled such thoughts from my mind now that I know I am going to die. In the parish prison I never overlooked an opportunity to preach to the young criminals the doctrine of clean living. . . . Now that I am about to die I want to hold up to the young men who are tempted to do wrong to take warning from my experience."

Bocchio was silent for a moment, but then he produced a letter he was writing to a reporter friend. As he read the letter the reporters were again impressed by his excellent English and good vocabulary.

"If my eyes have wept," Joe read, "I say that they have not wept for me, but for my mother and those close to me. As for myself, I'm free from any inquietude, and I find a peaceful rest in this clause: 'The sovereign will of God, ever just, ever adorable, be in all things, be praised and exalted in all eternity.'"

"Please say for me," Lamantia interjected, "that I want to thank the friends who helped me. I don't think, however, that I am going to die, but whether I live or die I forgive all my enemies. I want to thank the people of Tangipahoa who strived to save at least four of us from the gallows."

Since the reporters were in the cell area, Giglio and Rini asked to speak to them again. Giglio said that he expected Amite residents to be jubilant and he was surprised to hear that so many townspeople regretted that all six had to hang.

"Capital punishment is terrible and should be abolished," Rini added. "It has no place in a civilized country. And I hope that there will never be any more hangings or executions. Innocent men go to death—the laws kill them."

Giglio, standing on the other side of the cell, nodded his approval.

"Put it down on the paper and put it in the newspaper," Rini said. "Tell everybody why there should be no more capital punishment."

Giglio nodded again. "That's right," he said, looking straight at the *States* and the *Item* reporters.

"We—are," Giglio said, "we are—we help do away with hangings with our lives."

The *States* reporter returned to Bocchio's cell to tell him good-bye. As the newspaperman walked down the corridor, Leona shouted unintelligibly.

"You have no kick coming," Rini snapped. "They've got you right, but we are going to hang for a crime that you alone committed.

"Well, old boy," he said to Leona, "I hope I'll see you in Heaven, but I'm not so sure of getting there."

Joe thought for a moment and said jokingly, "Say, maybe if I throw my coat over the golden gate I can sneak in afterward."

After reporters left, Bocchio and Lamantia were depressed. Only Deamore did not drink the whiskey brought by the guards. As midnight approached they asked for more.

Beckler, the New Orleans policeman, talked to Deamore for several minutes. In the next cell, Leona listened quietly.

"Come here," Leona said. "That night—the night—you know the night I shot because my life was in danger," he said, again accepting responsibility for the murder. "I think I get killed if I do not shoot. So I shoot, and Mr. Calmes, he died.

"But in my heart was no murder," Leona said sadly. "No, no, only I shot because I think I get killed.

"I just want to tell you that, Mr. Beckler, just-a that," he said, stretching his hands through the steel grating. Beckler held them tightly for a moment. Then he walked down to Lamantia's cell to make a final search.

After midnight, several of the prisoners gave souvenirs to the guards and then asked for something to eat. No restaurant in town was open, so Surcouf and a national guard captain went to the camp kitchen to prepare sandwiches.[12]

After eating, Bocchio was still distraught over the fact that he and Deamore would be hanged first. "A reprieve might come after I was dead," he repeated in a stupor. Lamantia tried to cheer him up, but Bocchio again slipped into a deep depression.

Deamore slept for a while; every now and then, he burst out crying. Leona, who was alone, continually paced in his cell. Listening to Bocchio complain about the order of the executions, Lamantia also became depressed. Rini and Giglio smoked, talked, and took occasional naps.

At 1:00 A.M. Friday, May 9, the prisoners asked that the prison kitchen prepare chicken gumbo for their last meal. Surcouf said he would make the arrangements in the morning, and he ordered the guards not to bother the prisoners for the rest of the night.

"Well, Roy," Rini shouted to Leona, who was still pacing, "it's a tough break. We're dying because we stuck to you, but it's all right. I'm glad we stuck with you, and we'll stick with you to the end."[13]

The state of Louisiana made final preparations to hang six men for the murder of one man. And in Kentucky, for the first time in the state's history, three murderers convicted separately were to be electrocuted. These were not the only states making decisions about executions, and the condemned men often belonged to ethnic minorities. In February, for example, the warden of the state prison in Huntsville, Texas, had resigned rather than be the first to use electricity to execute five black men. In Carson City, Nevada, four prison guards resigned in protest over the first use of the gas chamber. In an editorial the New York *Times* condemned hydrocyanic acid gas as the most hideous of all known poisons.

12. New Orleans *Times-Picayune*, May 9, 1924; New Orleans *States*, May 8–9, 1924; New Orleans *Item*, May 9, 11, 1924; Chicago *Daily News*, May 9, 1924.
13. New Orleans *States* and New Orleans *Item*, May 9, 1924; Hearsey, *The Six Who Were Hanged*, 19.

Furthermore, the *Times* was critical of Nevada's using the gas chamber to execute an Oriental when a white man, condemned to die in the same manner, had his sentence commuted at the last moment.[14]

Probably unaware of these executions, Rini and his comrades hoped that they would not go to the gallows, but they must certainly have realized that all legal means to escape the execution were now exhausted. Fortifying themselves with prayer and whiskey, they spent a restless night.

14. New Orleans *States*, New Orleans *Item*, Shreveport *Journal*, and Louisville *Courier-Journal*, May 9, 1924; Washington *Post* and New York *Herald Tribune*, May 10, 1924; New York *Times*, February 8–9, May 10, 1924.

18

Eleven Lynched and Six Hanged

On Friday morning, May 9, the sun rose at 6:00 A.M., and the grass and the courthouse square were suffused with light. As the Washington Artillery broke formation, Troop G of the 108th Cavalry arrived in ten automobiles to patrol the courthouse square. With the additional troops, there were now ninety national guardsmen. Several soldiers used fire hoses to fill the moat, and the first group of spectators gathered at the street corner. Other guardsmen directed the traffic that began at 6:30 A.M.[1]

Shortly after sunrise, Leona asked to speak to a national guard captain. "We don't want to see any newspapermen anymore," Roy said. "Don't bring 'em in. Just have us let alone. We've got nothing to say and don't want to talk to anybody. Just let us alone, will you?"

As Father Casimir Munichia conducted a special mass for the six prisoners at St. Helena Church in Amite at 7:00 A.M., Fred Beckler and Paul Surcouf escorted Rennyson to the prison. Dr. McClendon told the deputies and other officials that Sheriff Bowden, who had recently had a heart attack, wanted Rennyson in charge of the execution.[2]

At 7:30 A.M., Joe the Hangman arrived, and Rennyson hurried him into the prison kitchen, the only private room in the downstairs area of the jail. The executioner seemed uneasy, so Rennyson picked up a bag, which probably contained the black hoods, and directed him to Bowden's office, where he would be safe. Rennyson took special precautions because of a telegram received earlier that morning from Shreveport. Addressed to "Nick the Greek," the message read: "For the sake of your countrymen, please refuse

1. New Orleans *Times-Picayune*, May 10, 1924; New Orleans *States* and New Orleans *Item*, May 9, 1924; Hearsey, *The Six Who Were Hanged*, 22–23.
2. New Orleans *States* and New Orleans *Item*, May 9, 1924; New York *Herald Tribune*, May 10, 1924; Hearsey, *The Six Who Were Hanged*, 21–22.

to spring traps and get someone else to do it. If you [are] after money, we will help you—A FRIEND."[3]

At 8:00 A.M., Rini and the others heard the keys clang against the steel doors. The chief deputy and three other officials had come to read the death warrants. Bocchio, probably believing it was time for his execution, became hysterical and fainted.

After the death warrants were read, Father Munichia and Father Zephirinus Martinez from Independence arrived to administer the last rites. Held in the cramped quarters of the Amite jail, the ceremony was nevertheless impressive, and the six prisoners, who all received Communion, seemed deeply affected.[4]

After the service, Bocchio lay fully dressed on his bunk. He was motionless and he said nothing. Joe's eyes were glazed, and he stared straight ahead.

"Come on, Joe," Lamantia said. "Here's some coffee. Take a little of it. It will give you some pep."

Joe refused the coffee and breakfast. While the others ate, Lamantia tried to get Bocchio to talk. Joe would not respond, and Andrea finally gave up.

After 9:00 A.M., Tangipahoa officials realized that the large crowds they had expected would not materialize. The last train from New Orleans arrived, and an *Item* reporter counted only seventy-seven people in small groups around the courthouse square. Most of the early spectators were men who stood near the water-filled ditches, and many were from towns in Mississippi. According to the *Item*, Tangipahoa residents showed little interest in the hanging. The "spirit of vengeance" had waned in the last three years, and many now sympathized with the six men.

A *States* reporter claimed that he "felt the pulse of the people . . . and the response seemed to be almost one hundred per cent that the law has been a little too severe in this case. That two of the men should be hanged and the other four given life terms seemed to be the feeling of at least fifty per cent of the people of Amite and surrounding country. That Joe Bocchio alone should be

3. New Orleans *Item*, May 9, 1924; New Orleans *Times-Picayune*, May 10, 1924.

4. New Orleans *Times-Picayune*, New Orleans *Item*, New Orleans *States*, and Louisville *Courier-Journal*, May 9, 1924; New York *Herald Tribune*, May 10, 1924; newspaper clippings, in Dallas Calmes Scrapbook; Hearsey, *The Six Who Were Hanged*, 22.

spared and the others hanged was the way perhaps 95 per cent viewed it."

Although there were fewer spectators than expected, the courthouse still resembled a fortress. National guardsmen with automatic rifles and sidearms stood at close intervals all around the grounds and on the roof. The three machine guns were in place. Guardsmen were near the bridge over the moat. No one entered the area without a pass.[5]

While the newly arrived spectators were gathering, Sal Rini visited his son for the last time. Leona completed his final letter to his wife. He gave it to a deputy and pleaded with the guard not to open it or reveal the contents to the newspapers. Feeling sorry for Leona, the deputy agreed.

Shortly after 9 : 00 A.M., the hangman joined Bowden, who was feeling better, and Rennyson on the scaffold. He wore a black mask with two crude slits for his eyes and one jagged opening for his mouth. The hood fit so badly, his moustache protruded.[6]

Deamore's ornate bronze casket arrived by truck. Four men carried it to the gallows area on the south side of the jail and put it in the small shanty where the bodies of the men would be placed later. Four other caskets on the truck were made of stained and varnished wood. The sixth casket was a plain pine box, probably provided for Bocchio by William Warrington and Mrs. May, who had guaranteed his burial expenses.

Bowden and Rennyson announced the list of official witnesses: J. F. Westrop, R. L. Hilburn, Dr. Jesse H. McClendon, Dr. Eddie McGehee, and three New Orleans reporters—Allen Dowling of the *States*, Herman B. Deutsch of the *Item*, and George Vandervoort of the *Times-Picayune*. Sheriff's deputies would be present, as would Rene Calmes, who, according to one reporter, "showed only a spirit of kindness and forgiveness for the unfortunate six."[7]

5. New Orleans *Item* and New Orleans *States*, May 9, 1924; New Orleans *Times-Picayune*, May 10, 1924; Crowell, "Stern Justice Took Six Lives for One," 1 – E; newspaper clippings, in Dallas Calmes Scrapbook; Washington *Post*, May 10, 1924.

6. New Orleans *States*, May 9– 10, 1924; New Orleans *Item*, May 9, 1924.

7. New Orleans *States*, May 9– 10, 1924; New Orleans *Item*, May 9, 1924; newspaper clipping, in Dallas Calmes Scrapbook; Hearsey, *The Six Who Were Hanged*, 29.

At 10:00 A.M., a group of Orleans Parish deputies who had guarded the six prisoners for the last three years made a special visit to the Amite jail. They found Leona dictating a farewell letter to another relative. Bocchio was unconscious. Giglio was cheerful as he sang an old ballad—the refrain was "Nobody knows, and nobody seems to care." Rini showed signs of losing his composure. Deamore surprised everyone and remained calm, as he had since receiving Communion. Lamantia and Leona were impassive.

After the Orleans deputies and the two sisters from the Sacred Heart Mission left the cell area, Giglio asked a deputy to get him more wine. While he waited he saw that Rini was near total emotional collapse. Earlier, Rini cheerfully waved farewells to spectators, but as the noon hour approached he became distraught. The guards inside quickly sent word to Bowden for help.

"I'm going to be with my mother in three days," Rini said. "She's buried in Chicago and they're going to take me there—back to my mother—in the grave next to her."

Rini looked at a guard intently. Calling for a doctor, he slumped to the floor and finally lost consciousness. Giglio, who was in the same cell, was calm and cheerful. But at the sight of Rini, he sat on his bunk, buried his head in his hands, and mumbled to himself. Then he got up and walked over to the window. Seeing the rows of tents that stretched from the jail to the moat, he repeated Rini's last words before he fainted.

Deamore continued to amaze everyone—he was quite composed. Leona was quiet but nervous. He paced his cell continuously, his footsteps sounding like the ticking of a loud clock. Although he no longer complained about his wounds, his bandages were still visible above the open collar of his khaki shirt. He would acknowledge no visitors. He spoke only to a national guard captain, the two priests, and the nuns.

Dr. McClendon tended to Rini, and Lamantia lay silently in his cell. He was neither cheerful nor bitter. Showing no emotion, he seemed the least likely to cause problems at the execution.[8]

At 11:00 A.M., a deputy brought in a large porcelain bucket filled with chicken gumbo. The prisoners wanted to eat their final

8. New Orleans *Item* and New Orleans *States*, May 9, 1924.

meal alone, and the guards left the area. Deamore refused to eat because he had drunk large quantities of milk during the morning. Leona sat on the floor and ate heartily. But Lamantia hardly touched his meal, and Bocchio, still in a stupor, could not eat. Giglio enjoyed the meal and called for some more liquor. It was nearly 11:30, and Joe hoped to get one last taste of whiskey.

"We are out of it," a deputy said, "but have sent to Hammond for some."

"That won't do any good," Giglio snapped. "A man can't drive to Hammond and back in thirty-five minutes, and by the time it gets here we'll be gone."

The guard knew Giglio was right, so he sent another deputy into town to find some liquor. Near the train station, where some farmers were loading their strawberries, the deputy found a local Italian bootlegger who had a gallon of strawberry wine at his farm.

Meanwhile, the official witnesses and local authorities gathered in the main room at the jail. After they synchronized their watches, the chief deputy collected the officers' weapons and gave them to the Louisiana National Guard. He ordered the deputies to clear the area of all spectators.

Just before noon, Orleans Parish deputies made a final visit to the cells. Rini asked one of the officers to give a religious picture to a girl in New Orleans. Leona finally told Rennyson that he had kept the knife behind the standpipe in such a way that it could not be seen. When the warden asked how he had gotten the weapon, Roy refused to answer.[9]

On the streets below, a *Times-Picayune* reporter estimated the crowd at only one thousand. The spectators stood quietly on the sidewalks around the courthouse or across the street. They heard the cries of newsboys from New Orleans selling the latest editions—a strange sound in a rural town.[10]

A few minutes before noon, a deputy rang the courthouse bell

9. New Orleans *Item*, May 9–10, 1924; New Orleans *Times-Picayune*, May 10, 1924; Shreveport *Journal*, May 9, 1924; Hearsey *The Six Who Were Hanged*, 22; interview with John V. Baiamonte, Sr., May 10, 1980.

10. New Orleans *Item* and New Orleans *States*, May 9–10, 1924; New Orleans *Times-Picayune*, May 10, 1924; Shreveport *Journal*, May 9, 1924; Hearsey, *The Six Who Were Hanged*, 22; interview with John V. Baiamonte, Sr., May 10, 1980.

to signify the start of the execution. Abandoning the announced order because they did not want to disturb Bocchio's or Rini's composure, officials went first to Leona and Deamore. As the deputies bound their hands Deamore sighed heavily but neither said a word.

As they walked down the narrow corridor Leona twisted his arms to shake hands with certain deputies and soldiers. He unashamedly kissed one of the Orleans Parish deputies who had guarded him for three years. Just before he went up the stairs to the gallows, Roy shook his head at J. A. Johnson, the Tangipahoa Parish jailer. "Nothing to say, Mr. Johnson."

Father Martinez and Father Munichia, giving absolution, preceded Roy and Natale up the stairs. "I am going to heaven," Deamore said and began to weep. "They hanga me," he cried. "They hanga me. Oh Dio, they hanga good man."

When Deamore reached the gallows, he looked up toward the glare of the noon sun. Although the day was rather mild, it was warm on the scaffold. Deamore was pale, and he had a slight beard. His eyes filling with tears, he sobbed, "Pray for me everybody. Oh, pray for me hard!" A deputy directed him to stand on the trap on the east side of the gallows.

Running up the stairs three at a time, the hangman went immediately to Deamore. He stood impassively while the executioner tied the rope around his legs and attached it to his manacled wrists.

Leona watched the hangman prepare Deamore. He listened closely to Father Munichia's prayers. But Leona said not a word. Then the hangman tied Leona's legs to his wrists with a rope, and Roy finally began to repeat some prayers with Father Martinez. Just before the hangman placed the hood over his head, he kissed a crucifix.

"Oh Dio," Deamore repeated, from under the black hood, "when they hanga me, they hanga good man. Oh Dio—."

The executioner chopped the cord holding the double traps at one minute past twelve o'clock. The traps flew open with such an unusually loud thud that people more than four hundred feet away heard the sound. Deamore and Leona fell simultaneously; the sudden jerk visibly stretched their necks several inches. Their bodies swung slightly and then were still. The priests sprinkled holy water on them. Terrified at the sight of his first double execution, the hangman collapsed on the scaffold and was carried into the prison kitchen. Awaiting the next pair, he again drank heavily from a jug of strawberry wine.

State law required that an executed man hang for twenty minutes after the trap dropped. Dr. McClendon stood below the gallows and waited. He declared Deamore dead at 12:13 P.M. Leona was pronounced dead at 12:16 P.M. But Dr. McClendon did not order the bodies removed until 12:21 P.M.

And during the prescribed twenty minutes, the deputies brought Giglio and Rini to the steps of the gallows. They stood silently, waiting.

"They have kissed the others good-bye," Surcouf said to witnesses there. "They are composed. They are not crying. They are ready for death."

Deputies placed the bodies of Deamore and Leona in the shanty near the gallows. A carelessly thrown cigarette ignited the cotton sheets that covered the crude structure. The deputies extinguished the blaze quickly. But several officers remembered Deamore's shouts of "Fire."[11]

While Rini and Giglio waited, a nun was praying in front of Bocchio and Lamantia's cell. She watched Lamantia fumble with his watch pocket. He took out a small knife, opened it, and repeatedly stabbed himself in the heart. The terrified nun immediately called for help. Before Deputy Johnson could get there, Lamantia stabbed himself at least a dozen times, and blood welled from his wounds.

"I wanta die, I wanta die, I wanta die," Lamantia chanted. He jammed the knife fiercely into his chest several more times. Lamantia carefully extended his hands, knelt, and then stretched out on the floor. He stabbed himself two or three more times. Finally, he threw the knife into the farthest corner of the cell.

11. New Orleans *Times-Picayune*, May 7, 10, 1924; New Orleans *States*, May 7, 9, 1924; New Orleans *Item*, May 9–11, 1924; Shreveport *Journal*, May 9, 1924; *Florida Parishes Times* (Amite City), and San Francisco *Chronicle*, May 10, 1924; St. Louis *Dispatch*, May 8–9, 1924; New York *Herald Tribune*, May 10, 1924; newspaper clippings, in Dallas Calmes Scrapbook; Hearsey, *The Six Who Were Hanged*, 23.

"I wanta die, I wanta die," Lamantia cried. He was bleeding profusely. Staring in total disbelief, Bocchio was horrified.

Dr. McClendon began a hasty examination and found at least twenty-seven stab wounds. Finding no pulse, McClendon knew that within minutes Lamantia would die. The Tangipahoa coroner ordered that Lamantia and Bocchio hang immediately, and Rini and Giglio returned to their cells.

Four deputies carried Lamantia, unconscious, down the corridor. His head lolled. Bocchio, supported by two guards, walked slowly. When they reached the bottom of the scaffold, Lamantia's fancy silk shirt was covered with blood, and Bocchio could barely walk up the stairs. On the gallows, Joe was almost unconscious and had to be held by a deputy and Father Munichia, who whispered prayers to Bocchio. Joe stumbled and fell. Surcouf put his arm around Bocchio's waist and assisted him to the trap.

The deputies placed Lamantia in a chair over the trap Deamore had occupied. When they handcuffed his hands behind him, Andrea slumped. His chin rested on his chest, and his legs sprawled. One of the priests spoke to him, but there was no response. Lamantia appeared to be breathing, and after a few moments, he opened his eyes and moved his head from side to side. He was bleeding again, and drops of blood fell on the trap.

Bocchio had a vacant stare as he stood on the trap. His knees buckled and he began to sway. Father Munichia offered him support. Almost unable to repeat the priest's prayers, Joe spoke in such a weak voice that the witnesses could hardly hear him.

While the hangman prepared Bocchio, Lamantia regained consciousness. He looked at Joe. As if offering a farewell gesture, he blinked his eyes. Then his head fell forward again.

A plane from Gates Flying Circus flew over the courthouse to photograph the scene. In addition, Clement Hearsey, a veteran police reporter from New Orleans, and a photographer on a nearby rooftop took pictures of the hanging. Sheriff Bowden's strict orders had been in vain.

The scene on the gallows was somber and terrifying to the witnesses. The executioner finally lifted Lamantia's head to place the hood, and he then turned to Bocchio.

"My God, hurry," whispered a deputy. "Let's get it over."

The hangman chopped the ropes for a second time at 12:36 P.M. The bodies fell instantly beneath the platform, and the chair tumbled to the sawdust floor below. McClendon declared Lamantia dead at 12:44 P.M., but it took thirteen minutes before Bocchio's pulse finally stopped.

Sixty-eight miles away in New Orleans, Joe Rini's father and brother were seeking an interview with Chief Justice O'Neill. Sal Rini, who reportedly had mortgaged his property and had spent $15,000 in legal fees for his son's defense, pleaded tearfully with the Louisiana Supreme Court clerks to see the chief justice, but O'Neill had left for his home at Franklinton. Sal had hoped that O'Neill would intercede and stop the execution of his son. But the old man finally realized that his efforts were futile. He sat on a courthouse bench and wept.[12]

At 12:57 P.M., the deputies put the bodies of Bocchio and Lamantia in the shanty, where an employee of Valenti's Undertaking was responsible for collecting their personal belongings. When he reached into Lamantia's inside coat pocket, he received a severe cut on his right index finger. Carefully searching again, the undertaker discovered a razor blade hidden in the lining. Although authorities never discovered how he had obtained the knife and the razor blade, a sympathetic soldier or law-enforcement officer probably passed them to Lamantia.

As Rini and Giglio waited their turn they heard a tapping noise coming from the cupola above their cell. One of them asked, and a deputy told them about the telegraph installed by the newspapers.

"Have they sent out the news that we've been hanged?" Rini asked. "You know they started out with us and brought us back."

"No," Deputy Johnson said. "They haven't done that."

"They might hang us twice, you know," Rini said, smiling.

Giglio heard the sound of a key in the heavy steel door at the end of the corridor. "They come for us again," said Joe. "Now there will be no wait."

12. New Orleans *States*, May 9, 1924; New Orleans *Times-Picayune*, May 10, 14, 1924; Shreveport *Journal* and New Orleans *Item*, May 9–10, 1924; San Francisco *Chronicle*, New York *Times*, New York *Herald Tribune*, and Washington *Post*, May 10, 1924; newspaper clippings, in Dallas Calmes Scrapbook; Hearsey, *The Six Who Were Hanged*, 24.

Giglio was totally composed, and he thanked Johnson for his kind treatment of them all. Rini insisted that only Leona fired the shots and that five innocent men were to hang. But he said he forgave everyone. "And my prayer is that my people will live to see capital punishment abolished in all this country," Rini said. "That ours will be the last hanging ever in the United States." He gave his gold watch to a captain in the Washington Artillery, in appreciation for his kindness.

Outside on the gallows, the hangman set the traps again and prepared a third pair of nooses. "All ready, Cap," he said to Rennyson, who notified a deputy to bring Rini and Giglio.

Giglio threw away a half-smoked cigar and nervously brushed his sleek hair back from his forehead. "It's all ended now," he muttered.

The deputies were ready to shackle them. Rini and Giglio faced each other. They embraced heartily and kissed. Then they offered their hands behind their backs. Shackled but showing no signs of fear, they shook hands awkwardly with several deputies.

As Giglio left his cell he whistled a popular tune, but he stopped when the priests met him in the corridor.

"Five innocent men!" Rini cried in a loud firm voice just before he went up the stairs to the gallows. "I hope everybody's satisfied." Rini then removed his shoes.

"I'm going up innocent," Giglio added. Climbing the stairs, he shouted, "They've butchered four of us, and now they are going to butcher two more. They'll be satisfied in five minutes when we are dead."

"That's right, Joe, five innocent men," Rini said. "We go innocent. God knows we do."

When they reached the platform, the deputies escorted Giglio to the west trap, where Leona and Bocchio had stood. Rini walked to the east trap. He saw Lamantia's blood.

"Governor Parker ought to get himself six more Italians," Giglio shouted. "He got us six and he had eleven before. That makes seventeen. He ought to get some more!"

While the hangman tied Rini's legs, Joe paid him no attention. He looked at the two airplanes circling one hundred feet over the jail. Despite Toombs's orders and protests from parish residents, the planes passed directly over the gallows in three attempts to photograph the hanging. Many Italians in the countryside around Amite interpreted the flights as attempted surveillance of the Sicilian communities.

"Who shot Calmes?" McClendon asked Rini.

"The man who confessed first," Rini said. "Leona did it. He told the truth."

"Governor Parker has now made it seventeen Italians," Giglio interjected bitterly. "Eleven lynched and six hanged."

"Then who was the seventh man?" McClendon asked. Although the prosecution had ridiculed Gulotta's seventh-man defense, Tangipahoa authorities were convinced that someone helped plan the robbery and turned out the lights in the bank on the night of May 7, 1921.

"Who helped you in Independence?" Beckler demanded. "Who was the seventh man in the crime?"

Rini lowered his head and refused to answer.

"You're going to your God, Rini," McClendon said. "You're going to die right now. Go straight, go clean, tell the truth."

Rini did not reply for several moments. "Every bone in my body is straight," he said finally, "as straight as a candle. The man who did the shooting confessed. He paid for it first, but I'll tell nothing. I'm straight and I'm honest.

"I'd never have told you anything," he said, holding to *omertà*, the code of silence. "Never have told you who did the shooting. But Leona confessed himself."

The hangman finished binding Rini's legs and placed the noose around his neck. He tried to put the black hood on Rini. But Rini angrily pulled away and shouted, "Wait a minute, you. Can't you see I'm talking." Probably astonished by Joe's brashness, the executioner waited.

"We're guilty of attempted murder, but—," Rini said.

"No, Joe," Giglio interrupted, "not murder but attempted burglary. There is no murder."

"Make yourself right with your God," advised one of the priests. "Get ready to die. Be composed. Strike out hate and anger from your heart."

"Bother, bother, all bother," Giglio snapped. He shook his head fiercely as if to get the priest to leave him alone. But the priest began a prayer and pleaded with Giglio to be calm.

"Yes, Father, yes, Father," Giglio murmured. He appeared to be composed. The hangman placed the hood over him, and he straightened his head.

The hangman turned to Rini. "Wait," he said loudly. "Wait with that thing." The executioner stepped back for the second time.

McClendon, thinking that Rini was ready to confess, placed his hand on Joe's arm and said, "Who was the seventh man who put the light out in the bank?"

"Leona told you the truth," Rini insisted. "I'll tell you nothing."

"Again and remember," he said a few moments later, "I'm going to die innocent. Going to my death now and I'll stick by my story."

"But—," McClendon tried to protest.

"No," Rini said. "I've told all there is. Every bone in my body is straight—straight as a candle, and I go to die now."

Giglio angrily cursed everyone on the platform, but Father Munichia reminded him to pray for forgiveness. Joe bowed his head. "That's right, Father," he said, "I forgive them all."

The executioner finally put the mask on Rini and went back to his position. Giglio and Rini were facing west. For several moments, neither man spoke.

"Good-bye, Joe," Rini said clearly.

"Good-bye, Joe," Giglio replied. "Good-bye, good-bye."

Kneeling, the hangman fumbled for his hatchet. He quickly slashed the ropes for the last time. The double traps dropped at 1:15 P.M.

With a sharp jerk the bodies stopped. Rini's body was almost still, but Giglio spun around twice. He let out a deep groan; his chest heaved and his shoulders contorted. He groaned again. There was a wheezing gurgle in his throat. Trying desperately to breathe, he twisted his wrists convulsively to free himself from the manacles. Giglio slowly strangled to death. After a few spasmodic twitches, the body seemed to become limp. It swung slightly before coming to rest.

At 1:30 P.M., Dr. McClendon pronounced Giglio and Rini dead. Although he insisted that Giglio died from a broken neck,

237

the reporters knew that they had witnessed a hideous strangulation. Deputies removed the bodies, ending this unprecedented execution which would later be described as one of the most unusual and most bungled hangings in American history.[13]

13. New Orleans *States*, May 9–11, 1924; New Orleans *Item*, May 8–11, 1924; newspaper clippings, in Dallas Calmes Scrapbook; Crowell, "Stern Justice Took Six Lives for One," 1–E; Shreveport *Journal*, May 9, 1924; Louisville *Courier-Journal*, New Orleans *Times-Picayune*, Washington *Post*, New York *Herald Tribune*, May 10, 1924; interview with John V. Baiamonte, Sr., May 10, 1980; Hearsey, *The Six Who Were Hanged*, 26–28; Negley K. Teeters, *Hang by the Neck* (Springfield, Ill., 1967), 178–80; Charles Duff, *A New Handbook on Hanging* (London, 1954), 109–11.

19

I'm Glad It's Through

Silence prevailed in Amite until 2:00 P.M. on May 9. Then people on the courthouse grounds began to speak in hushed tones, and small groups of spectators gathered on the corners. Later that afternoon, officials permitted the crowds to enter the gallows four at a time. Some picked up strands of rope, thinking they had part of the hanging rope. But those were packing cords left by the soldiers. The one hundred feet of rope used by the executioner disappeared a few minutes after Rini and Giglio were hanged.

By midafternoon, the strawberry and truck farmers were back to their normal routine. Loading their crops to be shipped by rail to northern markets, some Italians were discussing the execution. They were not laughing and joking as usual. "I'm glad it's through," one farmer said, but most of the Sicilians at the station preferred not to talk about the hanging.

The four cells used to house the six men were quiet. There were prayer books; clothing was piled in the corners; crumpled blankets lay across the mattresses. There were letters from relatives and friends; some fruit; a partially eaten sandwich. A religious candle burned. In Giglio's cell were his half-smoked cigar and a plug of chewing tobacco.[1]

The hangman took the evening train to New Orleans. When it stopped in Hammond, representatives of Thomas Funeral Parlor were there with the bodies of Leona, Giglio, Lamantia, Bocchio, Deamore, but not Rini. According to a reporter who viewed the bodies, Deamore's neck had been almost severed. The undertakers had to use more than a hundred pounds of ice to reduce his horribly swollen and discolored neck.

1. New Orleans *Times-Picayune*, May 10, 1924; New Orleans *Item*, May 9–11, 1924; newspaper clippings, in Dallas Calmes Scrapbook.

The bodies had been embalmed in Hammond, and once the train reached New Orleans, the wake for Giglio, Bocchio, Leona, and Lamantia began almost immediately. Nearly five hundred onlookers had gathered at Valenti's Funeral Parlor. In the chapel, candles burned at the head of the four caskets. Friends and relatives kept a vigil through Friday night until dawn. Throngs of people came to the wake, and the police assigned a special detail to the funeral home. In another part of New Orleans, Deamore's wake attracted several hundred mourners.

By Saturday morning the crowds were still so large at Valenti's that the police remained on duty. The special detail directed the crowd through one door, past the coffins, and out another door. According to the *States*, most mourners and spectators wanted to see Bocchio, whose casket was covered with wreaths and bouquets without cards. At Schoen Funeral Parlor, another large crowd gathered to view Rini's body, which finally arrived from Hammond just before ten o'clock.[2]

Before Bocchio's funeral began on Saturday afternoon, Patrina Fanucci arrived. She stood beside the coffin and repeatedly kissed Bocchio. She was calm, and she spoke to no one.

A gray hearse carried Bocchio's body to St. Mary's Italian Church for the 2:15 P.M. service. A small gathering of friends and acquaintances were there. Outside the church, three hundred people tried to view the casket. After the church service, the hearse and five cars went to the St. Vincent de Paul Cemetery, where there was a large crowd, mostly men. After a brief graveside service, Bocchio's body was laid to rest in an elevated vault. An unidentified woman silently placed a wreath and walked away.

Deamore's funeral was at 3:30 P.M. It was so large that there was a special police detail to control the crowds. The service was at St. Mary's Italian Church, and more than one thousand spectators jammed the streets outside. When the cortege reached the cemetery, there was a large crowd at the gravesite, only a few yards from Bocchio's.[3]

2. New Orleans *Times-Picayune* and New Orleans *States*, May 10–11, 1924; New Orleans *Item*, May 10, 1924; Hearsey, *The Six Who Were Hanged*, 29.

3. New Orleans *States*, New Orleans *Item*, and New Orleans *Times-Picayune*, May 11, 1924.

On Saturday evening, the bodies of Lamantia, Giglio, and Leona were returned by train to Brooklyn for burial on Tuesday, May 13. All three were waked at the same Manhattan mortuary. The funeral procession was enormous. More than thirty cars and several police escorts proceeded through Brooklyn's Little Italy to St. John's Cemetery.

At almost the same time in Chicago, a band played "Nearer, My God, to Thee" as Rini's body was carried to the hearse. According to the press, Rini was buried with the "pomp usually accorded a distinguished statesman or great public benefactor." The newspapers also said that the funeral was as lavish as Frank Capone's.[4]

A few days after the funerals, the board of directors of the Prison Reform Association of Louisiana announced its support of a legislative bill to allow capital punishment only in cases of premeditated murder. The association believed that the bill would pass because the graphic details of the execution in Amite had shocked the public.

The New Orleans *States* said in an editorial that "it has been said that the six gunmen executed in Amite the other day might prove martyrs to a cause—the abolishment of capital punishment. We doubt it. We have expressed our regret that, though under the law in this instance all six were equally guilty, so many men should pay the extreme forfeit for the killing of one." The editorial concluded that the "Tangipahoa tragedy" would not "change the attitude of Louisiana in regard to capital punishment."

The *Times-Picayune* carried a pro–capital punishment editorial, and the *Item* said that "one reaction to the hanging of the six murderers of Calmes is an agitation for the limitation or abolishment of capital punishment." Although the *Item* did not endorse capital punishment, the paper urged the state legislature to examine the life-sentence statute before abolishing the death penalty. The *Item* complained that a man sentenced for manslaughter in Louisiana could spend more time in prison than someone who had committed first-degree murder.[5]

4. New Orleans *States*, May 11, 14, 1924; New Orleans *Item*, May 10, 16–17, 1924; New Orleans *Times-Picayune*, May 10–11, 14, 1924; newspaper clipping, in Dallas Calmes Scrapbook.

5. New Orleans *Times-Picayune*, May 15, 1924; New Orleans *Item*, May

While the New Orleans press debated capital punishment, friends of Bocchio made plans to exhume his body and send it back for burial in Sicily. Later, Patrina visited the mortuary to ask about sailing schedules and cost. Since she and her friends did not have enough money, she said that she would try to get donations. Patrina never returned.[6]

After three years, *Rini et al.* was no longer part of the banner headlines in the New Orleans newspapers. The case did not reappear in the press until January, 1951, when Senator Estes Kefauver's hearings caused the rediscovery of the Mafia. An Associated Press reporter said that Kefauver's investigation of "organized crime" raised Mafia activities in New Orleans to a height unseen since the Hennessey case. The *Times-Picayune* and the Baton Rouge *Morning Advocate* felt compelled to publish during this period fairly accurate articles on *Rini et al.* One *Item* reporter, however, wrote about Hennessey and the Mafia of the 1890s in a series of articles that can best be described as a blend of fact and fiction, with an emphasis on the latter.[7]

Rini et al. surfaced again in 1975 when David Chandler, a former New Orleans reporter, added to the Mafia myth. In his book *Brothers in Blood*, Chandler provided without documentation a totally inaccurate account of *Rini et al.*: "Almost every community within a two-hundred mile radius of New Orleans had its resident Mafioso. As in Sicily, there was a strawberry Mafia, an orange Mafia, a vegetable Mafia, each of which levied tariffs on Italians growing and selling these products. At the same time, the country Mafias kept their hands in with an occasional bank robbery or truck hijacking. At all times they were under the control of the New Orleans family, which had guns and prestige to back its authority. These country Mafias were eventually destroyed by a prosecutor in Amite, Louisiana." According to Chandler, Amite "was not the type of place one expected to find a Mafia. Or so the

18–19, 24, 26, 1924; New Orleans *States*, May 13, 1924; newspaper clipping, in Dallas Calmes Scrapbook.

    6. New Orleans *Times-Picayune* and New Orleans *States*, May 14, 1924.

    7. New Orleans *States*, March 2, 1951; East, "Six for One," 3, 12; "Six Who Were Hanged," New Orleans *Times-Picayune*, *Dixie Roto Magazine*, March 2, 1952, p. 10; New Orleans *Item*, December 2–7, 1951; New Orleans *Times-Picayune*, January 26–28, 1951.

town thought. In 1923 the Amite bank was robbed and a guard killed." He erroneously maintained that the "six young Sicilian immigrants [were] members of a local Mafia that, it was revealed, had been secretly extorting strawberry farmers for twenty years." Chandler said that the "local Mafiosi" from Amite and New Orleans offered numerous bribes to District Attorney Matt Allen, who ordered that the six men be hanged all at once, "panoramically."[8]

In the spring of 1981, a veteran Tangipahoa newspaper editor and publisher contributed to the distortion of *Rini et al.* In the middle of his article on strawberry farming, he brought up the case. He said, incorrectly, that all of the "six Italians" were from Chicago and that the Mafia "tried to stir up the local Italians against their 'redneck' neighbors, which didn't go over so well either." In addition, in September, 1982, a longtime Tangipahoa law-enforcement official misrepresented the facts of *Rini et al.* He claimed that a capture occurred at Natalbany, rather than Albany, and that all six men were from Chicago. He also incorrectly described the wife and the girlfriend of two of the defendants as Bourbon Street prostitutes.[9]

Undoubtedly, *Rini et al.* has left some unanswered questions, which will probably continue to foster many myths and falsehoods about the case. For example, if Roy Leona truly recanted his confession in the May 7 letter to his wife, then who shot Dallas Calmes? Who turned out the lights in the bank? Was there a "seventh man"? If so, what did he do in the early morning of May 8, 1921? Many Tangipahoa Parish residents and others have their own theories in answer to these questions, especially who the "seventh man" was. Despite some convincing arguments, which were partially but not conclusively supported by the evidence, suspicions and conjectures were not included in this study because speculation is not within the historian's realm.

8. David Leon Chandler, *Brothers in Blood: The Rise of the Criminal Brotherhoods* (New York, 1975), 174–75.
9. Hammond *Daily Star*, April 8, 1981, September 3, 1982.

Bibliography

Primary Sources

DOCUMENTS

Charter Book No. 1. Tangipahoa Parish Clerk of Court Office, Amite City, Louisiana.

Correspondence in Relation to the Killing of Prisoners in New Orleans on March 14, 1891. Washington, D.C., 1891.

Deamore, N., *et al.*, File So. 311.6521. Department of State, National Archives.

Forni, Fara. "Gli' italiani nel distretto consolare di Nuova Orleans." *Bollettino Emigrazione*, No. 17, N.p., 1905.

Indictments, Appearance Bonds, and Court Summons, 1896–1937. Tangipahoa Parish Clerk of Court Office, Amite City, Louisiana.

Moroni, Giacomo. "Gli' italiani in Tangipahoa (Louisiana)." *Bollettino Emigrazione*, No. 7. N.p., 1910.

———. "La Louisiana e l'immigrazione italiana." *Bollettino Emigrazione*, No. 5. N.p., 1913.

LEGAL CASES

Joseph Rini et al. v. *State of Louisiana.* 44 Supreme Court Reporter 230 (1924).

State v. *Rini et al.* 91 So. 665 (1922).

State v. *Rini et al.* 95 So. 400 (1923).

State of Louisiana v. *Joseph Rini et al.* Transcript of Appeal, No. 24,914. 4 vols. State of Louisiana Supreme Court Archives, New Orleans.

State of Louisiana v. *Joseph Rini et al.* Transcript of Appeal, No. 25,583. 4 vols. State of Louisiana Supreme Court Archives, New Orleans.

COLLECTIONS AND DIARIES

Bocchio, Joseph. "Last Days of a Condemned Man." Edited by Herman Drezinski. New Orleans *Item*, January 27–February 10, 1924.

Calmes, Dallas. Scrapbook. In possession of Mrs. Betty Salter, Denham Springs, Louisiana.

Ellis, E. John, and Thomas C. W. Ellis. Papers. Department of Archives, Troy H. Middleton Library, Louisiana State University, Baton Rouge.

Hearsey, Clement G. *The Six Who Were Hanged.* N.p., n.d.
Parker, John M. Correspondence. Department of Archives, Troy H. Middleton Library, Louisiana State University, Baton Rouge.
———. Papers. Southern Historical Collection, Walter Royal Davis Library, University of North Carolina, Chapel Hill.
———. Papers. Southwest Archives and Manuscripts Collection, Dupré Library, University of Southwestern Louisiana, Lafayette.
Robinson, W. D. Papers. Southern Historical Collection, Walter Royal Davis Library, University of North Carolina, Chapel Hill.
Vertical File, "Crime and Criminals." Rare Book Room, Troy H. Middleton Library, Louisiana State University, Baton Rouge.

NEWSPAPERS

Amite City *Advocate,* 1905–1906
Florida Parishes Times (Amite City), 1908, 1921–24.
Amite City *News-Digest,* 1960.
Tangi Talk (Amite City), 1969.
Amite City *Times,* 1917–20.
Atlanta *Constitution,* 1924.
Baton Rouge *Daily Advocate,* 1890.
Baton Rouge *State-Times,* 1922–24.
Chicago *Daily News,* 1924.
Hammond *Daily Courier,* 1932.
Hammond *Daily Star,* 1981–82.
Hammond *Vindicator,* 1930–44.
Kentwood *Commercial,* 1900–1901.
Louisville *Courier-Journal,* 1924.
New Orleans *Daily City Item,* 1891, 1893.
New Orleans *Daily Picayune,* 1881–1910.
New Orleans *Daily States,* 1888–91.
New Orleans *Item,* 1921–24, 1951.
New Orleans *States,* 1920–24, 1951.
New Orleans *Times-Democrat,* 1890–1910.
New Orleans *Times-Picayune,* 1916–24, 1935, 1950, 1982.
New York *Herald Tribune,* 1924.
New York *Times,* 1899–1900, 1922, 1924.
Ponchatoula *Enterprise,* 1921–24.
San Francisco *Chronicle,* 1924.
Shreveport *Journal,* 1924.
St. Louis *Dispatch,* 1924.
Washington *Post,* 1924.

INTERVIEWS

Baiamonte, John V., Sr., May 10, 1980.
Calmes, Dallas, Jr., April 7, 1980.
Purser, John, May 14, 1984.

Bibliography

Secondary Sources

BOOKS

Alexander, Charles C. *The Ku Klux Klan in the Southwest*. Lexington, Ky., 1965.

Blok, Anton. *The Mafia of a Sicilian Village, 1860–1960: A Study of Violent Peasant Entrepreneurs*. New York, 1975.

Chandler, David Leon. *Brothers in Blood: The Rise of the Criminal Brotherhoods*. New York, 1975.

Duff, Charles. *A New Handbook on Hanging*. London, 1954.

Hair, William Ivy. *Bourbonism and Agrarian Protest: Louisiana Politics, 1877–1900*. Baton Rouge, 1969.

Hess, Henner. *Mafia and Mafiosi: The Structure of Power*. Translated by Ewald Osers. Boston, 1979.

Higham, John. *Strangers in the Land: Patterns of American Nativism, 1860–1925*. New Brunswick, N.J., 1955.

Horan, James D. *The Pinkertons: The Detective Dynasty That Made History*. New York, 1967.

Howard, Perry H. *Political Tendencies in Louisiana*. Rev. ed. Baton Rouge, 1971.

Ianni, Francis A. J. "The Mafia and the Web of Kinship." In *An Inquiry into Organized Crime*, edited by Luciano J. Iorizzo. New York, 1970.

Jackson, Joy J. *New Orleans in the Gilded Age: Politics and Urban Progress, 1880–1896*. Baton Rouge, 1969.

Leuchtenburg, William E. *The Perils of Prosperity, 1914–32*. Chicago, 1958.

National Association for the Advancement of Colored People. *Thirty Years of Lynching in the United States, 1889–1918*. New York, 1969.

Nelli, Humbert S. *The Business of Crime: Italians and Syndicate Crime in the United States*. Chicago, 1976.

Reynolds, George. *Machine Politics in New Orleans, 1897–1926*. New York, 1936.

Sindler, Allan P. *Huey Long's Louisiana: State Politics, 1920–1952*. Baltimore, 1956.

Teeters, Negley K. *Hang by the Neck*. Springfield, Ill., 1967.

Williams, T. Harry. *Huey Long*. New York, 1969.

THESES AND DISSERTATIONS

Baiamonte, John V., Jr. "Immigrants in Rural America: A Study of the Italians of Tangipahoa Parish, Louisiana." Ph.D. dissertation, Mississippi State University, 1972.

Botein, Barbara. "The Hennessy Case: An Episode in American Nativism, 1890." Ph.D. dissertation, New York University, 1975.

Carroll, Ralph Edward. "The Mafia in New Orleans, 1900–1907." M.A. thesis, Notre Dame Seminary (New Orleans), 1956.

Bibliography

Carroll, Richard L. "The Impact of David C. Hennessey on New Orleans Society and the Consequences of the Assassination of Hennessey." M.A. thesis, Notre Dame Seminary (New Orleans), 1957.

Harrell, Kenneth Earl. "The Ku Klux Klan in Louisiana, 1920–1930." Ph.D. dissertation, Louisiana State University, 1966.

Phillips, Spencer. "Administration of Governor Parker." M.A. thesis, Louisiana State University, 1933.

Scarpaci, Jean. "Italian Immigrants in Louisiana's Sugar Parishes: Recruitment, Labor Conditions, and Community Relations, 1880–1910." Ph.D. dissertation, Rutgers University, 1972.

Schott, Matthew James. "John M. Parker of Louisiana and the Varieties of American Progressivism." Ph.D. dissertation, Vanderbilt University, 1969.

Williams, Ernest Russ, Jr. "The Florida Parish Ellises and Louisiana Politics, 1820–1918." Ph.D. dissertation, University of Southern Mississippi, 1969.

ARTICLES

Alwes, Berthold C. "The History of the Louisiana State Lottery Company." *Louisiana Historical Quarterly,* XXVII (October, 1944), 964–1118.

Buel, Clarence C. "The Degradation of a State: Or the Charitable Career of the Louisiana Lottery." *Century Magazine,* XLIII (1892), 618–32.

Coxe, John E. "The New Orleans Mafia Incident." *Louisiana Historical Quarterly,* XX (October, 1937), 1067–1110.

Crowell, Charlotte. "Stern Justice Took Six Lives for One." Baton Rouge *Sunday Advocate,* May 10, 1964, p. 1–E.

Cunningham, George E. "The Italian: A Hindrance to White Solidarity in Louisiana, 1890–1898." *Journal of Negro History,* L (June, 1965), 22–36.

East, Charles. "Six for One." Baton Rouge *Morning Advocate Magazine,* January 28, 1951, pp. 3, 12.

Kendall, John S. "Blood on the Banquette." *Louisiana Historical Quarterly,* XXII (July, 1939), 819–56.

———. "Who Killa de Chief?" *Louisiana Historical Quarterly,* XXII (April, 1939), 492–530.

"Louisiana 'Ring Rule' Smashed." *Literary Digest,* LXIV (February 7, 1920), 18.

Marr, Robert H., Jr. "The New Orleans Mafia Case." *American Law Review,* XXV (May-June, 1891), 414–31.

Nelli, Humbert S. "Italians and Crime in Chicago: The Formative Years, 1890–1920." *American Journal of Sociology,* LXXIV (January, 1969), 373–91.

Perisco, Joseph E. "Vendetta in New Orleans." *American Heritage,* XXIV (June, 1973), 65–72.

Scarpaci, Jean Ann. "Immigrants in the New South: Italians in Louisiana's Sugar Parishes, 1880–1910." *Labor History,* XVI (Spring, 1975), 165–83.

Shanabruch, Charles. "The Louisiana Immigration Movement, 1891–1907: An Analysis of Efforts, Attitudes, and Opportunities." *Louisiana History,* XVIII (Spring, 1977), 203–26.

"Six Who Were Hanged." New Orleans *Times-Picayune, Dixie Roto Magazine,* March 2, 1952, p. 10.

Wiggins, Richard H. "The Louisiana Press and the Lottery," *Louisiana Historical Quarterly,* XXXI (July, 1948), 716–844.

Index

Index

Vandervoort, George, 228
Vernon, Norman P., 116, 156

Walmsley, T. Semmes, 196–97
Warrington, William, 147, 161, 178, 202, 208
Westrop, J. F., 228

White Caps, 2, 151
White Farmers Association, 15
White Farmers Co-operative Association, 15
Williams, George, 192
Wilson, Robert, 92
Wyckliffe, John C., 5–7